FLAMENCO STRINGS UNCORKED

A Callinda Beauvais Mystery, Book Four

Patricia Steele

Patricia Steele

FLAMENCO STRINGS UNCORKED

Copyright @ 2018 by Patricia Steele
Plumeria Press
Casa Grande, Arizona, USA

This is a work of fiction. Names, characters, businesses, places, events and incidents are either the products of the author's imagination or used in a fictitious manner. Any resemblance to actual persons, living or dead, or actual events is purely coincidental.

ISBN 9780996606349

Illustrated by SelfPubBookCovers.com/
TerriGostolaPhotography
Cover Design by Christopher Howard at blondesign

First Printing, March 2018
Visit the author website: www.patriciabbsteele.com

FLAMENCO STRINGS UNCORKED

Also by Patricia Steele ~
"Living with Cystic Fibrosis" in *Your Health Magazine*

Standalone Fiction:
Tangled like Music
Cloisonné

Fiction Series: Callinda Beauvais Mysteries:
Shoot the Moon, 1
Wine, Vines and Picasso, 2
Thorny Secrets and Pinot Noir, 3
Flamenco Strings: Uncorked, 4

Travel Memoirs:
A Roundabout Passage to Venice
Mind the Gap in Zip it Socks

Cooking DRUNK (and wine tasting 101), a cookbook
Goodbye Balloon, a children's story

By Patricia Ruiz Steele
Spanish Pearls Series:
Book One: The Girl Immigrant
Book Two: Silván Leaves
In Progress: Ruiz Legacies

FLAMENCO STRINGS UNCORKED

ACKNOWLEDGEMENTS

Some people walk through our lives to make a difference in ours. Sometimes those people change us in the way we think and the way we live our lives. Often, their words, or the way they say them, stay with us and I find a perfect fit for them within my stories.

This story is based in Spain. I walked through the Spanish village streets in this story, I drank their wine and *café con leche* and I painstakingly spoke their language.

Many thanks to:

My mother, Neyda Bettencourt – I always tried to get the long straw.
Rina Rien, Who shared her enthusiasm for Spain.
Janet Russell for teaching me to speak the Spanish language.
Roberto Wilcox, for self-defense techniques and creating bad guys.
Tina Heller, for her medical expertise
Jeannette Rhodes for her support and advice
Lana Walsh, Cindy Patterson and other CCC members who love Callie
Darla Leimeister whose name I borrowed for my story
Lyn Murphy for sharing *la casa redonda* (literally)
Saidie Owen for acting as my wine-cellar steward
El Carro – my Renault Clio that drove me through the Spanish villages
My readers, who asked me to write more Callie Beauvais adventures.

AND a special thank you to my beta readers!

ONE

Callie whispered, "Olivier still looks shell shocked."

Cendrine, chuckled. "Sex is an iffy thing. It was easier the first time because we both guessed correctly. But this time, there was only one." She snickered. "He's still getting used it."

Warmth seeped into the living room as the spring sunshine slipped through the large glass window. The tightly-swaddled infant fit into Callie's arms like a well-worn shoe. Large blue eyes stared into chocolate browns that began to puddle with emotion. The child stared, blinked, stared and blinked again. And then turned to root for the breast that Callie knew would never drip milk. Her heart thumped hard with the knowledge. She touched the soft, downy cheek with a finger and marveled at the golden tufts of hair that covered the child's small head. Lifting one tiny finger at a time, her hidden-heart hurt multiplied as she thought of the many times she'd ached to hold a child of her own. She smiled suddenly when the child's fist tightened around her smallest finger and Callie's melancholia turned to a perfect joy. She hadn't seen the older twins when they were one week old. This one, this little miracle, had already taken her broken heart and put it back together again. Blinking away tears, she lifted her head to smile at her niece.

Callie laughed and reached a hand toward Cendrine, to push a swathe of dark golden hair out of her eyes. Looking into her face, Callie whispered, "You are the child I never had, *ma chère*. And this child will ease the pain of the last few weeks. A new breath of life is exactly what we all need after learning the truth about your uncle's death. She will give everyone that special lift, *oui*?"

Cendrine's eyes filled and she nodded her head before letting it drop against the pale blue wing chair across from Callie. The women gazed at one another.

"Laurielle Chloe Benoit is a big name for such a tiny baby though..." Callie felt the amazing little package squirm, root for her breast again and knew it was time for *maman* to take over.

"We've called her Lulu for months. I didn't want to confuse the poor little one by calling her something else, so we had to find a full name." Cendrine's eyes twinkled as she lowered the child's rosebud lips to her breast and unloosed her bra flap to reveal her nipple.

Both women laughed when they watched little Lulu, who knew exactly what to do with it. Her pink cheeks rose and fell with the gulps of milk and her blue-tinged eyelids closed in abject contentment. Each of her fingers seized and expanded as if they were keeping time to music only she could hear.

"Now, when is the wedding?"

"Oh." Excitement warred with anxiety and Callie had difficulty swallowing. Questions could wait because the answers were complicated. How could she tell Cendrine her stomach was in a fist of confusion, or give her niece answers that she didn't have herself? How could she confront her own questions? Her head hurt. She wasn't ready to confront or explain. She just wanted to enjoy her little family and then she would drive to Spain. Jules had been patient, but she knew he had his own questions with little answers. She knew she had to talk with him. Soon.

"Callie?" Cendrine sat forward in the chair. The question lingered in the air; her forehead creased. Her blue eyes grew round and her golden hair fell across her cheek as she waited for Callie to respond.

Instead of answering, Callie leaned forward with open arms. "I think it is my turn to snuggle Lulu." She ignored the look on

FLAMENCO STRINGS UNCORKED

Cendrine's questioning face and pulled the child's now-sleeping body into the warmth of her neck.

Callie bit her lip. Returning to France was her priority now that she'd solved the mystery of her husband's death, sold her houses and assets in Oregon and agreed to be the trustee of Pablo Picasso's dream. Now she would concentrate on tiny Lulu, the twins, Francois and Bernadette, and her relationship with the lovely Jules.

"Jules." She leaned her dark head back onto Cendrine's couch cushion and closed her eyes. A swathe of silver bangs fell over one eye and she pushed it away with a brush of her wrist. As she listened to the tiny gulping sounds that Lulu made when she swallowed her mother's milk, she thought her heart could not expand with an ounce more of emotion. Jules' last kiss was still warm on her lips and her body quivered. Flashbacks pummeled her mind and she couldn't stop the tiny smile from spreading across her lips.

Cendrine scrutinized Callie's face. She shifted to a safer topic. "Are Spanish lessons helping you, Callie?"

Callie heard the laughter in Cendrine's voice and her eyes popped open. Pulling her thoughts away from bedroom memories, she rolled her eyes. "*Hablar Español es muy difícil.*" To speak Spanish is very difficult.

When Cendrine clapped her hands with delight, Lulu nearly rolled off Callie's lap. Her mouth formed an O as she moved the swaddled infant to her mother's breast. The tiny mouth latched onto the nipple and both women laughed in wonderment.

"You speak Spanish! *Viola!* What is your plan now, Callie? Olivier tells me the solicitor in Fuengirola has the papers ready for you, but you will stay a few days here first, *oui*?" She slipped one finger across her daughter's soft cheek and then ran it through her dark hair as it lay near her ear. The child was focused and her eyes started to drop like a curtain and then pop open for a second and then down again.

Callie's lips quivered before she gave her niece a tremulous smile. She covered Cendrine's hand with her own where Cendrine hugged her child. "You couldn't pull me away from here with a ten-foot pole, *ma chère*. This dream of Picasso's has waited many years. It can wait a little longer. I had hoped to speak better Spanish before I arrived in Algodonales. Jules promised to help me, but he's been away from his computer business for nearly two weeks and I know he will be busy with the catch up. He could find a Spanish tutor for me if I wanted one. But I am going to go just as I am. And then…"

"…And then you go to Spain? Olivier is very happy you are willing to do this. It has been filling his head for weeks thinking about helping his father fulfill Picasso's dream. It is still so hard for us to believe they were friends. When I think of all those brandy bottles…"

Callie shook her head at the enormity of the job she'd set for herself. "The bottles must be sold first, *ma chère*, or we will not have the money to follow Picasso's wishes." She pursed her lips. "And now there are men who think the brandy money should be theirs…" Callie took a deep breath and blew it out slowly. She fought the heaviness that had invaded her senses ever since she'd learned about the men trying to stand in the way of the guitar school. Shuddering, she shook her head slowly and licked her lips.

"Olivier is worried about you. These men read about the brandy bottles and your plan to sell them for Picasso's music school. They think we are stealing from their family." Cendrine's face was mottled with frustration.

"I have been speaking with the people at *Guitarras Valeriano Bernal*. They will help me. That family's attorney showed them a copy of Picasso's letter. He told Olivier that the men steamed out of his office afterward, very angry. I doubt we've heard the last of them."

"Oh, Callie. This project sounded perfect when we read Pablo Picasso's letter and we knew the brandy bottles could make a difference. But, now with these Spaniards pushing their way into the equation, it has become so complicated and a little frightening. Maybe you should...."

"I am going. Over the past year, I have allowed people to push me around. These Spaniard brothers are wrong. Picasso's word stands. The attorney in Fuengirola seems to think we have a very strong case to move forward. And I want to create that guitar commune in that little village in the mountains. I have already rented a lovely apartment in Algodonales called Casa Baraka. I am told it's near the main square of the village by a massive church...and an easy walk to the flamenco guitar shop." She dropped her folded hands in her lap as if to put a period on the end of her sentence. Her eyes bored into Cendrine's and her lips pursed together tightly.

Cendrine's face changed from interest to impishness. "And you will marry Jules before or after you return from Algodonales?" Her eyes challenged her aunt for an answer again.

Callie raised an eyebrow. "Tell me about your cousin, Veronique, and her interior design shop. And I will tell you about Lily in America. I can help you prepare the downstairs bedroom for her arrival. She's anxious to meet you and anxious to learn how to make wine." Callie was quiet before murmuring, "She's had a rough time."

"When can we get her here?"

"Not until the middle of August. Her mother is still trying to get adjusted to the idea of her daughter spending her last year of high school in France. "You are sure that Lulu won't keep you from working with her?"

"Always room for one more, Callie. This little girl will fit into that snuggly thing *grandmére* gave me. I won't slow down. You know me. Wine is my middle name. Sparkling wine is part of my DNA. It is amazing how much this industry touches me. If I can be a part of Lily's passion to make wine, I will share my own with her and we will make it happen. I know you have a special interest in this girl. When you told me how her uncle abused her, my heart cried. Maybe one day you will tell me why this girl matters so much to you."

Callie blinked at her niece's canny perception.

"I know there is a story there, auntie." Cendrine face stilled.

"Yes, there is. One day I will tell you when it's quiet and we've finished drinking one of your *Chloe Rosé* bottles." Callie's eyes brimmed with tears and she gave a sad chuckle.

Cendrine didn't question her further.

"Sometimes there are secrets we hold inside that are better kept there, deep inside where no light can touch it. I was able to stretch my head around my own troubled past by helping Lily with hers. She is a good girl and her mother is very sweet. I am anxious for you to meet her." Callie's eyes cleared and she patted the blanket folds around Lulu.

Cendrine tucked the yellow blanket around her tiny daughter and then lifted her eyes to her aunt. "And I can hardly wait to mentor her with my wine-making skills. Between me and Papa, I think we can make that young lady a winemaker."

Callie's face clouded for a moment before nodding. "But first, the brandy. The flamenco guitars. Lily. And Jules."

TWO

Two hours earlier, Callinda Beauvais and Jules Armand had flown into Aix en Provence, France from Oregon. Driving to Pertuis felt like a dream. She was anxious to return to the village where she'd lived with her late husband, Francois Beauvais, where they had renovated a large, old mill house to make it their own. They had eventually added a guest cottage apart from the big house. Now that cottage would be her new home.

She was in France again, home at last. She'd left behind her friends, her American memories with Francois and a few pieces of her heart. She'd brought fresh dreams across the ocean. And now she sat beside Jules, a man she had not known well until a few months ago. He had wrapped up her heart like a tidy gift, a *regalo*. She laughed as she realized she was beginning to think in Spanish.

Jules looked at her when he heard her chuckle. "What?"

She lifted her hand to squeeze his arm. "We are coming home."

He placed his hand over hers and smiled warmly. "*Oui.*"

When his eyes returned to the winding road that would take them from Aix to Pertuis, Callie's mind had wandered again. She knew that her life would be very different now. She would miss friends in Oregon. She had WhatsApp on her smart phone. She could call Livvy, her best friend. That is, once she got the time difference worked out in her head. She'd already sold one of her houses and hoped her beach house would sell soon. She had a deposit slip in her purse from both estate sales. Her boxes would arrive in a few weeks filled with everything she refused to leave behind.

"What's going on in that pretty head of yours, *ma chère?*" Jules chuckled. A car passed them. The countryside was aflame with wild flowers and there seemed to be magic in the air.

FLAMENCO STRINGS UNCORKED

"Just thinking...and planning...and...."

Jules laughed out loud and eased his foot off the gas pedal as he made another sharp turn toward the Beauvais Vineyard. His dark hair was laced with silver and his strong jaw was tight with thoughts of his own. He drove on quietly. Callie knew his office manager had been running the business during Jules' absence. She also knew Jules was clearly anxious to get back to his computers so he could relieve his manager.

Callie looked down at the tightly clasped hands in her lap. She wore one ring on her right hand, a gift from Francois on their twentieth anniversary. She touched the onyx stone with a finger and felt the tears well up in her chest. They had been happy and when he died, she had been devastated, never imagining she could love again. She turned to look at Jules' profile. Warmth filled her from the inside out. She loved him. So, why was she questioning herself? He was charming, beautiful, kind, and funny. He made her laugh. He was quick witted and she hadn't felt such peace in a long time.

Before he arrived in Oregon to spirit her away a few days earlier, she'd learned the greatest, most important thing about herself. She knew who she was and that she was quite capable of being independent. She had the freedom to do exactly as she pleased. But despite the fact that he made her feel shiny new again, she needed to put her mind in order. She'd finally come to terms with Francois being murdered, but it hadn't been easy. His killer was in prison. That thought gave her a bittersweet jolt of happiness. But Francois was still dead.

When the car jerked to a sudden stop, Callie was thrown forward and Jules' arm automatically pulled her back. The French oath he whispered surprised her. He looked at her apologetically, shook his hand at the rude motorist, who had stopped in the roadway without alert blinkers, and swerved past him.

"I am sorry, *ma chère*. I should have pushed him into that ditch. Maybe I should go back and do that, but not today." He pushed the gear shift into second and the engine whined before it got to third. His lips strained against his teeth.

Callie laughed. "Thank you for that, Jules."

He chuckled, his mood reverting back to normal.

"I will need to leave immediately after taking you home, this is alright? Claude needs me at the offices and..."

"But, of course! I have a baby to meet, hugs waiting and plans to make." The air in the car seemed to swoosh around them.

"And the biggest plan is to set a date for our wedding?" He whispered the question.

Callie's heart stilled. "*Sí, señor.*"

He laughed and patted her knee where black, gray and white leggings molded her legs. The long black tunic fell in folds past her thighs and her shiny black ring glittered in the sunshine.

"*Bon.* Olivier will show us the newspaper article tonight at dinner about the vineyard people in Spain hoping to cash in on the brandy. Is that why you've been so quiet since we got off the plane?"

She turned toward him. "No. My mind is whirling about many things, Jules. That is just one of them. These descendants were not part of the flight to smuggle Picasso's brandy bottles to France. Some people may have died in the process. These men are distant relatives of Picasso's partner, not beneficiaries of his will. They can't stop us...can they?" Her voice wavered only a heartbeat before she answered her own question. "No, they cannot."

Jules smiled. "That's my girl."

French sweet music filtered through the car's stereo and Monet-like vistas outside Callie's window returned her heartbeat to a crawl. She laid her head back on the seat and closed her eyes. Touching French soil had always filled her with peace. This time she was moving home again. Why wasn't the expected peace finding its way into her mind? Why was she questioning her feelings for Jules now? Maybe she wasn't ready to give up her independence? Or did she want to live in pause position until her Spanish adventure ended?

She heard flamenco guitar music in her head and realized how anxious she was to get to the little village. She'd only seen photographs of Algodonales on the internet and then she had rented the little apartment. Her Spanish dictionary was stowed in her bag. The Spanish translation APP on her phone was accessible off line and Spanish words fluttered around in her head like jumping beans. She took a deep breath. Her gypsy blood was thrumming and just maybe this one last adventure would put things right again. Until then, she had a new baby to meet.

Jules' tires crunched over the loose gravel beneath the arched stone entrance to Beauvais Vineyard. She glanced up and smiled, waiting for the cottage to come into view. They passed several large trees and the mill house that she and Francois had refurbished years earlier. The vista of bright, early blooms flew past her window in a blur. The sky was blue, welcoming. It was spring and her life felt brand new.

Callie lifted a finger to blot the puddle that filled her eyes. The sweet connection moved over her like a tornado. She felt disembodied, caught between the far past and the near future.

And there it was.

The house.

The cottage.

Home at last.

Suddenly, she felt calmer than she had in many days.

THREE

Anticipation hung in the air a few hours later when Callie walked into the mill house with Jules. Olivier greeted her with kisses on both cheeks. She shared a startled look with Jules, when Olivier immediately thrust a crinkling newspaper into her hands. The Olive Press headline from Fuengirola, Spain stared back at her, outlined in bright red ink. "Picasso's Aged Brandy Found in France."

"Mateo Rosa Trascasas sent this to me a few days ago. I am glad his law firm is handling the paperwork for the foundation, Callie. He said these men do not merit part of the cash from the brandy sale." Olivier dropped onto the couch beside her.

Jules sat next to Callie's chair to read the article over her shoulder.

Callie's breath hitched a moment before she read the words aloud, "The great-grandsons of Jose Luis Alonzo Mesa learned recently that bottles of brandy from the now-defunct *Colinas Ocultos Vineyard*, are to be sold by a foundation purportedly based on a letter left by Pablo Ruiz Picasso years ago. The brothers, Eterio and Ruben Alonzo Fernandez, say the proceeds should be theirs. They admit they were unaware of the existence of this brandy until the story came to them through their friend, Demetrio Martin Salas, from Jerez. It was mentioned that the label showed a Spanish señorita riding a cork like an American bucking bronco. An unknown French woman is involved in the complicated arrangements. The Alonzo brothers do not know who she is or why she is part of this foundation."

Cendrine walked into the room. Lulu's face was buried into her neck, sound asleep. Three sets of eyes turned toward her.

"What?" Her eyes shifted between Callie and Olivier as she pushed golden-blonde hair from her eyes with a free hand.

Olivier's eyes nodded toward the newspaper in Callie's fist.

"Oh." Cendrine frowned and raised her eyebrows.

"How could this have happened? Before we've even begun, it's blasted across the news." Callie shook her head as she traced the words on the paper with her finger. When Jules squeezed her shoulder gently, she lay her cheek over his hand before clenching the paper again.

"There's more, Callie. I didn't want to tell you until you arrived…" Olivier shook his head at them.

Wary, she lowered her head and shook it slowly as if to say, what else?

"These Alonzo brothers want to sue the foundation for the money once the bottles are sold. Their attorney contacted Mateo two days ago. He told me they should have no rights to the money because of Picasso's letter. I believe him. But, when the brothers find out they will receive nothing, they'll probably fight you."

Callie's face cleared and she smiled with the face of a rebel. "And I will be ready for them."

"Alone?" Jules voice sounded like steel.

Callie didn't answer him, but instead, raised an eyebrow.

Jules cleared his throat. "I can't worry for your safety, *chère?*"

The room grew quiet as her eyes swung toward him. "Of course you can. But right now my concern is getting to Algodonales and preparing for the music colony. After the bottles are sold you can worry about me. *Oui?*"

A look of impatience crossed his face for an instant before he sighed heavily. "So, it sounds like our wedding will not take place until after the big Spanish plan?"

Callie looked at him beneath lowered lashes and bit her lip. "Yes, I think that is best. There is so much to do there and I want our special day to be clear of all the complications that lay ahead."

Cendrine and Olivier exchanged a look at the same time Lulu began to whimper and the spell was broken.

The room was warm and seemed to spin around her. Jules' fingers lay on her arm. She'd promised to marry him after they returned to France. Where had this uncertainty come from? She'd hurt his feelings, felt it through her body like a burning coal. But when her truth meter had peppered her with questions, she had listened.

When Cendrine snuggled Lulu into her bassinet, she hastened into the kitchen to finish preparations for dinner. Jules and Olivier walked outside, leaving Callie alone where the warm room engulfed her and tossed the complicated worry game inside her head.

She'd fallen in love with Jules several months earlier, when she'd finally accepted that Francois' was dead and buried physically and mentally for her. Jules had been Francois' best friend and the sweet connection wasn't lost on either of them.

Now, learning that Francois had been murdered, after receiving a letter from Jules' attorney, had changed something inside of her. She knew Jules hadn't approved it. And she wasn't being fair to him. But a bit of numbness had crept into their relationship.

Callie rubbed her eyes, daring them to seep tears. She had enough of tears. Her husband's killer was behind bars. She had sold the house and left tangible assets behind her. Why then, was she carrying this ball of sadness around with her and blaming Jules for her distress? She'd erased the anger that had engulfed her over Veronique, the daughter Francois hid from Callie for twenty years. She was enchanted with the girl. It was her mother, Jules' sister who'd sent Francois the letter. Aurore, the attorney. Why couldn't she forgive Jules? What did she have to forgive him for? He was everything to her, but...

Callie slipped out the side door toward her cottage. She needed a little time away from everyone. The air was sweet with fragrance.

FLAMENCO STRINGS UNCORKED

She walked slowly, stopping every now and then to sniff the scented blooms. Once inside, she turned to stare out the windows into her flowering gardens. Spring was upon them, the vineyard had fledgling green shoots across the way. She squeezed her eyes shut against the hot tears that promised to puddle and cascade down her cheeks. Sniffing loudly, she slipped inside the house and turned to press her back against the kitchen wall. Her eyes fell on the bottle sitting on her counter. The Spanish *señorita* had flowing black hair as she rode a cork across the label. Callie's breath caught. Those bottles started her life rolling down a long hill filled with adventure a few weeks earlier. Now her pace was increasing at breakneck speed. And those bottles had given her Jules.

She loved Jules, dammit. Then, why??

When she saw him walking toward her through the window, she felt a knot of desire, complicating her thoughts. When he looked up and smiled at her, she went weak inside. When he walked into the door and held her close to his chest, a whimper stumbled out of her when he kissed the top of her head.

"Dinner, sweetheart. Do not over think this. Let's take one day at a time, *oui*? Baby steps." He gave her a smile of surpassing sweetness and she was sure she'd never loved him quite as much as she did that moment.

Arm in arm, they walked back to the mill house. Once inside, they were nearly knocked over by Francois and Bernadette's small hugs. Their squeals of laughter neutralized her melancholy and she melded into the craziness of family life again.

Dinner aromas teased her taste buds. Cendrine's father, Andre, grinned at her with two bottles of his new wine in each hand.

After more hugs and cheek kisses, she was enchanted before the food was on the table. She would think about the crazy Spaniards and Picasso's dream later. For now, she would enjoy the moment.

FOUR

In Spain, a leather bag was slung over his shoulder as Mateo Rosa Trascasas walked past the Mercadona Market and took the steps two at a time into the abyss of the Fuengirola train station. He lifted the cuff on his shirtsleeve to reveal his sports watch. Despite being ten minutes late, he knew Gérman would wait. Sure enough, the smiling young man stood inside the entrance as he'd expected. After a swift exchange of papers two minutes later, Mateo retraced his steps back onto the street and found his car parked along the motorbikes just outside the door.

Within minutes, the attorney was on his way toward Jerez, a two hour drive westward. He'd been jerked into irritability earlier that morning with a phone call from the Alonzo brothers' attorney and he wanted to put an end to their suit against the Jose Luis Alonzo Foundation. A phone call or email wouldn't satisfy Mateo. He wanted to look into their faces and put Olivier's fear for Ms. Beauvais to rest.

Once he was on the A-7, his fingers loosened on the steering wheel. He drove along the jagged Mediterranean coast past Miraflores, Cala de Mijas, Calahonda and then he saw signs to Marbella. The Mediterranean Sea sparkled like diamonds as the sun shone into its turquoise depths. He adjusted the volume on the radio. His body relaxed when *Cuando Calienta el Sol* played through the speaker; he sang along with the singer and smiled.

He prepared his conversation while traffic zoomed past him. These people wanted the proceeds from the brandy bottles they didn't deserve. Their ancestor's vineyard was no longer in business and they weren't part of that either. His mind reached for possibilities, wondering who leaked this story to Señor Martin in Jerez. The only

FLAMENCO STRINGS UNCORKED

people who knew about the bottles were Olivier and his family, the woman, Callinda Beauvais, and the prospective buyers. Mateo shook his head. They wouldn't want anyone to know because of the competition. There must be someone else who wanted to interfere. His eyes zeroed in on the turnoff northward toward Seville. Or did the buyers hope to cause a complication? His eyes narrowed.

He took the exit to Jerez de Sur and wound his way up the mountain road going straight at each roundabout. His GPS led him to the Alcazar District. Parking next to the Casa Grande Hotel near the square, he grabbed his leather satchel. The massive eagle that stood watch on a tall column greeted him. Squaring his shoulders, he walked in the direction of the *plaza mayor* where he'd agreed to meet the men's attorney, Cristóbal Navas Garcia. When he passed a small bar on the left, he promised himself to stop for a sherry afterward. He'd probably need one.

Mateo lifted his face to the warm sun. When he reached the square, he found the restaurant easily. The tables and chairs were strewn across a patio of *El Chicarrón* like drunkards looking for a stool. The *Plaza Arenal* was a flurry of activity. Tourists walked in and out of shops while others licked dripping ice cream cones at the *heladería* (ice cream shop) across the way. He glanced around. A man in a silver-toned suit beckoned toward him with a lift of his hand.

"Mateo?" The older man's hooded eyes looked sympathetic.

"*Sí*. Cristóbal?" Mateo dropped into the chair next to the man and ordered a *café con leche* before placing his leather satchel on the table near his right hand.

They talked about everything but the reason they were meeting in the square while they drank their coffees, as is the way of the Spaniards. Time was stretchy there and he knew he'd probably spend part of the day. He glanced around, wondering where the great grandsons were lurking. Surely he would talk with them before he returned to Fuengirola.

FLAMENCO STRINGS UNCORKED

When he finished his coffee, the attorney opened their conversation. "Thank you for taking my call seriously this morning." He pulled a piece of paper from his inside vest pocket and laid it on the table. Pressing his fingers over it to smooth it out, he looked up as if he had all the answers.

Mateo was amused. Without a word, he lifted the flap on his satchel. Mirroring the man's movements, he placed his own papers beside the lawyer's and stared at the man. "It seems we have a complication. I want to take care of it immediately so my client can get back to his business."

"His business includes my clients, *señor*."

"No, it does not. The Alonzo brothers should not be involved with this situation." When he saw Cristóbal twist his lips in disagreement, he hurried on, "These men are not linked with the *Colinas Ocultos Vineyard*. Picasso owned the defunct vineyard with Jose Luis Alonzo Mesa. I did some checking and learned that these men are the grandsons only by marriage. They are not blood relatives."

Cristóbal touched the table with two fingers. While barely containing his impatience, his face showed surprise.

Mateo had counted on that and said nothing.

"But they *are* great grandsons of Jose Luis Alonzo and they *should* be part of the sale from these valuable brandy bottles. I looked at the records for the vineyard and the winery. The partnership was never dissolved. Picasso was in France permanently after 1905. The vineyard and winery was created in 1911, so I surmise he and Alonzo were friends...a friend who needed help. Picasso was a poor painter, so there couldn't have been much of a monetary exchange. The papers show money was given to Alonzo in pieces over the years. I looked further, but I could not find anything." The man's fingers gripped the piece of paper as he spoke.

Mateo pressed his lips together before dropping his bombshell. "Picasso and Alonzo were cousins. They'd always been interested in grapes, vines, and wines. They hoped to farm the grapes even though Picasso's first love was painting. So, if your boys think they should get the money from these mysterious bottles, they should be aware of Picasso's descendants. If they pursue this, they would have nothing. Picasso wanted the money to open an art colony in Alonzo's home village to help poor kids learn to play the guitar. It's a noble dream. What would your boys do with the money?"

Cristóbal Navas squinted his eyes in the bright sun even though the umbrella partially shaded his face. "Cousins? That changes things."

"When will I meet these brothers?" Mateo shifted in his chair.

"They are sitting at the table across the courtyard right now. Shall I bring them over to talk with you? The older one is hot headed. The younger one is a follower."

"Do you think they will listen?"

"Probably not."

Mateo turned slightly when the man nodded his head toward two men at the far end of the square. They looked ready to move toward the *El Chicarrón* restaurant. He couldn't see their faces clearly because of the bright sun, but he couldn't miss their aggressive postures. The crowd surged forward and he lost the line of sight. When the area cleared, the table sat empty. He turned toward Cristóbal with a question on his face.

"I don't think you have seen the last of them. They are furious. They think this is family money. I'm not sure if their *bodega* bar is suffering or if it's just the principle of the thing to have money from the old vineyard that they can't touch."

"So, you believe they will continue to harass the foundation?"

"*Sí.*" Cristóbal reached a hand to shake Mateo's. "I believe Picasso's dream is a good one. I would like to see it happen as he hoped, but as you know, an attorney acts for his clients. I did my best. Personally, I agree with the woman trying to make this a reality."

The men stood up, shook hands again and nodded goodbye.

Mateo headed back the way he came, with an eye out for the Alonzo brothers. When it was clear they were avoiding him, he detoured over to the bars he'd passed on his way to the square. The *Bar Corredera* was empty, but the *Abaceria Tio Peña*, next door, was alive with music and a group surrounding the entrance.

A woman with a red, fringed shawl covering her shoulders tapped out a flamenco dance on the tiles. Her toe-heel clicking steps were accentuated with the toss of her head and the sharp swing of her arms. She reached her hand upward and twisted her fingers as if plucking an apple from a tree. He grinned. And then she brought her hand down in a sensuous gesture to her mouth as if eating the dripping fruit. Her fingers danced continually.

Three men clapped in the cadence, called *palmas*, used for this type of dance and everyone whispered, "*Olé.*" Mateo watched her move sensuously as she stomped her feet, making her own music. When everyone clapped, he saw her blush.

His day felt complete when he lifted the small glass of *fine* to his lips. The taste of the golden colored sherry was pleasant while he shared a smile with the woman. He reached for a plump green olive.

Her eyes lingered on him. While her feet tapped against the tiles, she swept her arms up and over her dark head, beating out a sensuous tempo as her hair flew around her serious face.

Mateo sipped more sherry and tracked her with his eyes. She seemed to glow as she swirled around the small area. While the men clapped, her eyes rested on Mateo's face, clearly interested.

After a small nod, he set down his empty glass and left the group. Mateo's heart was still too sad to look at women, even when they were as sensuous as this one. He bowed his head as he walked to his car. One day, he would surely get his mind right again.

FLAMENCO STRINGS UNCORKED

Three hours later, Olivier's phone rang. When Cendrine heard him laugh, she jerked and Lulu's mouth became unlatched from her nipple. Bernadette giggled when she heard the popping sound and saw Lulu's eyes blink open with surprise. The little girl had been sitting next to her mother, thoroughly enthralled with the view of her baby sister suckling her mother's milk.

Olivier was still chuckling when he joined his family in the salon. His thick hair fell over his forehead when he sat down on the couch across from his wife. Rubbing his fingers over his face, he scratched his chin and ran his hands through his red hair. He chuckled again.

"What?" She gently guided Lulu's mouth back to her milk. Running her hand softly over her older daughter's head beside her, she smoothed the fine strands of hair behind her ear. The baby had her fist wrapped around Cendrine's smallest finger so tightly it was nearly numb. Suckling sounds filled the room.

"Mateo said he told the other attorney that the Alonzo brothers should drop their interest against the foundation because they would not receive much money." He dropped his mobile phone on the table and turned toward his wife. His eyes blinked back more laughter.

Her eyebrows nearly met in the center, clearly interested in what could be so funny when this was such a serious issue.

"Pablo Picasso and Jose Luis Alonzo were cousins. He told him about the other Picasso descendants who would try to get the money from the brandy bottle sale if they pursued it."

Cendrine's eyebrows shot up. "They were cousins?"

"No, that's why I laughed. It is a possibility only. Their attorney believed him. The man also told Mateo he hoped the guitar school flourishes and Picasso's dream becomes a reality. But even though he's happy about the guitar school, he also said he was sure the Alonzo brothers won't give up easily."

The young couple shared a look.

"I don't like the last part. Callie will be in Spain alone." Cendrine hugged her infant daughter to her chest and gazed toward her husband. Bernadette tapped her feet against the edge of the couch, her eyes still on her baby sister's lips.

"She will meet with Mateo before she goes to Algodonales. He will go over everything with her and I know he will watch over her. I'm more nervous that Callie does not seem to be taking the warning seriously. Has she always been so headstrong?" He twisted his lips with vexation and took a deep breath.

Cendrine laughed. "She has always had the spirit of a dragon. So, your answer is yes."

"Well, these men might be more than a dragon can handle."

Lulu nuzzled her breast again. Bernadette watched the baby with fascination. Francois, on the other hand, drove his truck across the floor, oblivious to the workings of babies and how his mother fed them. His voice hummed as his truck sped along the ceramic tiles.

When he came close to the couch, he drove it up Bernadette's leg, who squealed and pushed it out of his hand. He scowled at her and picked it up again, teasing her with hand motions. She pulled her legs up beneath her and he swooped away in the other direction.

"I hope you're wrong, Olivier. No matter how important this flamenco guitar school is, Callie is more important." Cendrine's arms circled her baby in a protective gesture and her face clenched.

"Yes, me too, *chère*." He smiled as his wife nursed his new daughter. Their family life had changed rapidly over the past months. Worrying about Callie added a complication, but she seemed ferocious in her new role of trustee for the estate. She was learning Spanish and was adamant to cement Picasso's dream.

"Will anything stop her from bulldozing her way forward?" Olivier sounded conflicted with the decision he'd made weeks earlier when he asked Callie to go to Spain.

"She has Jules even though the wedding is on hold. He won't let anything happen to her." The baby whimpered and she pulled her close.

"Well, she'll be in Spain. He'll be in France, not somewhere beside her. And she wants to do this alone. That worries me too."

Olivier whistled through his teeth and shook his burnished red head. "I hope she can do this without putting herself in danger..."

Five

"I thought you were going to fly directly to Malaga."

Callie heard the expected frustration in Jules' voice. She bit her lip. Her journal pages held detailed travel information. She'd researched the miles, Airbnb rentals, contacted Fernando in Malaga and set the date to meet Darla Ruiz. Now, she had to convince Jules. She turned toward him and handed him the book in her hand.

He stared between the journal and her face, poured some red wine into stemmed glasses and sat down next to her. Sighing noisily, he raised an eyebrow in her direction and opened her small book.

She watched him turn each page, knowing he would read every word. Callie knew he wouldn't like her driving over the mountains from France into Spain without him. However, she was looking forward to the silent trek on her own. She wanted to listen to her music and concentrate on the job ahead of her, not their relationship. But she also wanted his approval because it was important to her.

"So, it appears you have prepared your journey…" He lifted his glass. "…without me."

She looked at him over the rim of her glass and took a sip. "Jules, I have been thinking about it for a while. I know you can't leave your business and I have people along the way who can help me if I have a problem. And remember, I'm a white belt in Tae Kwon Do."

He laughed indulgently. "Uh-huh."

She took another sip of wine. "It's only five hours from Pertuis to Barcelona. I've reserved an Airbnb near *Las Ramblas* and *Plaza Catalunya*. I might spend a day there before going onto Cartagena, which is only six and a half hours away. I have a friend there who has invited me…well, I invited myself to stay with him and his wife. He tells me the fish in the port town is the best and wants me to try *boquerones en vinagre*. That's anchovies in vinegar," she said proudly.

He didn't comment, but pointed to a scribbled map on the page.

"From there it's only four hours to Malaga. I'm eating *la comida* (dinner) with Fernando Sanchez and Crescéncia at two o'clock. And then Darla is meeting me afterward. I'll follow her to the round house her father built many years ago in a small village not far from there."

"How long have you been planning this big road trip on your own?" A muscle jumped below his ear and his gray eyes turned dark.

Callie sighed and blushed. "After Olivier asked me to be the foundation's trustee, I thought about it. When I was in America getting the houses ready to sell, the plan seemed to bloom and came together one piece at a time. Darla told me about renting an Airbnb in Barcelona instead of a hotel, so I did it."

"Without me." He said again, clearly upset.

Callie placed her wine glass on the wicker coffee table and reached for his glass. When she'd placed it next to her own, she turned into his arms and he automatically embraced her. "Jules. You know I am hard headed. You know I'm independent. And you know that I love you. This is an exciting adventure. After jumping off the emotional roller coaster at the beach when we learned Francois was killed... I need this."

He groaned into her hair.

She smiled against his chest.

Sitting up again, he wrapped two fingers around the stem of his glass and handed her the other one with a big sigh. "Tell me about your friend, Darla."

"Darla Ruiz Molina and I have known each other since high school. She wasn't raised with her Spanish father because her parents divorced when she was young. He left California to live his dream in Spain where his parents had immigrated to America in the early 1900s. He built a two-story round house she calls *la casa redonda*. He begged her to visit, but she never found the time or she didn't make the time. Then, he died. An English woman bought the house. Now it's a B & B. Darla met her a few years ago and they became good friends. She wants me to spend time with her at *la casa redonda* before I go to Fuengirola. I couldn't say no." Callie looked at him through her eyelashes trying to gauge his reaction.

"That's several days away. And then, what's your plan afterward?"

He was thawing out, but she had another hurdle to jump over. "And then I meet Mateo Rosa in Fuengirola. From there, it is a short drive to Algodonales, which is just beyond Ronda, where people were thrown off a cliff in Ernest Hemingway's book, *For Whom the Bell Tolls*."

Jules whistled between his teeth. "I've heard of Ronda. There's a military base there in the mountains. Are you going to stay there?"

She counted to three. "I've rented an apartment in Algodonales for a month, Jules."

He choked on his wine and sputtered, "What?!"

Her fingers rubbed against his muscled thigh. "Jules, I can't drive into the village, meet people at the guitar shop and then leave immediately. You and I talked about this. A place needs to be leased. A guitar teacher must be hired. And then there's the marketing to advertise the music school. I will need someone to filter the applications." She lifted her empty glass toward him.

Jules took both glasses into the kitchen. She watched him stare out the window for a moment. He filled both glasses and then he turned toward her. His eyes crinkled with a reluctant bubble of amusement.

"So, my darling, when do you leave?"

She grinned mischievously at him. "In four days."

"Four days. Okay then. Drink your wine. We have a lot of cuddling to do between now and Monday. His voice turned amorous and his eyes made promises she was instantly ready to explore. She licked the rim of her glass to catch the red drop that slipped down one side. And when he took the empty glass from her fingers, she raised them toward his hair. When she was pulled into his arms, her last thoughts were simple. She'd worry about all the other stuff later. For now, this was exactly where she wanted to be.

~

The next few days flew by. She packed a bag and stuffed a swimsuit and sunscreen inside at the last minute. It would soon be hot in Spain. Her passport was tucked into her red purse and an extra pair of sunglasses were in the glovebox of her car. She wanted to have all that ready so she could spread herself thin between Cendrine and the children, Lulu, her in-laws and of course, Jules.

Saturday night, she and Jules drove to their favorite restaurant, *Gadoline's*. Veronique hadn't arrived yet. Callie was anxious to see her step-daughter and wanted to hear about her buying trip in Paris. Once inside, soft music lulled them into a romantic pause as a full moon shone into the window and bathed them with enchantment.

Several moments later, Veronique leaned toward them. "Ah, the lovebirds have returned." Her voice was laced with laughter. The candlelight bathed the young woman's face in a healthy glow and her eyes glistened.

Jules and Callie lifted their faces to receive her hugs and kisses on each cheek. Jules' niece was more beautiful than Callie remembered. Her honey-colored hair flowed past her shoulders and the white leggings were blinding against the lime green and yellow tunic that flowed around her slim hips.

"You look like a breath of spring, my darling." Callie pulled her down beside them. She squeezed her hands and lifted them to her lips for another quick kiss.

FLAMENCO STRINGS UNCORKED

"And you two look like you are ready for a bridal magazine. When? When?" Veronique's eyes moved from one to the other.

Jules' eyes swung toward Callie.

Callie's eyes smiled, but she didn't answer.

Veronique looked at Callie first. "Well... you know the wedding reception must be in my shop, *oui*?"

Everyone relaxed.

Candlelight swathed Veronique's round face softly and shadowed Callie's jaw. Music played low, just loud enough to know it was there, to enjoy, but not loud enough to blot out conversations.

Jules reached across the table to hold his niece's hand. "You, *ma chère*, have our word."

Callie put an arm around her shoulder. "I've missed you."

Veronique looked at each of them in turn. "Okay, please tell me what is happening. And I'll tell you about Paris. And then let's eat. I am starving."

The waiter brought a bottle of red wine to the table with three crystal glasses. After he placed menus in front of them, he filled their glasses. While sipping their wine and in between lots of laughter, Callie's adventure was outlined for Veronique.

"And then I will go to Malaga and swim at midnight in the pool on a hill in the village called Los Nuñez. My friend has bragged about doing that for weeks. I'm anxious to meet Elvira Smiffy and live among the Spanish, although this woman is English. Darla told me she uses many English words she doesn't understand. And that I will love it all."

"Swimming at midnight?" Jules raised his eyebrows. She knew where his mind was going and he chuckled when he saw the look on Callie's face.

Veronique clapped her hands with delight. "I knew you were going to do this, Callie, but I didn't know you would be leaving so soon. I guess the sooner you go, the sooner you will return to us, *oui*?"

FLAMENCO STRINGS UNCORKED

"That's one way to look at it," Jules drawled.

Over dinner, her potatoes grew cold and she shuffled the pork medallions around on her plate with an idle fork. Callie watched Veronique's animated face as she talked with Jules. The girl was so much like Francois. If he had trusted Callie's love, they would have been able to share this girl before he died. A burst of anger clung to her throat before she could tuck it down again. She loved Veronique. That was the important thing. She'd answer her questions about her father and be a surrogate parent. It would have to be enough.

Hopefully, Aurore, would allow it. Always hopeful, Callie remembered the tentative camaraderie they'd shared at the opening of her daughter's shop, Hybrid Designs, a month earlier. Callie took a deep breath inside her mind. She knew she'd have to work on that one.

~

Sunday afternoon, the entire family gathered at the manse at Beauvais Vineyard. Janine Beauvais yanked open the door. As soon as Callie was within reach, she hugged her so hard, her bones hurt. The older woman's softness and warmth made her feel steadier on her feet.

When Janine turned toward her infant granddaughter, she folded Lulu close to her chest. The baby immediately snuggled into the folds of Janine's apron and started rooting for her breast. Everyone laughed and the house settled into contentment.

Olivier and Jules walked toward Michel, who appeared pale and did not rise from his easy chair. They shook his hand and sat down.

The old man's eyes followed Janine. And then his lips stretched into a smile when she brought him the infant. Janine leaned down toward her husband and placed the sweet-smelling baby on his lap.

Old, gnarled fingers gently rolled over the swaddled child and he laughed when Lulu stared at him and made a gurgling sound.

Callie noticed he was paler now than before she'd flown to America. Something wasn't right. She noticed how carefully Janine handed him the child. Her elbows bent and her face was taut as if she fought against tears. Callie swallowed and turned toward Cendrine with a question on her face. Cendrine closed her eyes and nodded slightly, before swinging her eyes back to her grandmother.

Callie watched the way Michel held the baby. She wasn't imagining it; he held Lulu aloft, away from his belly and instead, gingerly held her head and body across his lap. His fingers caressed the tiny bundle while his eyes glistened with unshed tears. Callie took a deep breath and looked across the room to find Janine staring at her. The women shared a significant look before her mother-in-law turned away and reached a wrinkled hand to push hair from her face.

Little Francois and Bernadette pulled out their toy basket and the adults sat in the large salon. Andre, Cendrine's father, wandered in a few minutes later with his hat in his hand. His eyes swung to the baby and a smile slid across his features. He seemed to be counting the minutes, waiting his turn to hold his new granddaughter.

Callie thought that Andre had changed since Olivier had been abducted a few months earlier. He seemed more humble and spent more time with his family. He didn't hide his feelings in a corner of his heart as he had done for years. He laughed now when before, he had only smiled. Family seemed more important to him. No, Callie thought. It wasn't more important. Family had always been important. Andre knew if he didn't embrace his family, they could disappear at any moment. Like his wife and son. And now with Lulu in their lives, it was more central than ever before. She felt her heart flutter against her tunic and brought a hand up to hold it still. So many changes were happening for everyone. And now Michel was...?

"Callie, how is your Spanish coming along?" Andre's eyes crinkled in his tanned face. He'd watched her struggle with French when she'd married Francois years earlier. In fact, he'd helped her stumble through the language. He grinned at her.

Callie gave an embarrassed chuckle before glancing around the room. She saw Janine walking toward them. Love permeated the manse from every corner and she was too hampered by emotion to answer his question.

Janine pulled Callie into the large kitchen and nodded toward the tray. Two chilled bottles of *Chloe Rosé* sparkling wine were ready to pour. Callie picked up the accompanying tray of crackers and fruit to follow her mother-in-law into the salon where conversation rose and fell like a pendulum.

Jules inched toward Callie. She lifted her fluted glass in the air as Michel said, "Welcome, children. May this be the beginning of a new life now that we have Callinda home again." All eyes turned toward her. And the emotion rushed up to catch her unaware.

Jules gave her his handkerchief to blot tears.

Six

Olivier knew he was closer to fulfilling his father's promise after he hung up the phone. The *Sueño España* bottles were packed solidly against breakage and tomorrow they would sail from Marseille, France to Fuengirola, Spain. The paperwork was complete and fifty-seven bottles of seventy-year old brandy were now gone from his cellar.

He sighed with relief. He was anxious to get back to his life as the accountant of Beauvais Vineyards and his family responsibilities. He wanted to hand the reins for the estate's art colony creation to Callie.

Grinning, he realized how easy it had been to enlist Callie's help. Her Spanish language skills had something to be desired, but she was trying so hard that he laughed when he thought of it.

The night before, she'd proudly displayed her language talents to a group of Frenchmen who had no idea what she said, except for Jules. When Olivier watched his face and realized she didn't have the words quite right, they all laughed.

"Well, I am working on it," she'd said and then hit Jules in the shoulder with a mock punch. "Let's try again..."

She wasn't giving up and now she was leaving tomorrow. He wasn't happy about her driving solo. Everyone disagreed with her, but as Cendrine said, she had the spirit of a dragon. And she was not changing her mind.

Olivier picked up the phone again and dialed their attorney. Mateo Rosa Trascasas would be accepting delivery for the brandy. There were two buyers vying for the bottles; Olivier was flattered. The more competition meant more money. He knew the Jose Luis Alonzo Foundation would need all the help they could get to make

Picasso's dream come true. Whispering in the back of his mind was the knowledge that he needed ongoing donor funds to keep the school alive. For now, he'd concentrate on the village and the school.

Algodonales was a small, white village in the region of Andalucía. Olivier knew it was the perfect place to open the guitar school. He was stunned when Callie told him she already rented an apartment. The owner had agreed to help her gather people together to get started. He knew she was anxious to leave. He also knew that Jules was not happy about it. Olivier was sorry for that.

Mateo's voice broke into his thoughts. "*Hola*, Olivier."

"Mateo, I received notice this morning that the bottles are on their way. I will email you the paperwork, so you can accept delivery. They will arrive the same day Callie begins her drive to Spain."

"What? The woman is driving here from France? Please tell me she isn't driving alone." Mateo's voice showed his disdain at the idea.

"That is exactly what she's doing. Nobody can change her mind. It appears she has an itinerary that is tightly woven around her friends. She plans to stay a few days with one of them in a small village called Los Nuñez, near Malaga. She plans to contact you from there."

Mateo Rosa sighed loudly. "I hope she knows what she's doing. It is a long way from Pertuis to Fuengirola on unfamiliar roads. But, once she arrives, you can be sure I will watch over her. Please email me her phone number with the paperwork. I have already made plans to go with her to Algodonales."

Olivier's shoulders relaxed. "I hoped you would do that. Now, what is the status of the buyers you have for the brandy?"

"Before we talk about that, please tell me what Callie thought of the Alonzo brothers' claim to the proceeds? Also, I have been contacted by the Picasso Estate. They agreed to step back when they read Picasso's letter. I was stunned and relieved, of course. But, these Alonzo people have me concerned. They are going to make trouble.

Olivier was thoughtful for a moment.

"Olivier, are you still there?"

"Yes, and I'm thinking. Maybe sending Callie to Spain isn't a good idea. She's headstrong and sometimes doesn't recognize danger when it stares her in the face."

Mateo laughed. "I will watch over her, *señor*. Now, the prospective buyer's information...I will send through email as soon as we hang up the phone. And I will wait for your instructions. This is something you must decide, not me. I will guide you and make suggestions only, *sí*?

"Yes. I'll share the information with Callie. And please call when you have the bottles safely stored."

"Agreed."

Ten minutes later, Olivier read the names of both men who hoped to buy Picasso's brandy. Each man had outlined his company information and the reasons why they thought the brandy should be in their hands. Olivier groaned. "I will let Callie decide." He chuckled. He wanted to get back to his job, so he'd push this one away to her too.

Earlier that morning, Callie had spoken with her friend to finalize the specifics of her arrival in Malaga. She hadn't seen Darla in more than ten years. She was looking forward to renewing their childhood friendship. Darla's father's unique round house had been a place she'd visualized for years. Now, she was anxious to step foot inside the house to feel its charm.

Callie pulled out her map of Spain and spread it over the dining room table. With a yellow highlighter pen, she inched the marker along the road from Pertuis toward Spain. When its nib reached Barcelona, she pushed it south toward Valencia and eventually finished the yellow line at Malaga. She looked for the town of Puerto

FLAMENCO STRINGS UNCORKED

de la Torre. Darla said it was near Fernando Sanchez's home in Malaga.

She paused a moment, dropped the marker pen and sat down in the chair. As she slipped on its lid, Callie thought back to several months earlier. Fernando's first visit to Olivier had uncorked a mountain of adventure. It had been the beginning. He'd given Olivier a photograph and a letter from his deceased father. Olivier had finally opened a wooden box his father left him and it had, in turn, opened a hornet's nest. Callie had asked Jules for help and they'd found the bottles of brandy. She had fallen in love again. And then they were running from a lunatic who wanted the bottles. Now, there were other men who wanted the money from the bottles' sale.

She turned to gaze outside her cottage window where a rogue limb danced and scratched against the glass. The sky was blue, cloudless. Beyond that, she saw the mill house where Cendrine was possibly feeding her children, probably nursing the new baby girl.

Glancing at the map of Spain again, she picked up the marker pen. It would be fun to reminisce with Darla about their high school days, Napa Valley, the vineyard, old boyfriends; their lives that were filled with laughter and good times. Their mothers had been alive and neither of the girls could have imagined they'd lose them within a month of one another thirty years later. Yes, it would be good to catch up. She took a red marker and circled the village of Los Nuñez. She knew the round house sat on a winding road leading toward Almogia.

She circled another town along the Mediterranean. Fuengirola. The attorney was unsure she could handle the estate work in Algodonales. She could and vowed to tell the man she wasn't going to let him take over because she was a woman. It wasn't lost on her that many Spaniards thought women couldn't handle the important things. She chuckled, gathered up the map and folded it carefully. She planned to let him know that immediately.

Sometime later, Olivier knocked on Callie's cottage door. When she opened it, they kissed one another's cheeks and he held up a packet of papers. "Do you have time to look over the prospective buyer's information? I'm taking them inside so we can talk about them over lunch. I think Cendrine may be knee deep in children." He laughed at the look on Callie's face.

She lifted an eyebrow. "Of course, I have time. And if Cendrine is knee deep in children, I'll jump right in the middle of them." She grabbed her reading glasses and latched the door.

Within minutes, Callie held a tiny, sleeping girl in her arms while she boosted Bernadette into a chair beside her brother. Cendrine brought plates of sandwiches and then the adults sat around the dining table with a glass of wine and munched on a *cassoulet*. The steam drifted up from the casserole. After their forks slipped it into their mouths, they tried to talk around mouthfuls of the chicken and mushrooms.

"This man inherited a vineyard from his fourth great grandfather. He thinks he deserves the bottles because he was a vintner during the time Picasso's friend produced the brandy. He included a photo of the vineyard then and now." Olivier read the name aloud, "Pedro Jiménez Gil."

Callie reached for the photo. "Jiménez Bodega y Vino. I like the letter he included. Who's the other man?"

Cendrine pushed the second envelope toward Callie. "Salvador Alejandro Trujillo writes that he believes we should allow him to buy the brandy because Ruiz is one of his ancestor's names. Since Ruiz is also Picasso's family name, he's sure it would make an impact on anyone who was interested in buying the brandy from his winery."

"His winery is in the hills above Jerez where the brandy was produced all those years ago. I think the Jiménez Bodega y Vino is nearer Ronda. I like the idea of selling the brandy to someone where the brandy was produced in the first place…" Cendrine tapped her finger on the table.

Callie studied both letters. "Both men seem perfect. Can we sell half to each of them?" She tapped the letters and grinned.

Olivier laughed. "And make a difficult situation more complicated? Please do not suggest that to Mateo, Callie."

She took a deep breath, pushed more *cassoulet* into her mouth and washed it down with her red wine. "You are right, of course. Maybe we can just let them draw straws?"

Cendrine and Olivier's faces looked blank. "Draw straws?"

Callie held her fork in mid-air. "When I was little, my mother offered me choices if we couldn't agree. She broke a toothpick and then she put both pieces between her fingers so that they were exactly the same height in her hand at the top. If I chose the longest straw, I won."

Cendrine clapped her hands. "I like that."

Olivier crunched down on his crusty bread. "Grown men would not make a binding business deal based on the length of a toothpick. Especially when it involves so much money. Originally, we thought we might receive about 1,000 euros for each bottle." He tapped his finger on both letters. "But now we may have a bidding war. Negotiations will be kicked into high gear. No, a toothpick would not work." He shook his head with a chuckle and swallowed more wine. "Let's ask how much they are willing to pay. You notice that neither man gave an offer?" He chewed thoughtfully.

"Hmmmmm. That would definitely make it easier to choose," Callie mused. "Can you send an email to Mateo and ask him to contact these men again and ask them to make the estate an offer?"

Olivier grinned. "I'll do it today."

Seven

The village of Trebujena lies to the north of Jerez, bordered to the south by gently rolling countryside and on other sides by the marshlands adjoining the Guadalquivir River.

Eterio Alonzo Sepulveda kicked a stone aside at the base of the windmill. From the round structure's elevated position on the outskirts of the village, he often climbed up the hill to enjoy extensive views over the picturesque rooftops and beyond. Today, his face was creased with anger. His brother's uncertainty toward the Picasso brandy was getting harder and harder for him to accept.

They'd agreed to fight the people who found the bottles, together. Now, Ruben was showing signs of weakness and Eterio wasn't moving an inch in that direction. So what if they weren't directly related to Picasso? So what if Jose Luis' vineyard was no longer active? When the brandy was produced, it was alive and functioning. And those bottles came from Alonzo grapes. The proceeds should stay in the Alonzo family's hands.

Eterio and Ruben were proud of their lineage, proud to toast the arrival of the *mosto*, juice pressed from the first grapes of the season. They shared the old man's name. And they should share the old man's legacy. Just because Picasso had written a letter years ago, it didn't give him the right to dissolve the Alonzo family's heritage.

Money. A lot of money. And he needed it. If Ruben knew why Eterio was not giving up the fight, his brother would explode. He'd promised Ruben when they opened the restaurant *bodega* that he'd go straight. And Eterio had tried to keep that promise.

He kicked another stone with his shoe and watched it bounce off the round stone column, the only part of the old *Molino de Viento* that remained in the sanctuary. He rammed both hands into the pockets of his jeans and sat down on the broken wall. He'd imagined after his friend Demetrio Martin talked to the journalist at The Olive Press newspaper that public opinion would be on their side. They were Spaniards, after all. Eterio couldn't let some French woman keep all of the proceeds to use for a guitar school or anything else.

He groaned. So, what if it was supposed to be built in Algodonales, the village of his ancestors? He pursed his lips. After talking with his distant cousin, Javier Alonzo Ruiz, and hearing the excitement in his voice about Picasso's dream coming to Algodonales, he was angry at both Javier and Ruben. He stood up, kicked the stone wall with the toe of his shoe and headed back down the hill. Today the windmill no longer felt like a sanctuary. Today, he would figure out how to stop the woman and get what belonged to the Alonzo family.

But first, he had to find out where the brandy was stored. He had been thinking about it too long to give in to Ruben's worries. And Javier was an old man. Surely he'd see reason once Eterio talked to him face to face. Besides, he wanted to taste that brandy himself. He should drive to Algodonales. Soon.

He chuckled as he began to jog back toward Trebujena.

~

The Alonzo brother's attorney, Cristóbal Navas Garcia, flinched when his secretary told him Eterio was on the phone. He'd hoped the brothers had heeded his warning a few days earlier. There was really no basis for their suit. And Cristóbal had secretly hoped they would disappear. He let out an agitated breath and picked up the phone.

"Dígame." Talk to me.

"This is Eterio Alonzo. We still want the money from those old brandy bottles. What should we do next?"

"I told you, Eterio. There are many Ruiz descendants who are closer to Picasso than you are. Do you think you and Ruben are more important than the Ruiz people?"

"Those grapes were from an Alonzo vineyard. It's easy to understand. Why are you fighting us? Just because the foundation wants to stop the suit? We pay you, not that attorney from Fuengirola."

Cristóbal rolled his eyes skyward. "Let me do some more checking into prior cases to see if anything like this has happened before. If I can find a precedent, I will work on it. If not, there is nothing I can do."

"Do you know where the brandy bottles are stored? Are they in Spain yet?" Eterio's voice was loud and a little belligerent.

"I do not. I told you that before. And don't start thinking about that brandy, Eterio. Don't get yourself in a muddle. Last time, I had a hell of a time getting you out of your troubles. This would be much worse, I think."

Eterio's sharp intake of breath was not lost on the attorney. "Claro. That's clear. If you can't do anything, we will." He hung up.

Staring at the phone in his hand, the attorney shook his head in despair. They weren't going to stop. He'd look for precedents, but he was sure there was nothing to find. He should call Mateo again to warn him. The French woman might not be safe from them. Cristóbal shook his head slowly. He should never have accepted the Alonzo brother's case. He knew that. But since he did, it might allow him the opportunity to keep his finger on the pulse of their emotions, their movements and possibly guide the woman's project toward Picasso's last dream.

He called his secretary into the office and gave her research instructions before he lifted the phone again and dialed the attorney in Fuengirola.

~

Across the miles, Mateo Rosa sighed heavily after speaking with Cristóbal Navas and propped his chin beneath his steepled fingers. Staring at the ceiling, he lined up his thoughts and moved his schedule around. He'd planned to drive to Algodonales with the woman. Now, he wondered if he should also spend the night. Keeping her safe wasn't part of his job, but it had become personal for him.

He'd always had a fondness for Picasso's life story and some of his paintings, especially his Classicism Period. Cubism wasn't a favorite, but once he saw the Guernica painting about the small village that was decimated during the Spanish Civil War, it had become personal for Mateo. Now, with the challenge involving aged bottles of brandy and the artist's dream to help indigenous students learn to play the flamenco guitar? Yes, it damn well was personal and these hoodlums weren't going to put a cog in the wheel if he could help it.

He tapped a pencil on his desk top and thought again about the painting that hung in the Sofia Reina Museum in Madrid. He'd seen photos of the painting, read the history and always thought it was a screwed-up piece of work; everything was in pieces and nothing made sense. And then he saw it and felt the emotional tug of war between his brain and his soul. It was known as an anti-war symbol, a reminder of the tragedies of war. It had been a terror-bombing exercise by the Germans and the painting depicted Picasso's love of his native country, even though he expatriated to France and never returned to Spain.

Mateo knew the Guernica was definitely a war painting. World War Two would begin two years after he painted the visual account of the devastating impact of war on both men and women. It revealed victims, living and dead. And there were the animals, especially the bull which is the symbol of Spain.

~

At the Alonzo Bodega in nearby Trebujena, the crowd was noisy like usual. It was about two in the afternoon. Margarita, their cook, worked tirelessly to keep up with the Menu Del Día dishes, menu of the day. The bartender filled tapas plates and glasses with beer and wine.

Today's *raciones* (tapas/portions) sat beneath a clear, plastic enclosure on the bar. There was a cold potato-fish salad, shrimp in garlic oil, bread slices with tomato, ham and green olives, boiled eggs, chorizo and tuna salad.

When an American walked into the *bodega*, he ignored the arrangement on the bar and instead, ordered Avocado and Tuna tapas, red wine and crunchy bread. Eterio forced a smile and gave Margarita the order. But his mind wasn't on food or the American. He replayed his conversation with Cristóbal in his head. He mentally kicked another stone from his path and removed his apron.

"Ruben. Tell Margarita I will return in about an hour." He ignored Ruben's disgruntled snort and pushed the back door open. The hot sun flared against his eyes. He reached into his pocket for his sunglasses. But he'd left them inside the *bodega*. He paused a moment, shook his head, and moved away from the restaurant squinting his eyes against the sunny onslaught.

Five minutes later, he entered his house and went straight to his bedroom. He pulled a carpet bag off his closet shelf, pushed clothes inside and at the last minute pulled the knife out of his bedside drawer. He meant business and wouldn't let his brother or the attorney stop him. His jaw hardened and he scratched the black stubble that scraped against his hand.

His cell phone rang. He stared at it and his heartbeat sped up. Should he answer it? He knew the man was trying to scare him. And, he thought, he was doing a pretty good job of it. When the phone rang again, he tapped the button.

"*Digame.*" Talk to me.

"Eterio. Eterio. Is that how you talk to your friends?"

"You are not my friend, Manolo."

"That's not what you said when you needed me."

"I told you to stop calling me. I'm working on the deal. I told you! I've done everything you want me to do with the girls. I need more time to get your money," he whispered into the phone.

"The French woman is driving to Spain today."

"This is my plan, not yours. And how in hell do you know that she's on her way to Spain, Manolo? Do you also know if she has the brandy bottles with her? If she's driving, maybe they're in her car."

Manolo chuckled.

"I can deal with this. Let me do it."

"Eterio. Eterio." The man's laughter sounded like a cough and then he hung up the phone.

Eterio was shaking all the way down to his toenails. After locking his front door, he tossed his bag into the trunk of his car, filled the gasoline tank and returned to the *bodega*. He pushed past the planters of bright flowers hanging from the patio's overhang. Paco de Lucia's flamenco guitar music thrummed in the air from inside.

Ruben was wiping tables and cleaning up the bar when his older brother returned. He tossed the rag into the bucket of water, put down the spray cleaner and followed him into the back room. His brother's face was pale. Ruben filled a glass with draft beer. When he placed it into Eterio's hand, his brother stared at the glass. When he swung his bloodshot eyes upward, one eye looked in one direction and his good eye stared at Ruben. His hair was a mess. The beard growth made him look like he'd been in a fight.

"*Gracias.*" Eterio's voice sounded gruff and a little deflated. His hands shook as he picked up the beer and slid his fingers down both sides to linger over the condensation. The cold glass tugged at his thoughts and he stared at it.

"Eterio, what's the matter with you? Why won't you talk to me?" Ruben's face changed from concern to frustration as his brother's miss-matched eyes darted around the small room.

Eterio couldn't answer his younger brother's question. Or maybe he just didn't want to. He'd slid down farther than he'd ever been with Manolo. This time he was unsure if he knew the way up again. He lifted the cold beer to his lips without saying a word.

Ruben sighed, put a plate of food in front of his brother and returned to the front. There was a lot of work to do. The sounds of crockery and glasses were muted over the loud conversations inside the *bodega*. Business was good and so was the food.

Eterio slammed his fist on the table. When would Manolo leave him and his family alone? He seemed to overshadow everything they did. He'd done it many years. He hadn't wanted to get involved with the prossie ring. Some of the young girls had been his friends in school and he'd had to harden his heart to hand them over to Manolo. They weren't prostitutes but his choices put them there. Marbella was a long way from Trebujena. And Manolo knew Eterio would give him what he wanted because his money, in exchange for the girls, was good.

His eyes swam and the beer glass wavered in front of him. He slipped a hand across his forehead and lifted his hair, making it stick up in all directions. His beard stubble itched and his stomach rumbled. He should eat some more, but he'd have to face his sister and brother if he did that. And he was sick of being on the defensive. Couldn't they see how important this was? No, the *bodega* didn't need the money from the brandy bottles, but it would help them. Why couldn't they understand that this was Alonzo money?

He scooped up the remainder of the chicken before washing it down with the now-tepid beer. His head hurt trying to tamp down his anger at Manolo. The man scared him. He had always scared him. Now he thought he could stand up to him. Eterio was the man of the house. He had to steer away from Manolo's hold on him. If only he had not borrowed that damn money to gamble.

Margarita is the oldest in the family. She should be the one to fight for this brandy. But of course, she won't. She was like a shadow lately. His sister used to be in charge of everything. She had been their rock since they were young. But lately, he had not paid attention and he wondered why she'd been so quiet. He pondered the questions in his head as he sipped the last of his beer. But, he had other things to worry about. He could figure out Margarita's moods later.

He tipped his beer, smoothed back his hair and adjusted the sunglasses on his face. When he backed his Renault out of the back parking lot, neither Margarita nor Ruben saw him leave.

Eight

Earlier that morning, Callie couldn't stop grinning. One bag was in the car. "*Maleta,*" she whispered. Suitcase. *En el Carro*. In the car. She slipped her finger inside the make-up bag and shoved the mascara deeper to force the zipper closed. Cendrine had a cooler bag full of food. She'd also given her ten bottles of water, a blanket, pillow and flashlight.

"What do you think I'm going to do, go camping over the Pyrenees?"

Cendrine laughed. "You must be prepared, Callie. We love you, so you must let us worry. That is what we do." She hitched the baby closer to her chest inside the carryall and pushed another cup of coffee across the table.

"If I drink any more coffee, I'll have a low-panic moment and I will need to pee before I get out of Pertuis."

"Maybe you should take a small jug with you."

"A small jug?"

"*Oui.* You would have your personal toilet with you."

"Ha-Ha." Callie grinned and shook her head.

"You have your maps. The car has GPS. You have money. And you have the address for Mateo Rosa in Fuengirola?"

"Yes, I have everything except Jules." Her face grew pensive.

"What is wrong, Callie? You have not told me why you decided to go to Spain before marrying Jules. He seems very disappointed and you aren't talking." Cendrine's forehead creased as she stood swaying to and fro to calm Lulu's fidgeting.

Callie looked at Cendrine. "I don't know, darling. I love the man. But I'm not ready to make the jump yet. I'm hoping the silence of my own thoughts during the drive to Spain will push out all the cotton I've stored in my brain about it. I can't stop thinking about that horrible letter Aurore sent to Francois with Jules' signature. Part of me resents both of them. I know it's unfair, but I can't stop the words from darting around in my head."

Cendrine's eyes grew round. "But, Callie, Jules didn't..."

"I know! That's just it. I must get my head straight. This journey is not only about brandy bottles and creating the music colony in Algodonales. It will be a journey from the inside too."

When Callie saw Cendrine's face, she reached up and kissed her on both cheeks. "I am fine and I will be much better after I think everything through without Jules at my side. *Mejorido.* Much better."

They were both laughing at Callie's Spanish when Jules drove into the driveway. His face looked sad when he opened the car door. Callie walked out of the house to meet him. When he kissed the top of her head, she moaned softly. "I will miss you, Jules."

"Not as much as I will miss you, *ma chère.* When are you leaving?"

"Now. My car is packed. I promise to call you every day." She reached up on her tip toes to kiss him soundly. His warm lips opened and he touched her lip with his tongue. As she leaned into him, she welcomed the connection and tried to tamp down her worries.

He pulled away from her and then opened her car door. When she slipped inside, they didn't take their eyes off one another. Swallowing hard, she threw him another kiss that included Cendrine.

She backed out of the driveway. And then she smiled. She could do this. She promised herself she would enjoy every minute. Then, she would return to her real life. "After my big adventure."

Callie pushed the Spanish language CD into the player and threaded her way out of Pertuis while listening and repeating Spanish words and phrases.

Her journey had begun.

~

FLAMENCO STRINGS UNCORKED

As Callie drove westward that day, Mateo Rosa Trascasas walked along the boardwalk toward the port in Fuengirola. He had the transport papers in his hand. The storage area was prepared in his own cellar, several blocks from his law office. He thought back to the time when Olivia and Bram had first met with him over the Christmas holidays. It had been during their honeymoon. He grinned as he remembered thinking it was never too late for love. The couple had greying hair and eyes only for one another.

Mateo remembered that Olivia was Callie Beauvais' best friend. So, he wondered if Callie was also about the same age. About his age then. When they'd explained why they needed an attorney who spoke French, Spanish and English, because of a letter Picasso had left behind years earlier, he'd been intrigued. Now, he realized he was much more than intrigued. He was excited. And he hadn't felt like this for a long time.

After his wife succumbed to cancer five years earlier, he had buried himself in his work. The law firm had grown, he'd hired two more lawyers to help him and he'd pretty much tossed away his personal life. When he heard the Picasso story from Olivia and Bram, he had been fascinated.

He chuckled softly. Now he'd evolved from that workaholic attorney who wanted to make this dream real. Yes, that was it. His mind set had changed that day. And the law firm was no longer his life. He missed Elisa, of course. They'd been married twenty years. He didn't have a child to turn to, so of course, his child was his law firm. But now, there was more to consider.

He reached the end of the pier and found the boat, Oleander, waiting at dock ten, just as the papers promised. A young man was mopping the deck. He heard a clinking sound where the chain held it firmly to the cleat, a fixture shaped like a wide and short capital letter T. He saw the A line. The loop on the end was wound through the legs and secured over the horns of the cleat.

FLAMENCO STRINGS UNCORKED

Mateo stopped to enjoy the beauty of the turquoise sea and leaned on the steel railing. The boat rocked in the water and the clanking sounds of nearby boats sounded almost musical. The day was perfect and calm.

The man acknowledged him with a wave. "Señor Rosa?" The sailor pulled his hat from his head and slapped it against his hip to remove the water that surged from the rim. He was a big guy, tall, not fat. His hair curled around his ears and an earring protruded from the lobe of his ear. Tattoos swirled along his forearms. He smiled and walked toward Mateo with a hand extended.

"Yes. I have papers here." Mateo pushed them into the man's hand. The man scanned them and then glanced around, "And you are going to lift these heavy boxes and carry them...where?" The sailor's lips twitched.

Mateo gave him an answering grin. He pointed to the two men leaning against the large SUV behind him. "Do you think they can handle it?"

The sailor laughed. "I'm Ben, captain of this vessel. They look like they can lift the heavy wooden boxes just fine."

Mateo's helpers answered his wave and jogged to the boat. When Ben invited them onto the deck, the men pulled on heavy gloves and followed him. They were both strong young men who worked at Mateo's favorite restaurant on the beach who specialized in fish grilled on sticks. When he'd offered them fifty euros to carry the boxes and load them into his cellar, they'd agreed immediately.

Thirty minutes later, each man had made five trips to and from the SUV and Mateo was behind the wheel driving away with brandy worth about 142,500 euros. The boys followed him in an old Volkswagen. He'd done his homework. He knew the bottles were sealed in glass containers and must be stored on their sides to keep the cork wet. They should be airtight and stored in a cool, dark environment away from direct sunlight and exposure to high

FLAMENCO STRINGS UNCORKED

temperature fluctuations. He didn't know where the bottles had been stored when they'd been found. But surely the men who hid the bottles years ago knew that brandy should touch their cork to keep them from drying out. Since the best place to store the bottles were in a cellar or closet away from outside walls, that's exactly what he planned to do.

The boys, Ricardo and Esteban, hauled the pine boxes from the car efficiently without bending beneath their weight. Their muscles bulged through their tee shirts and Mateo wondered how long it had been since he had moved with such agility. Getting old, he thought.

Once the boys left, Mateo walked down the stairs into his cellar. The lightest box had seven bottles instead of ten like all the others. He pried it open with his hammer; he wanted to see the label that had intrigued him ever since he saw Olivia and Bram's photo a few months earlier. He pulled a bottle into his hand.

"Oh, my God. Yes, you are quite beautiful, *señorita*." The label was unique and reminded him of an art nouveau poster. The Spanish woman's long black hair flowed behind her as she rode a cork like a bucking bronco. He caressed the label with his fingers and translated the label aloud, "Spanish Dream."

And then, he carefully placed each bottle on their side where they would remain until the buyer retrieved them. As the thought ran through his head, he mentally reminded himself to ask Callie if he could buy one of these beauties for himself. And that thought took him to the next item on his agenda.

Which buyer would she choose? Pedro Jiménez, whose family had a vineyard during the time Picasso's friend bottled the brandy? Or Salvador Trujillo whose family had the Ruiz name in their ancestry? A bidding war was still in process and the Olive Press journalist had been hounding him for a story. His first article had been a horrible idea; it awakened the sleeping giant with the Alonzo brother's greed.

He knew Callie had her hands full even without the newspaper's story. He'd managed to avoid the journalist so far. He wondered if the arrival of the bottles had been leaked. If so, he had to be very careful. On the way out his front door, he set his house alarm. He'd made sure the boys had no idea what was in the boxes. He'd known Esteban for months. Ricardo was a new guy, but they seemed to be good friends. He trusted them, but boys talk. He knew that; he'd been a boy once himself and knew how easy it would be to brag about Picasso's brandy.

Nine

One of the main things Callie enjoyed when she left Pertuis was the scenery along the way. She wanted to appreciate the view, not drive straight through and miss the panorama. An hour after leaving Pertuis, she drove through Arles. Afterward, she passed ochre mountains, pristine lakes, villages nestled into valleys so tightly she wondered how the builders pushed the houses together. Lavender fields. Mustard fields. She'd changed the CD from Spanish words to sweet music. French songs floated through the car as she sped along the highway.

After Arles, she approached Montpellier and remembered Jules telling her that it was considered the most seductive city in southern France. Their trams were sexy, he'd said. She laughed softly. How could a tram be sexy? Her mind veered to Jules again and the kiss they'd shared before she'd left him standing on the porch beside Cendrine and Lulu. Now *that* was sexy.

She was hungry. Weaving her car into the city, she pulled over to the curb and studied her new tour book. She pinpointed the main square and locked the car. Heading north on foot toward the Esplanade, she saw the promenades and trees extended into the square. There, she would find the *Café de l'Esplanade.*

Upon arrival, the only thing that intrigued her was its terrace. Their hamburger menu turned her face to a grimace. She glanced around until she saw *Chez Boris*, which was absolutely French. She snagged a table and ordered an omelet and salad. The breeze danced through her hair as she watched tourists scamper around the square. She was half way to Barcelona. She wouldn't tarry, but the freedom she felt was delicious.

Three hours later, she'd skimmed the coast, driven through Girona and fought traffic leading into Barcelona. She tapped the address into her GPS for the IBIS hotel. Delighted, she found a parking spot on *Calle Pamplona*. The timing was perfect as she pushed open her hotel room door because her phone jingled, showing her Jules' smiling face on her screen.

"Hey, you. I am safe. *Y no estoy perdido*." And I am not lost.

His voice purred with laughter. "*Bon*! Olivier said the brandy arrived safely and Mateo has the bottles. The men are still bidding against one another. At this rate, you may never need any more money to continue that guitar school."

Callie smiled. "How are you, Jules?"

"Missing you." His voice was low and sensual.

"I know. And I love you for that."

He didn't answer immediately.

"Jules?"

"I'm here, *ma chère*. I'm happy you are safe. Get some rest now." The phone quietly clicked off and he was gone.

She sat a moment. She'd wanted time and he was giving it to her. Unsure how she felt about that, she pulled off her clothes.

After a hot shower, Callie sat on her bed and pressed the hotel's wrinkled street map of Barcelona across her lap. The Metro was on the end of the block. She followed the street names with her fingernail. "Okay, morning breakfast in the lobby and then explore the basilica at *Sagrada Familia*. Gaudí was on the agenda for tomorrow. She purchased a ticket online and then sank her head against the pillow.

The next morning in the lobby, the coffee maker was frustrating. The large cup didn't fit beneath the espresso spout. Huh. She pulled a smaller paper cup off the shelf above her, glanced around for help. Nobody noticed. So, she shoved the undersized cup under the spout and punched the 'White Coffee' button. The pot dripped coffee. And it dripped and dripped some more. She wrenched the small cup from the spout when it overflowed. *Well, that was fun.* She filled her tray with yogurt, thinly sliced ham, cheese, fresh fruit and a croissant. She sipped coffee and studied the Metro map while she ate.

Thirty minutes later, she stared at *Casa Milá's* façade along with hundreds of other tourists. Her neck hurt as she craned it upward to see the curious artwork and twisting, wrought iron balconies. Her first glimpse of the lobby, once inside the building was beautiful with art nouveau decor. The colors, design, shapes and feeling of warmth grabbed at her. The building was built between 1907 and 1910; Gaudí's last design for a private residence.

The roof terrace was astounding, but when Callie walked through the original owner's apartment, she was taken back in time. The beauty of art nouveau was on the floor, ceiling and walls. "I could move right in," she whispered. Each room was beautiful as well as utile. To think that this was built the same time historically that hundreds of Spaniards were leaving Spain because they were too poor to feed their families just didn't compute.

Across the city an hour later, she stood outside the walls of the *Sagrada Familia.* Statues embraced the front area of the immense cathedral. A bronze door, covered in intricately shaped metal leaves, invited her through the entrance. She snapped photos with her phone, but she knew photos couldn't tell the story.

When she walked into the basilica, she was transformed. The stained-glass windows whispered to her. Sunshine sparkled through each segment. The gigantic chandelier above the nave made her wonder if others were as dumbfounded with the beauty as she was. Were their eyes glazing over? Their hearts thumping in their chests? Sitting down on a bench along the wall, she was gratified to see her feelings reflected on other faces. It was that look that said, unbelievable, awesome, beautiful, reverent and much more. She knew she wasn't the same person who had walked through that leaf-etched door.

Her feet burned, but she forced her steps toward *Las Ramblas*. The arboreal-covered walkway stretched from *Plaza Catalunya* to the sea. It was, after all, the city where Gaudí left his mark everywhere. She stopped at a café and dipped hot, crispy churros into a cup of thick hot chocolate. Musicians played on the plaza. Children ran amok. It was magic. When she looked at her watch, she was reminded that she had a job to do.

She also had a road to follow south toward Cartagena. Mercedes and Jenaro planned to meet her on the outskirts of the city and lead her to their house. So far, her plan was going smoothly. And from there, she was only four hours from Malaga, her next destination.

She was hungry again. Once back in the hotel room, she checked her messages. One sounded very peculiar. The call was from Loli, the woman whom she'd rented the Algodonales apartment. She punched in her number and started removing her clothes.

"Loli? This is Callie Beauvais."

"Callie. I saw Javier Alonzo in the village this morning. Eterio Alonzo is agitated that Javier wants to help you with the Picasso project. He told me that he is angry about your visit."

"What? Javier is my contact at the guitar shop. Of course, he is helping me. What else did he say?"

"Yes, I know this. He wants you to be aware of the situation. He will talk with his cousin again. Are you still arriving next Monday?"

Callie grabbed her calendar and ticked off the days. "Yes. One week from today. The attorney might be with me. He thinks I need his help. I'm hoping the Alonzo brothers will stop causing problems and everything will be fine. Thank you for calling, Loli."

"You are welcome. See you soon, Callie."

~

Twenty minutes later, her hotel's phone rang. She wrapped a towel around her wet body after stepping from the shower.

The front desk clerk's voice said, "Ms. Beauvais? There is a police officer here. It's about your car."

"My car? It's legal to park on *Calle Pamplona*, isn't it?"

"Yes, but it is not parked on our street. It is near the Cristóbal Colon Memorial Monument near the port. Please come down to talk to him?" The woman's voice was apologetic.

Callie's heartbeat was galloping. "Yes. Give me five minutes." She was shaking as she pulled on underwear and then yanked a dress over her head. Her brain stalled. She slammed her hand against the wall as she pulled open the door and ran for the elevator. She could almost hear Jules voice in her head... But she pushed the thought away and punched the button for the lobby.

Two hours later, she stared at a woman with disheveled brown hair and dangling earrings that hung to her shoulder. Callie's heartbeat had leveled out, but her anger was still in piss mode. Her BMW had been driven into the side of a truck, totaled beyond repair. Pieces of metal had been jammed into the radiator and her CD player was damaged or missing. Her breath was coming in short gasps. She slid the paperwork toward the young woman and then allowed herself to be led away by the kind policeman who'd met her at the hotel. It was nine o'clock.

The rental car company would arrive in the morning with the car she'd rented online with her iPhone. She tried to calm herself down, but the thought of driving a Spanish car through an unfamiliar country was starting to unnerve her.

"Someone will return you to the hotel, Ms. Beauvais," the young policeman said in Spanish.

FLAMENCO STRINGS UNCORKED

The policeman had done everything he could to make the horror smooth out for Callie. She turned to him and laughed suddenly. "Oh my. I understood what you said. Thank you."

He looked at her thoughtfully before turning the key in his ignition. His lips twitched as he drove her back to the IBIS Hotel.

Her mind bounced back and forth between anger and adventure. Her beautiful little BMW was gone. But she was in Spain and would soon see the bone-white barren hills and lush olive groves as she headed south toward the shimmery gardens of Andalusia.

She decided that keeping this little secret from Jules and her family might be a very good idea.

Ten

Callie tugged the door of the Renault Clio open and slid into the soft seat. "Put it in neutral," she mumbled. "There's the brake and the clutch. The key?" She stared at the plastic card in her hand. When she punched the start button, a message told her to insert the key. Really? Exploring the dashboard with her fingers, she finally found the slot, pushed it in and pressed the start button again. She laughed. So far, so good. Now, where is the reverse gear?

Her mother had refused to let her get her driver's license unless she learned to drive a manual shift. She smiled at the bittersweet memory. "Someday you might have an emergency and will need to drive a stick shift." She'd laughed at her then. She wasn't laughing today.

She'd left her friends in Cartagena after a big breakfast of *Tortilla Española,* a potato and egg omelet, alongside crispy bacon and fresh fruit. Then she'd pointed her new little car toward Malaga. She'd wished she had time to visit the spectacular Roman ruins and the original Charles III rampart, but not this time. The car was still strange to her; she could not push it into reverse without panicking. She missed her GPS and using the clutch still gave her goosebumps.

She pointed the car toward the jagged Mediterranean coast of Spain. Putting her hand out the open window, she felt a breeze flow through her fingers. Without straining her brain on worries, she shied away from Javier Alonzo Ruiz's feuding cousins. He was excited about the Picasso guitar school project, but he was apprehensive too. She had heard it in his voice when she spoke to him that morning.

The mountain highway gently inclined upward for miles. Vineyards sprawled over the valleys below her, layered and tiered like an artist's painting. It was green everywhere, with patches of white where small villages nestled in the crux of the mountains.

Her excitement mounted as signs for Malaga came into view. She was anxious to see Fernando and his family again. And Darla. When her phone rang, she punched the Bluetooth button.

"Hola." Hello.

"Is this Callie Beauvais?"

She didn't recognize the number. "Yes," she responded slowly.

"This is Mateo Rosa Trascasas."

"Ah, the attorney. I should arrive at your office in six days. Is that still a good plan for you?"

She heard him chuckle. "Yes. I understand you are driving your own car, so I will follow you to Algodonales. I just spoke with Javier Alonzo in the village. He is very concerned for you because…"

"…Yes, I know about his cousin," she interrupted him. When she looked in the rear-view mirror, she moved into the right lane before the small Fiat jumped into her back window. When it whizzed by her, she relaxed again and slowed down.

"Did you also know he may be in Algodonales when you arrive?"

Callie's breath slowed. "No, I didn't know that. There will be people around me, so I will be safe. Do not worry please."

"I was told you would respond like this."

She bristled. "Oh, really? And who told you that, Mr. Rosa?"

"Does it matter? You must take this seriously. The brothers are angry and will try to stop you. The brandy bottles are in my cellar. I need your decision by tomorrow on which man is going to buy your brandy bottles."

"Why the rush? Olivier told me they are in a bidding war."

FLAMENCO STRINGS UNCORKED

"They want to stop playing games. Can you receive email attachments?"

"Yes. But not until tonight when I have Wi-Fi in Los Nuñez."

"I will send their final bids. Please call me in the morning." Mateo's voice echoed his frustration.

She bit her lip. "Yes, *sir*." She imagined herself saluting as if he was a general in the Army and tried not to laugh. She knew he was serious, but really? He sounded like a father chastising a child.

Mateo said, "Goodbye. I will see you soon."

She made a face. "Goodbye then..." She shook her head and wondered what the man was like if he could so easily be pushed into a corner. He probably had a bald head and beady eyes. Why do these Spaniards think I'm helpless? Well, there is the car thing, but...

Suddenly, she drove beneath an overpass and bam! A large bird pooped on her windshield. Not only poop...but several lumps of yuck filled her screen so badly, her first instinct was to turn on the windshield wipers. So she did. "Oh no! Where's the water spray to make it go away?" She had absolutely no idea. None of the buttons gave her water. So, sticky poop scraped back and forth in front of her eyes until she could barely see the road.

And this happened when cars sped by at 120 kilometers per hour. It was difficult to calculate because in America, the speed was listed as miles per hour. It was driving Callie mad. She was used to seeing signs showing 50, 60 or 75. The mangled bird poop stripped her sight from the road. She was frantic. She squinted to peer between the shiny stuff and the glass. But not for long.

Callie knew she must take the next exit. She saw a roundabout. Exit 1? No. Exit 2? No. Exit 3? Maybe. Uh-oh, she realized she needed Exit 4. Rats. The dang bird poop... She'd stopped counting the hundreds of roundabouts. She disliked the circles and arrows pointing to a city and began to grumble.

FLAMENCO STRINGS UNCORKED

She could no longer squint through the shine. She had to turn around. About a mile farther, she found another roundabout and headed back the other way. The first exit looked wrong, so she skipped it. The next one had a roundabout. Yes! Wrong. She knew it as soon as she saw the huge statue leading to the beach. She jerked her car into the first gas station she saw and filled the tank. When she saw the water spigot nearby, she grinned. The machine swallowed one of her euro coins but at that point, she would have paid more. She sprayed her windshield, scrubbed it clean. When she turned around, she saw a man staring at her.

"That water is for your radiator, not washing cars."

"Really? Well, my radiator is just fine. The bird poop wasn't," she snapped at him.

He looked between her and the car before bursting into laughter. "Okay," he said with a snicker.

Callie raised an eyebrow, returned the hose and got in the car.

The traffic in Malaga was thick and fast. She pulled over to look at her map. She wished for the hundredth time that the rental car had GPS. She mentally kicked its tires. The little gray car was an enigma without an instruction manual. After getting lost for more than an hour, she trudged on, but the streets were narrow, winding and convoluted. A view of the Alcazaba, one of Spain's iconic landmarks, pierced the sky. Callie recognized the area because Jules had driven her there a few months earlier. The city had a penchant for flamenco and more tapas bars than bus stops. Her mind stilled at the memory. She couldn't have done any of this without him. Callie's face softened.

She found the street five minutes later. It was all luck. A parking space was half a block away. She slipped in, just barely missing the motorcycle skewed in between the curb and the street. Cars were parked on the sidewalk and some spots that weren't parking spaces at all. Relieved to arrive at last, she grabbed her dangling purse and locked the car.

When Crescéncia opened the door, she saw Fernando's toothy smile behind her. Both reached out their arms and pulled her into an embrace, each kissing both of her cheeks. "*Encantada.*" Delighted.

The aroma of delicious food made her stomach yawn. She noticed a tray was centered on the coffee table where a bottle of wine, three glasses and plates of green olives and potato chips waited. She grinned at them and reached for their hands.

"*Estoy muy feliz de verte.*" I am very happy to see you.

Fernando's eyes widened and he laughed. "*¿Hablas español ahora?*" You speak Spanish now?

Callie chuckled and held up a thumb and pointer finger with a half inch space between them. "*Un poquito.*" A little.

Crescéncia clapped her hands and the room erupted into Spanish. Callie started laughing and held up both hands. "*No entiendo. Hable depacio por favor.*" I don't understand. Speak slower please.

She pulled her mobile phone from her purse and switched on her translation APP. When she typed in the English words and they saw Spanish words pop up, they grinned at her like little children.

Crescéncia motioned toward the dining room after one solitary olive remained in the dish. She saw four places set on the table. The next moment, the front door opened and Francisco walked into the room. After a big hug, he swung her around like a child.

"Francisco! *Encantado.*"

The young man's eyes lit up. "*Muy bien*, Callie." Very good.

His grin set the mood for the rest of the afternoon.

With the aid of her translation APP and her fledgling Spanish, she brought them up to date on the brandy bottles, Algodonales, the crazy Alonzo brothers' claim to the proceeds and the bidders vying to buy the brandy.

FLAMENCO STRINGS UNCORKED

Fernando sat back in his chair and folded his wrinkled hands over his full belly. She saw that he was worried. She patted his hands and shook her head and they talked for another hour. Callie knew he felt responsible for the problems she'd encountered as well as the near death of his grandson, Francisco, over the brandy bottles.

Francisco stood to return to work. She hugged him tightly and kissed both of his cheeks. He was humbled. He kissed his mother and grandfather, patted Callie's cheek and walked out the door.

When her phone rang, Darla Ruiz's face filled the screen and then her voice chattered so fast, she could barely understand her. Crescéncia and Fernando smiled. Callie knew it was time to go. Their faces mirrored her own. They knew they would see one another again, but leaving was difficult.

Thirty minutes later, she was hopelessly lost. Driving through Puerto de la Torre seemed to take forever. She nearly cried when she saw a sign for the Jose Carlos Restaurant. And then she nearly kissed the ground when she stepped out of her car.

A blue-haired woman ran toward her and squeezed Callie like a plump orange. "You made it." Darla breathed into her ear.

They laughed like children.

"Yes, but I got lost!" Callie laughed, "And I nearly wore out the clutch getting here."

"A clutch? Ah, so your mother's prophecy came true?"

Callie laughed again.

"Well, now you need to follow me down the road from hell. Go slow. If you see a car coming toward you, slow down or pull over. It isn't far." Callie touched Darla's blue-striped silver hair. Ten years had changed her friend, but she still had a warm smile and kind eyes.

"Blue? What have you been doing for the last ten years? And what do you mean, I should pull over?" She looked at her friend's hair again and whispered, "Blue?"

Darla laughed. "Yes, blue and ballsy. Follow me."

Eleven

Callie stared after her. Ten years. From a complicit housewife to a striking hippie. *Oh, my.* She put the car into gear and followed her a short way. A sharp left led them onto a narrow, serpentine road. Blind curves, trees, ravines and a one-car bridge kept Callie's concentration at its peak. When another car came toward her on a road that surely was only meant for one, she slowed to a near stop and allowed the cream-colored Volkswagen to speed by. It hadn't slowed down. When Callie looked up again, Darla had left her in the dust.

Ten minutes later, her palms were sweaty and her heart was stampeding against her ribs. She slowed to a stop behind her friend. Darla turned right and led Callie to another bridge. This one was definitely built for only one car. Darla sped across its expanse with Callie on her heels. When she saw a road sign to Almogia followed immediately by another sign listing Los Nuñez, she sighed happily.

Well, not exactly happily. Two sharp turns later and her heart dropped into her belly again. The incline was steep. The road was narrow. The stone wall on one side of the road created a blind curve. Darla sped up. Callie followed close behind, but when she saw a car coming toward her at breakneck speed, her adrenaline spiked. She wanted to close her eyes and just let it happen. But then, the car disappeared and Callie was at the top of the hill staring into a convex mirror beside a large wrought-iron gate. She smiled. They had arrived at the round house.

La Casa Redonda was all Darla had promised. Once a private residence, it was now the *Redonda B & B* owned by an English woman named Elvira Smiffy. Several hairy dogs barked and jumped up and down like yoyos.

Darla hopped out of her car and opened the gates. Callie followed her down the inclined driveway to park beneath a pergola that would shade them from the intense sun of southern Spain. Before she could get out of the car, a woman and three dogs came to meet them. She tried to pull the excited dogs back from the cars, while speaking their names and grabbing at their fur-lined bodies with both hands.

She had short-cropped white hair, bleached from the Spanish sun. Despite being somewhere near seventy, she was spry and moved like a much younger woman. She grinned apologetically as her dogs nipped at her heels.

"Hello, lovey," the woman cooed at Darla before turning toward Callie. She reached forward to give Callie a kiss on each cheek. "You must be Callie and I'm Elvira." The dogs began to jump again. "And these little horrors are Scalli, short for Scalliwag, Pesky and Scamp. They come with the house." Her blue eyes twinkled against her deeply-tanned skin amid a smile that shone like a full moon in a clear night sky.

Within minutes, Callie's bags sat in a bedroom as large as her cottage's living room. Two tall windows looked out on a covered patio on one side and a glass door led outside near the long couch on the other. Callie found the curved walls fascinating and her breath caught with the beauty of it all. Tiers of orange trees and grape vineyards filled the landscape just past a small community of white houses that dotted the hill below the round house. As she stared across miles of vineyards, she heard roosters crowing, a burro braying and of course, the dogs still barking their welcome. She was enchanted.

When she came out of the bedroom, Darla led her outside through a *cortina*, which was a beaded curtain that hung in front of the Dutch door. The swimming pool sparkled in the afternoon sun. And the round patio table held a bottle of red wine and a number of small bowls filled with *tapas* on the sun-drenched terrace.

Elvira smiled and invited Callie to sit on the stone bench, after handing her a small cushion to sit on. She poured three glasses of wine and once Darla joined the ladies, Elvira lifted her glass in a communal toast. "Welcome to *La Casa Redonda*. Here's to your great expectations."

Callie clinked the edge of her glass to the others and thought how very English the woman sounded. In fact, she had to listen very closely to her words in order to understand her. Learning Spanish was difficult, but interpreting her English accent was no small thing.

She sipped the red wine and smiled at Elvira as she gazed into the deep-blue swimming pool and the endless, mesmerizing view. "This is very good. What is it?"

"*Ribera del Duero*. It's from the north. I think it is the best red wine that Spain offers. I saved it for your arrival." She winked at Darla. "I just purchased four labels of reds for the wine tasting tomorrow night. Saidie will be here about two for lunch. She's my good friend and our bartender," she told Callie. "She loves being in the wine cellar and talking about..."

Callie's phone rang and interrupted Elvira. She saw Jules' photo. "Sorry, ladies, but I must take this call..." She got up and walked to the edge of the pool and stood beside the Níspero tree. "Hello there."

Jules' voice was warm. "I'm missing you."

She smiled. Before she could respond, he continued. "I just got a call from Mateo. The buyers want a decision on who you are choosing to sell those bottles to. Have you decided yet?"

Callie groaned. "No. What should I do, Jules? They both have good reasons for wanting the bottles. And if I can't sell half to one and half to the other, I'm not sure what to do." Her voice cracked.

"Well, this might make it easier for you to decide. Olivier just told me that Pedro Jiménez called Mateo. He offered 2,500 euros for each bottle. When Mateo called Salvador Trujillo with Pedro's offer, the man hung up on him."

"Hmmmmm. Well, I want to sell them to a gentleman. So, that's easy. Pedro has the deal. That means...uh...it would add up to..."

Jules chuckled. "142,500 euros."

"Oh. My. God." Callie's eyes widened.

"One other thing. Mateo wants to buy a bottle and will pay the purchase price once you make the decision."

"Really? He was a little testy on the phone earlier today."

"Too testy to let him buy a bottle?"

She laughed. "Not if he's willing to pay 2,500 euros for it."

"God, I miss your laugh, *ma chère*. Where are you now?"

"I am at the B & B with my friend, Darla. The English woman who owns the round house has just served wine and tapas. Her dogs are circling the table. The smallest dog brings her a rubber toy that she tosses over the railing. When she retrieves it from the bottom of the hill, she brings it back to Elvira so quickly it makes my eyes swim."

It was his turn to laugh. "Call me later?"

"Mmmmmm... yes. Before I go to sleep."

"Well then..." His voice trailed off.

"Later." She smiled when she slid the phone into her pocket. 2,500 euros. She called and left a message for Olivier. Everyone would be happy except Salvador Trujillo and the Alonzo brothers. She pushed them to the back of her mind and returned to her wine, soft chatter, dogs and tapas. She had a week to unwind and she wanted it.

She and Darla talked until after midnight, each trying to catch up the other. Ten years was a long time and each of them had so many changes in their life, they kept interrupting the other. They'd been friends most of their lives and visiting one another for an entire week was a rare gift. Darla's blue hair was explained along with

Picasso's bottles of brandy. They went to bed laughing long after Elvira had retired.

Callie sent a text to Jules when she slipped into bed. "Still up?"

Her phone rang instantly. "Up as in awake...or up as in...?"

She chuckled. "Awake, you naughty man."

"I've been laying here a couple of hours trying to sleep. I'm glad you called. I've been thinking..."

"Uh-oh."

"I think you're holding out on me. There's something on your mind and you aren't sharing it with me. Tell me." His voice changed to a low rumble.

"Jules. I love you. That's number one."

"And number two?"

"You're right. I am having difficulty getting past the letter that drove Francois across the lake in the storm. I know it wasn't your fault. I *know* that. But, I'm conflicted." She caught her breath after saying the words aloud that had been rambling in her head the past two weeks.

Jules was quiet for a beat. "You love me, though."

"Of course."

"Then, we can work it out. Go to sleep, darling."

Callie lay her phone on the night table. She was glad she'd finally voiced her feelings, but she hated the thoughts that ran through her head. Could she ignore the resentment? Could she forget that Francois might still be alive if he hadn't raced across the lake with anger in his heart? She stared up at the gauzy curtain that hung above the bed for a long time. She wondered, idly, if it was mosquito netting.

From there, her thoughts ran rampant. A rock lodged in her throat and she swallowed several times. Pulling a hand up to cover her breast and feel the heartbeat thump beneath seemed to calm her just a little. She'd never known such an understanding man, nor loved one so well. Maybe that was her problem. She was afraid she might love Jules more than she had loved Francois. And for that, she felt guilty. "Oh, hell." She punched the soft pillow and burrowed her head deeply into its folds. She closed her eyes. A breeze rustled beyond her glass door and the shadow of trees blended with moonlight on the pane. The thump of her heart sounded loud, unbending, and foreign. Tomorrow had to be better.

~

After she had a complete tour of *La Casa Redonda* the next day, she was eager to enjoy the remainder of her week. Early that morning, she'd joined Darla and Elvira with the three dogs housed in the back of the woman's car. They drove across the narrow bridge and turned right at a restaurant called *La Pirata* to park above a dry river bed. The dogs jumped out and headed in tandem toward the orange groves. The women followed them, walked around the island...up inclines, around corners, through wild flowers and back down the riverbed. It felt good to exercise again and the dogs had given them plenty to laugh about. Their antics were funny as they sniffed everything in sight, stopped to pee and poop and then bark their heads off at other dogs along the way.

Elvira's big personality drew Callie into her world. The woman's accent was endearing and several of her speech patterns made her laugh. When she explained the brandy bottle situation, Elvira said Salvador Trujillo was probably pulling a wobbly. Callie's eyebrows shot up.

"A fit. Angry. A tantrum." Elvira said through laughter.

"Oh...I must remember to share that one with Cendrine. I like hearing your phrasal verbs that are so different from American or French. And your Brit sayings are so funny.

"And yours are strange too, but we shouldn't have any problems understanding one another." Elvira grinned at her. "Callie, let me take you up the apples and pears since we don't have other guests."

"Up the apples and pears?" Callie was flummoxed.

Elvira laughed. "Up the stairs." Marble steps led to the second floor. She showed Callie the solarium, a huge walk-in bathroom with a second shower and a round-shaped master bedroom. "You are welcome to come up here to read in the solarium or just sit and enjoy our lovely view across the hills."

That night the cellar would open for Elvira's monthly wine-tasting event. When Elvira's friend arrived, Callie was delighted to hear her laugh. It was difficult to differentiate between Elvira and Saidie's English accents; the same, only different.

Elvira set the dining table with a tuna salad and thick bread. Ice cubes floated in a light red wine inside three glasses.

"Saidie, what are *you* drinking?"

"Callie, this is beer mixed with lemonade."

"Lemonade and beer?" Callie made a face.

Saidie grinned. "It's called a Shandy in the UK, but here in Spain it's called *Clara de Limón*. It's refreshing. Simply mix your beer with lemon soda." She lifted it to her lips and sipped.

"And this?" Callie pointed to the red beverage in her glass.

"Ah, this is poor man's sangria called *tinto verano con limón*. You can make that too. Just pour a glass two-thirds full of red wine and a third with lemon soda or any other gas drink."

"Gas drink?" Callie felt like she was learning a new language in Elvira's house. She sipped and tasted bubbles on her tongue.

Everyone laughed. "*Con* gas or *sin* gas. That means with carbonation or without carbonation."

"Well, I definitely like it. I will tell Cendrine about this too."

Elvira rose to dish up fried chicken tenders swimming in garlic oil. Deftly filling four plates along with crispy potatoes, she resumed her seat. Afterward, the four women sat leisurely over their meal.

FLAMENCO STRINGS UNCORKED

At eight thirty that night, Saidie held everyone's attention downstairs from the outside terrace. Bright blue, *azulejo* tiles lined the wall behind the marble-topped bar. Callie was charmed to see a spigot for *tinto verano*, so Saidie spurted some into a small glass. Callie grinned when she saw it trickle as if it was draft beer.

"Before the others arrive, let me give you a taste of this wine. *Ribera del Duero* tastes better than *tinto verano* or *Tempranillo*."

She placed several small plates of crackers across the bar and piled napkins alongside them. After stacking clean wine glasses on the end of the bar, she pointed to the stool for Darla.

Saidie raised her eyebrows, or rather where her eyebrows should be. She had a condition called *Alpecia* and she'd lost all the hair on her head, her face and well, everywhere. She typically wore a wig unless the weather was too hot. She'd explained that to Callie as she'd pulled her short wig off her bald head.

"Now," Saidie said as her impish personality added adventure to the air. "This first wine is...."

Saidie replaced her wig when they heard footsteps on the stairs. When the cellar door opened, she raised a hand in welcome and turned toward Callie and Darla. "These are our friends, Bobbie and Mike from *Almogia*. And behind them are two couples who always show up at our tastings, Mari and Juani and Angela and José."

"*Hola*, Bobbie." Callie grinned at the small woman, whose blue eyes reflected her quick smile. Pushing a swathe of blonde hair from her face, she sat on a bar stool. Her husband, Mike, who was much taller than Bobbie, edged in among the ladies with a chuckle.

There were now eight in the group who tasted wines and lingered until after midnight.

The late hours were strange to Callie, but she didn't fade until the wee morning hours. Maybe she was becoming a Spaniard after all.

Twelve

Day seven arrived. Callie was relaxed, filled up with feelings of family. She knew she'd return to the *Redonda Bed & Breakfast.* Elvira had mapped out the directions that would lead Callie westward to Fuengirola. Darla was leaving on a plane back to California the next day. Saidie had just gone home after sharing a long breakfast on the patio beside the pool. And Callie felt uneasy about her meeting with the annoying attorney.

She'd woken up to the sounds of roosters crowing. She had laid in bed, spread eagled and naked, under the covers enjoying her last morning under the roof of the round house. It was like no house she'd ever seen. Elvira had become a friend, much more than just the hostess of the beautiful B & B.

"I promise I will bring Jules here one day."

Elvira's face perked up. "Jules?"

Callie winked at her. "My special gentleman friend."

At 11:30 that morning, Callie pulled into the city of Fuengirola. She marveled at the view of the turquoise sea behind the beautiful coastal panorama. She was happy she had found the place. Damn, she missed her GPS. She sat in the gray car and looked at the sign above the door. *Attorney*, Mateo Rosa Trascasas. She counted to ten and then got out, marched up to the office and opened the door.

The woman at the front desk looked up with a smile. Callie relaxed and she said in halting Spanish, I am Callinda Beauvais to see Mateo Rosa please."

The receptionist's lips twitched. Callie wondered if her words were in the wrong order again. Damn. *This Spanish language.* Before the woman could rise, a nearby door opened and a good-looking man walked out. He had a warm smile on his face that reached his eyes and encompassed her.

Intrigued, the man stopped. When he looked between Callie and the receptionist, he started forward. "Callie?"

"Yes." Darn it. She liked him. His eyes were kind and his welcome was sincere. She backed up a few steps and then reached out to place her hand in his.

"Please come in. I've been waiting for you."

His voice was deep and smooth, certainly not what she'd anticipated, but he spoke excellent English. She heard an unexpected gentleness in him. By the time they'd reached an agreement, she'd signed the papers accepting Pedro Jiménez's offer at 2,500 euros per bottle in exchange for the brandy.

In the meantime, she was anxious to drive to Algodonales. "I'd like to go to the village and meet Javier Alonzo now. If you want to follow me, that's fine. But if you'd rather drive up later, that is also agreeable. She saw his eyebrows go up half an inch.

"Please follow me, Callie. I will lead you right into the village. Cristóbal called me this morning to remind me that the Alonzo brothers are still very much against the foundation. He is worried they may know you are coming to the village."

"Who is Cristóbal? How could those men possibly know I'm coming to the village or when I'll be there? You make this sound like a double oh seven spy movie."

He took a breath. "Cristóbal is the attorney for the Alonzo brothers. He is a good guy, Callie."

"And he is worried about me? Or was he trying to warn me? Maybe he has an ulterior motive. Pretend he's on our side and then surprise us when he pounces?"

Mateo chuckled. "Now who's watching spy movies? Actually, he *is* on our side. He likes the prospect of having a guitar art colony in Algodonales. He told the Alonzo brothers they would not receive any part of the proceeds from the sale, but they would not listen. So, that is why he is worried." Mateo rubbed the side of his neck.

Callie's eyes tracked his tanned hand. No, he certainly wasn't the man she'd expected.

"The drive to Algodonales is two hours. Between Marbella and Ronda, the mountain road is very steep with many curves. Are you sure you do not want me to drive you there?"

Callie pulled her lips in. "No, I will follow you."

He laughed. "Okay, then. If you are ready, we can leave now. We can stop to eat in Ronda. This meets with your approval?"

She glanced at his face and grinned. "That sounds good."

He didn't say a word, but instead, led her out of his office. Mateo pointed toward the small silver Mercedes on the corner. "We will take the A-7 toward Marbella. If I lose you, please stay on the A-7, avoid the AP-7 and wait just past the exit toward Ronda. There's a small restaurant there called *La Latina*. I will wait for you. *Sí?*"

She nodded and jumped into her little Clio. She'd stick to the man like glue. Her mind ran in circles; she had made it this far, she wasn't planning on getting lost again. Callie watched him walk toward the silver car. It was an easy gait, comfortable. She shook herself, put the little car in gear and eased out onto the street. When she narrowly missed hitting an old man walking on the edge of the road, she took a breath. He'd been in her blind spot and it was close. She *must* pay better ttention.

As he wound his way out of the city, the traffic on the A-7 was fast. Cars flew past her as if she stood still. She throttled the car steadily and stayed behind Mateo as he sped westward. When they drove through Marbella, she saw the twinkle of the sea and remembered that is where Olivia and Bram had spent their honeymoon. She missed her friends and a smile spread across her face. She turned on the radio and found a classical music station. *Ah, that's what I needed.* "Slow and easy". When she saw the sign to

Ronda, she followed the attorney off to the right as the sounds of violin and piano filtered through her car.

And then he stopped. She inched off the road onto the lot next to *La Latina* restaurant. She watched him walk toward her and she lowered her window.

"Can I buy you a coffee?" His eyes were the color of a murky sea, almost the same color of his silver car. They seemed to speak volumes and she was knocked sideways. She wished he wasn't so damned good looking. Why wasn't he an old, crusty attorney? Why did this one seem to have a personal challenge in this project? Why had she never spoken with him after Olivia and Bram found him a few months earlier? It was as if he'd started a ball rolling and she was running to keep up. And she was thrown off balance.

Inside the small restaurant, he led her to a table by the window that overlooked a tiered valley. White houses meandered down toward the sea and the view beyond the roofs was mesmerizing. The south of Spain reeled her in and the man across from her was trying to also. His eyebrows were perfectly arched, almost too pretty to be a man's. His teeth were aligned. Braces? He had a dimple in the middle of his chin that changed when he smiled. And his hair was perfectly cut and hugged his head like a cap.

"Am I all in one piece?"

Callie looked up quickly. She hadn't realized she'd been staring, taking his face apart like a jigsaw puzzle. "Sorry. You just...aren't, well...exactly how I'd imagined you."

"Not the gruff old guy who told you to be worried about the Alonzo brothers?" He laughed when he saw the look on her face.

Her cheeks turned rosy. "You were a bit testy, Mateo. May I call you Mateo?" She accepted her *café con leche*, glad for the interruption.

"But, of course." His face turned serious. "Just before you arrived, I received another phone call from Cristóbal. He told me that

FLAMENCO STRINGS UNCORKED

Javier Alonzo called him this morning. He said he saw Eterio, the older Alonzo brother, in Algodonales today when he was in the square drinking coffee. When he turned around a few minutes later, the man had disappeared, without talking to him. He said it was very unusual because in that village it is sacred social behavior to reach out to friends and family in a situation like that. He's sure that Eterio is going to give you trouble; he's just not sure when or where." Mateo sipped his espresso, lifting it by the uppermost rim to avoid the hot glass.

Callie put down her cup, glad she'd asked for her coffee *en la taza*. (in a cup.) The first time she'd ordered coffee in Spain, it arrived in a glass and she nearly dropped it when it burned her fingers. "He can't possibly know I am arriving in the village today."

He huffed out a breath. "Callie, it's a small village. How many people have you been in contact with there? He has a lot of family in Algodonales and they are not all as kind as Javier."

She was thoughtful. "Loli knows I'm here and... Javier."

"Who is Loli?" His fingers tapped the table between them.

She huffed, "She owns the apartment I rented and we've become friends. She's been eager to help me. She was best friends with Javier's wife before she died."

Callie saw a shadow cross Mateo's face before he reached for his coffee. "And...? If they were friends, she's probably also friends with her friends and maybe they spoke to someone else..."

"Well, she's offered to help me find a place to lease for the guitar classes. I suppose she may have told her friends. I doubt she knows that the Alonzo people are fighting me on it. She said there's an empty studio near Bernal's. She's also going to take me to Ronda to purchase the things we need for the classroom."

"In that small village, I'm sure everyone knows the Alonzo brothers want that money. It's a different world here, Callie. Everyone talks to everyone about everything. You must be diligent.

FLAMENCO STRINGS UNCORKED

Be aware of your surroundings. He wants that money and money makes people do bad things."

"Stop trying to scare me, Mateo." She put down her coffee cup. "Let's go. I'm anxious to meet these people." She put her sunglasses on her face, picked up her bag and dug out a two-euro coin.

Mateo covered her hand with his own. "My treat, Callie."

His hand was warm and she pulled hers out from under it. She dropped the coin back into her purse and followed him outside. When she opened her car door, Mateo put his hands on the top of her car and dipped his head toward her. "Some drivers have expressed concern about the safety of this highway because there are many curves going up the mountain. This stretch of highway takes about an hour. This road does not have special lanes for overtaking, so we may be behind slow vehicles for long periods of time. Passing others may be dangerous because drivers get impatient. To be safe, be patient, and do not take any risks. There are 218 curves."

Callie stared at him. "Really? Two hundred and eighteen curves. You sound like a tour book."

He laughed. "Put Algodonales into your GPS if you lose me."

"*El Carro* doesn't have GPS and it's been driving me mad."

His face turned toward her dashboard. "Tap the screen there when you turn on your radio and look for navigation."

She rolled her eyes and punched the screen to prove him wrong. And then her heart bumped in her chest. "Holy shit. I've had it all along?"

She heard him chuckle as he turned toward his car.

Thirteen

The road up toward Ronda was, indeed, as bad as he said it would be. The sky turned dark with heavy clouds. She followed him up the serpentine road along hills and mountains that were layered one upon the other as far as the eye could see. There were olive orchards and grape vineyards tiered across the valley, and also isolated dips in the mountains littered with *casas blancas* (white houses) sprinkling the landscape. Pine trees decorated the roadside so thick that at times, she couldn't see through them. Deep gorges blocked her view over the sides of the cliff.

When Mateo rounded the next curve, he slammed on his brakes. Her breath hitched and her heart beat jumped up a notch. She stomped on her clutch and brake. Her hand sprang to her throat and she swallowed hard. She missed slamming into his bumper by mere inches.

An orange truck full of rocks was stopped in the middle of the road. No blinking tail lights. No cones to alert them. After pulling her heart back into place, she watched Mateo drive around him and then dodge the huge rocks that littered the road.

The mountain incline was steep. Callie pressed her foot on the gas all the way to the floor when she realized she was lagging behind Mateo. And the car kept slowing down. No compression. What? Not another car problem. Cars trailed behind her. After a few minutes' spurt of panic, she remembered to throttle down. When she dropped it from fifth into fourth gear, the car jerked forward. She let out a relieved breath. She missed her BMW and its automatic gear shift.

Small cars sped down the mountain toward them at full tilt. Some of the cars passed them on blind curves. Solid granite pointed into the sky on one side and the gorge fell steeply on the other. And

FLAMENCO STRINGS UNCORKED

then the sun came out and the sky loosened up to shine a welcome. Just before Ronda, a huge eagle soared through the gorge with its wide wings spread, dipping and gliding over them.

She was startled when Ronda came into view. Following Mateo was now more difficult. Cars came toward her from all directions. They circled a large roundabout and then another. They were now in a busy district; his arm popped out his window to point toward her right. She missed a pedestrian, nearly crashed into a bus and then slid into the parking lot. She was shaking.

Mateo was knocking on her window. Dazed, she grabbed her purse and opened the door to let him pull her outside. "We should have driven here in one car, *sí*?"

She glared at him. "Did we really have to drive into the city?"

"Are you hungry?"

She realized she was starving. When he reached for her hand to lead her down the street, she let him pull her along like a child. When she came to her senses, she pulled her hand out of his and scowled. *Good grief.*

They walked past a very old church and then she saw tall, black, grilled gates. Military vehicles stretched in a long line and camouflage-dressed men and woman scampered past them. Then, Mateo led her past the *Plaza de Toros*, the bullring, with its ochre walls teeming with history. A metal *toreador* sculpture swished his cape in the wind. She breathed it all in. She told herself she would return to see everything at her leisure. Although, maybe she'd ride a bus next time...

"We are almost there," he whispered. "But first, the cliff."

She didn't ask where *there* was. The cliff? The sun was now shining over them as the clouds had disbursed. She followed him closely. The narrow street was thick with people and she didn't want to lose him; she knew she'd never find her car.

When he touched her hand again, she allowed him to pull her across a stone bridge. When he guided her to the right, her eyes grew round and she pulled in a breath. The ochre-colored cliff seemed a mile down. She saw a trickle of water rushing far below. A river? A waterfall? She shook her head and a slow smile crossed her face.

"Amazing, right?"

She turned toward Mateo and nodded wordlessly. When he grinned at her, he pointed across the street and pulled her behind him. The other side of the stone bridge afforded a different view but no less dramatic. "Did you read Ernest Hemingway's book, *For Whom the Bell Tolls?*"

"Why, yes I did. I know this is the place. Her mind crawled back to remember the book, one she'd read about the Spanish Civil War. Sadly, she'd walked along these hills with the characters in the book.

"This is where the Republicans pulled the government officials out of their offices and marched them to the cliff."

"Yes, Oh my God. And they pushed them off into that abyss."

"Yes."

Her fingers clung to the top of the stone wall and she leaned against it. Looking over the edge, she peered down, down, down to see waterfalls and trees growing out of the side of the cliff. "You said you were going to feed me. I hope that includes wine."

He chuckled. They walked to the end of the stone bridge and he led her into the arched doorway of the San Miguel Hotel. They walked down the stairs where she came face to face with a Botero print on the wall, titled *Dancers*. It lightened the mood as she saw the oversized couple dancing across the floor. Botero prints always made her smile.

Within minutes, she had a glass of deep, red Ronda wine in her hand. As she took her first sip, her phone rang. She saw Jules' face smiling at her. "*Hola.*"

"*Hola, ma chère.* You are now with Mateo?" His voice sounded like velvet and suddenly the need to be next to him overwhelmed her.

"Yes, I followed him up the mountain to Ronda. We're eating lunch. We'll be in Algodonales this afternoon." Her eyes met Mateo's and her eyebrow asked him for confirmation. He nodded.

"Your friend, Javier, just called me. He tried to call you and Mateo but couldn't get through. Maybe the mountains... His cousin, Eterio, just left him. They had a big argument and Eterio pushed Javier into the wall outside his office."

"What?" She was horrified.

"Tell Mateo. He can watch for him. I am going to email you a photo of the man so you know what he looks like, *oui*?" The agitation in Jules' voice was obvious as it scampered across the line like a squirrel on a wire.

"I will watch for him too. Is Javier ok?" Her voice shook.

"Yes. He said to tell you that Loli will be waiting for you. He wants to meet with Mateo as soon as he arrives. I miss you."

"Me too." She felt warm. "Do you want to speak with Mateo?"

"No, just you. Call me later?" His voice lowered intimately and she was pulled into him.

"Mmmmmm. Yes." When Jules hung up, she picked up her glass and stared out the windows. She sipped her wine and looked at the bridge where she and Mateo had just stood. The massive stones curved into an archway affording a panorama that encompassed miles. Directly below them, a breathtaking view helped calm her nerves.

Mateo squirmed next to her and touched her arm. "What?"

She relayed the conversation and watched his jaw grow taut. A small muscle jumped in his neck. She was moved by his concern and admitted he was right.

This was getting more serious.

Fourteen

The road to Algodonales was easier than the mountain road leading them to Ronda. Within thirty minutes, they entered the village, passed the bus station and restaurant on the right and tidy, white washed houses on the left. When Callie saw the church steeple of *Iglesia de Santa Ana* above the buildings, she knew her apartment was nearby. No parking spaces. She wanted to go directly to her apartment. He'd argued. She'd argued back. She won.

She spied an opening on the second trip toward town. When she drove into the slot, she narrowly missed the motorcycle where it didn't belong. She smoothed her hair. Shrugging off apprehension, she showed a girl on the street the address to the Airbnb.

The girl gave directions in Spanish and pointed.

Callie was surprised to understand her. Walk down the main street, past the church, across the square by the restaurant. She let out a little laugh. She was becoming part of the landscape.

Callie wore a light jacket and scarf tied around her throat. Her purse was strapped to her back. She pulled her roller bag behind her and grew warm as she walked up the hill. By the time she got to the church, she couldn't find the *Restaurant Bodeguita*. She was sweating, tired and wished she hadn't worn her sparkle shoes. When another young woman walked out of a shop, Callie nearly flew at her. She'd overshot the street by four blocks. The girl led her back to the square. Once there, a Spaniard saw the girl point toward the restaurant with her in tow. He grabbed Callie's elbow, lifted her bag up four stone steps to the square and pointed to the restaurant.

Callie grinned her thanks. All uphill again. She walked until she couldn't walk anymore and then Loli stood in a doorway. Rushing to welcome Callie, she opened the metal door to number seventeen.

And she faced a hundred steps going upward. *Oh. Lord. No.*
"Welcome to Algodonales, Callie."

The woman lugged up the bag. Callie pulled herself up the steps by the handrail. After touring the apartment, Loli gave her a key and demonstrated how she must tug the steel rod in the door to unlock it. And then Loli left her.

The apartment was more than Callie had expected. The bedroom was artistically decorated, welcoming and very clean. Bright pillows were tossed on a white coverlet. White, gauzy curtains blew gently from the breeze that drifted through the partially-opened window. She twirled around like a dancer and kicked off her shoes.

Her kitchen-living-dining room was perfectly equipped, had a beautiful view of the mountain behind Algodonales and a bottle of wine welcomed her on the counter. How could this place possibly give her grief? Did the Alonzo man know she'd arrived? Would Mateo and Javier be able to calm him down? Would she have to face him today? Why did she have to face him at all? The questions flit through her head like marbles.

She'd worry about it later. She had a key to her new place, euros in her pocket and her iPhone. Right now, she wanted to explore and wander around without Mateo dogging her steps. Nothing could happen with so many people milling around the square, surely?

She wanted to step into the ambiance of the village. Slipping her shoes on again half-heartedly, Callie walked down *Calle Beatas* to the square. There was only one main street and one large square; she couldn't get lost. She loved the main street's neatly lined trees and charming shops. Baskets of pink flowers hung from a little *bodega* bar called *Mesón Tendido Cero*. She stopped and ordered a chilled glass of *tinto verano con limón*. Lofty trees held chirping birds. She covered her glass with her hand when one flew over the table; she didn't want any surprises. Worry about the Alonzo people was bad enough without finding poop in her wine. As she listened to the chatter around her, she felt at peace.

"I suppose I should look for Mateo," she mused and waved at the server. "*La cuenta, por favor.*" The check please.

He bent toward her. "*Uno, veinte.*" One, twenty.

Dazed, she asked, "*Uno, veinte*? *UNO*?"

"*Sí.*" He sounded insulted when she questioned the amount.

Callie was stunned. The wine cost one and twenty euros, which would be about $1.40? She paid him and smiled apologetically.

When she pushed back her chair, Mateo's voice stopped her,

"Callie, you're not taking this seriously!"

She narrowed her eyes, turned around and placed both hands on her hips. "Mateo, I don't expect danger on every street corner. This is a quiet village. You told me to be aware of my surroundings. And I am." She wanted to stomp her foot, but instead, she spread her hands toward the cobblestoned street and the open square. "Do you really think someone will hurt me here in the open while I drink a glass of wine?" Her eyes flashed. They stared at each other.

"Yes, I see you really do have the spirit of a...." His eyes softened for just an instant before he turned to the man coming up behind him.

"Callie?" She recognized Javier Alonzo Ruiz's voice immediately. With a swift smile, she was engulfed in a hug and kissed on both cheeks. He murmured, "*Encantada.*" Charmed.

She liked him immediately. His soft brown eyes were warm beneath thick graying eyebrows. His curly, dark hair was riddled with silver and tucked behind his ears. He wore a pale shirt with the top button loose and fashionable gray slacks. His enthusiastic smile engulfed her and he whispered, "I am happy to see you."

She smiled with delight at his English. He stretched his arm toward the square and the narrow village street. "Welcome to Algodonales. You will like it very much. And we will bring Picasso's dream alive."

She touched his hand, warmed by his words. Excitement mounted as emotion bubbled up into her chest. *If Jules could meet this man and feel his exuberance, he wouldn't be so worried about me.*

The men turned toward her empty table and motioned for her to sit down again. They pulled out chairs and Mateo ordered beers for both men. He stared at Callie. She hadn't forgiven his overbearing approach yet, but turned to order in Spanish. "One more *tinto verano* with lemon please."

When she turned back toward the men, she said, "Please tell me what happened, Javier." Slipping off her light shawl, she leaned back in her chair and then toed off her shoes. She lifted her wine and looked at him over its rim.

Javier pursed his lips and massaged his shoulder. Eterio is angry because I am helping you with the school. He said families should work with each other, not with strangers. I think his brother Ruben does not share his antagonism, but he follows Eterio. He didn't really hurt me, but I was surprised…"

Mateo made a sound that brought her attention back to him. It was clear that he didn't agree with the man's sentiments. "Where is Eterio now, Javier?"

"I believe he left town. After he pushed me against the wall, I think he was ashamed, especially after my daughter hit him." Javier laughed. "She is like a mother lion for me, I think."

Mateo cut in, "Did you see him drive away or are you assuming he left?" His shoulders were rigid as he raised the beer glass to his lips. "I don't want to leave town without knowing for sure. Callie is…."

"I'm what?" She could see he was worried, but she had friends here now. He didn't need to treat her like a child. Why did men always think women had to be coddled and watched over as if they didn't have a brain in their head? She swallowed some wine and licked her lips.

"I was going to say that you are alone and vulnerable. Your friends will not be with you every minute."

"And *you* are? Mateo, you and Jules are both treating me as if I am a piece of glass. I won't break. I promise." She drained her glass and placed it on the table top with a slight thump.

Both men shook their heads at her.

Mateo exhaled an irritated breath and looked at his watch. "I don't want to drive back down that damn mountain in the dark, so I'll spend the night. And then, tomorrow we can discuss this some more."

Javier spoke up then. "*Mi casa es tu casa*, Mateo." My house is your house. The breeze picked up as the sun dropped behind the far mountain. They nodded in agreement and finished their beers.

"Let's meet here at 9:30 tonight. I will buy your dinner." Mateo looked at Callie with a challenge in his eyes.

She was beginning to get a headache. Siesta time. She nodded to Mateo, pushed back her chair, but refused to allow the men to walk her back to her apartment. She ignored their looks and began her assent up the street beside the café.

And she promptly got lost. How could she get lost? She'd just walked down this street to the café, hadn't she? All the houses looked the same and she couldn't find the street she'd walked earlier. After fifteen minutes, she leaned against a building in the shade, clearly panicked. When a Spaniard rounded the corner at a trot, her heartbeat spiked. Eterio Alonzo? No, the man walked past her.

Nervously admitting defeat, she called Loli. "Why are the houses numbered to 16 and then jump to 27? I know the house is number 17. It's listed on my key."

FLAMENCO STRINGS UNCORKED

Loli chuckled. "Callie. What street are you on?"

"*Calle Beatas*...the street right beside the café."

"Ah...I think you're walking on a parallel street that connects to my street. That café is one street over from mine. Walk past number 27, and then turn left into the little alley. You're about fifty steps away. I will stand outside the door."

Her panicky feeling dissipated when she saw Loli waving. And she was relieved Mateo wasn't there after she was so determined to return alone. Callie called Jules the minute she was inside. And she felt better instantly. His voice soothed her fears. Of course, she didn't tell him she'd already gotten lost in the small village.

That night, she heard noises outside her window. She turned off the lights and gazed down into the street. She saw movement there. Eterio? Mateo and Javier's fears spun through her head. She looked at her watch. 9:20. It was dark outside, but the café was close. When the men's words reverberated through her head, she pushed the small ammonia-filled spray bottle into a pocket for protection. She walked downstairs to the metal door, jerked on the bar and walked outside.

"Right on time," The man's voice was close.

Callie jumped and slammed a hand to her chest. When she spun around, she heard him chuckle. Mateo.

"You didn't think I'd let you walk down to the café alone in the dark, did you? Even if you think you are Super Woman, I wouldn't have done that." She heard gentleness in his voice.

"You're right, Mateo. I didn't want to walk down the dark street alone. I am glad to see you," she answered grudgingly. "Is Javier meeting us?" He touched the small of her back and guided her down the cobblestone street. Brightness appeared far below like a beacon.

"He's saving us a table. And he has news for you."

"What is it?"

"His news, not mine. Are you always so impatient?" He laughed in the darkness.

"You mean, am I nosy? Why, yes I am." She answered him with a sniff. His hand was warm on her back and she was glad he was with her. Jules hadn't been thrilled to hear she was meeting him for dinner. Why hadn't she bought food at the market? Huh.

They wove themselves through the tables and chairs parked on the sidewalk of one noisy restaurant and moved toward the smaller café next to the old church. Javier had already ordered three glasses of red wine. *A man after my own heart*, Callie thought.

"What happened, Javier?" She sat in the chair Mateo pulled out.

"Let's drink wine and eat dinner before talking business, yes?" He raised his glass to hers as she picked up her wine.

Mateo nodded beside her.

"*Salud*," Javier whispered.

After eating rice with pieces of delicious rabbit, crunchy potato chunks and sliced tomatoes covered in olive oil, Javier turned to Callie. "Eterio's brother Ruben called me. Eterio returned to Trebujena, but Margarita said he won't discuss his visit here today. She has tried to talk to him about this, but he won't listen. When Ruben questioned him, he got very angry. I do not know if it is because he is tired of them fighting him about it or if he feels bad about attacking me today."

Mateo sighed loudly.

Javier continued after shrugging his shoulders toward Mateo. "So, tomorrow, we visit the flamenco guitar shop, Callie. This is good for you?"

Callie beamed. She tapped the rim of his glass and said, "Yes, it is very good. Tomorrow the fun begins. That is why I am here. The owner will tell me about flamenco guitars?"

"Yes, a big tour of everything," Javier said proudly.

"And I have good news for you also." She'd been saving the best for last. She was determined to make this journey a good one and would not allow one man slow down her project. Callie put on a brave front though, and did not want the men to suspect that she was worried about the Alonzo people. She grinned at the men.

Both men turned toward her expectantly.

Mateo's glass stalled half way to his lips.

Javier's eyebrows rose a half inch.

The church bell gonged beside them, deep and true. And a meandering guitarist strummed his guitar across the square.

"Money. The deposit was received from the Jiménez family in the estate's bank account today. Olivier called me this afternoon. They paid 140,000 euros for fifty-six bottles."

"Fifty-six bottles. There are fifty-seven, and I...?"

"...Yes, Mateo. Keep one bottle. Olivier and I agreed."

Mateo grinned at her. "*Gracias*. The label intrigues me. The *señorita* looks like she rides the cork up to the moon and back."

Callie laughed at the visualization. "I thought the same thing when Jules and I pulled the bottles from their hiding place."

Mateo and Javier both leaned toward her, clearly interested.

"The *Chateau de Jouques* was supposed to be built in the western part of the village. Vaults to support the Chateau Terrace were built to support the Monumental Staircase, but construction was stopped for lack of funding and the chateau was never completed. Picasso's map led us to find the brandy hidden in the medieval village. It is about an hour from Pertuis." She glanced up at them.

"It sounds like a pirate story." Mateo shook his head with disbelief. "And it is amazing that you found them...all of it."

Javier listened intently. "And my ancestor made this brandy, but he couldn't do it with Picasso's help. Now, we create the school."

Callie said, "Yes, and we can't let the Alonzo family stop us." Her eyes studied Javier.

He lifted his glass. "We will work together, Callie. We cannot allow anything or anyone to stop us."

Fifteen

The *Guitarras Valeriano Bernal* shop sat in the middle of a short block on *Calle Ubrique*. It was a well-hidden haven for those who enjoy the art of the flamenco guitar. The small sign above the door seemed demure based on the fact that it was world renown. People ordered their guitars from every corner of the globe and yet, the shop was humble and quiet, tucked down a backstreet that one probably couldn't find without asking for directions.

When Javier shouldered open the door to the shop for Callie, she stared around with interest. There was an intricate archway that mimicked the end of the headstock where the tuning keys are attached on a flamenco guitar.

It was a family shop. Javier introduced her to Señor Bernal's daughter, Chari, the woman behind the counter. Callie already knew that her husband and cousin helped run the shop with Rafael. She felt the family camaraderie in the tranquil atmosphere. When Rafael joined them, he led them up a bank of steps to the manufacturing part of the shop for a tour.

Callie was awestruck when she saw flamenco guitars in various stages of creation. Rafael explained each step to her. He said the cypress wood needed to be seasoned slowly. When Callie saw the beautiful decoration around the soundboard, he showed her the intricately created piece he'd sliced thin and inlaid into a groove.

"This Spanish cypress wood is used to cut out guitar pieces. Although rosewood is also used, it is generally between ten and thirty years old; the older the wood, the better the sound."

Callie touched the wood. "And these labels?

FLAMENCO STRINGS UNCORKED

Rafael pointed. "Each type of wood lists the model of guitar it is destined for. We create about 150 guitars every year. It takes about three months to make one guitar and we usually have ten guitars in progress at one time. They take between fifty to one hundred hours to produce. Our techniques are based on guitar making from 19th century Spain and most pieces are handmade."

"And the "S" shape?" She was fascinated.

"We heat the wood on the sides of the guitar to bend it to that shape. The back side of the top is braced with metal clips as much for harmonic tone as strength. Flamenco has a brighter tone than a classical guitar and the position of the clip is vital to attaining those sounds."

When Callie pointed to rough-hewn guitar shells flat on their backs in brackets at the center of the shop, he said, "These hold the glued pieces of wood together. They remain in these devices for two or three days."

He led Callie and Javier down several steps into an adjoining room where men were working on a guitar, sanding and gluing the wood. "After gluing the back of the guitar onto the body, we cut a strip of the trim edge to circle the guitar. And then we wrap the guitar in a long rubber band to sit for a few days. Afterward, a fingerboard and a bridge are placed on the guitar."

Callie had never seen anything like it. A small weight bloomed in her chest with the responsibility of Picasso's letter. She thought of the young people who would soon be part of this flamenco guitar world.

"And then?"

Rafael smiled at her enthusiasm. "And then, layers of varnish are added and they are sanded smooth as glass. The machine heads and frets are next and strings are placed on the guitar."

FLAMENCO STRINGS UNCORKED

Callie loved the smell of wood in the workshop, the sound of hammering and sawing, the lack of noisy power tools and the relative calm at which artisans went about their work.

Afterward, he led them downstairs again and Rafael picked up a guitar to plunk the strings. "The special sounds of a flamenco guitar are not heard on another instrument," he said as he strummed it.

Callie's feet began to tap. Her eyes closed. She imagined herself wearing black flamenco shoes and a red rose threaded in her hair. When he handed her the instrument, it felt good. She sat beside him and touched the strings to enjoy the warmth under her hands.

"We will teach you about the flamenco guitar. Maybe you will learn to play this instrument?"

Callie rolled her eyes.

"We know that Loli told you about the empty building two doors away from our shop. I spoke with the owner and he agreed to lease it to the Jose Luis Alonzo Foundation. Everyone is excited about your project, Callie." Rafael was talking fast, but she understood his Spanish.

"Everyone?" Callie wanted to acknowledge the elephant in the room.

All eyes turned toward her. Their faces mirrored her concern, but not with alarm. She knew they must be aware of Eterio and Ruben Alonzo's angst. Mateo's words came back to her. There might be friends or other relatives who agreed with the brothers. How could she root out the people who might be watching her and...?

"...Please, Callie. We will make everything okay. There is a lot of work to do, so tell us what you want from us to begin your project."

Callie was at a loss suddenly. She looked at Javier's face. The gap between his front teeth gleamed when he smiled at her. She knew he wasn't one of the naysayers; his eagerness to bring this project to fruition was obvious.

FLAMENCO STRINGS UNCORKED

When she turned toward Rafael, she saw a small scar running through his left eyebrow. His eyes seemed clear, honest. And his laugh was contagious. Callie knew instinctively she could trust these men.

The bell above the door jingled and a woman walked in pulling a wheeled marketing basket behind her. She had black hair tied in a twist at her neck. A large handbag dangled from her shoulder and her hands looked as if gardening was a favorite pastime. The men greeted the young woman with hugs and kisses on each cheek.

"Callie, this is Marina, my cousin," Rafael said.

Callie was kissed briefly in the Spanish way before the woman gave her an appraising look. She seemed to look through Callie, staring at her slim black pants that hugged her calves and the red and black tunic that hung above her knees. When the woman's perusal reached her black sparkly sandals, the woman's smile didn't reach her eyes.

The appraisal had taken only a few seconds. But it was enough for Callie to suspect the woman was not pleased to meet her. Marina gave Rafael a meaningful look before she turned and left again after a tense nod in Callie's direction.

Callie was left to wonder what she'd missed. Obviously, something was amiss. A family issue or was it more than that? The room seemed overly warm after Marina left.

Chari returned to the counter behind them and slipped a CD into her disk player. The strumming of a guitar and then a man's voice filled the room to break the quiet. "*José Monje Cruz* is better known by his stage name *Camarón de la Isla*, a Spanish flamenco singer. You will like it," Chari told her.

Callie grinned at her. And then everyone began talking again, as if Marina hadn't entered to blur the feelings in their midst. "Can I look at the building, Rafael? Loli will help me with the paperwork and get items for the classroom. But I cannot lease it without seeing it."

"*Vale.*" Okay. He bent behind the counter and called someone. After a quick conversation, he held up his hand to show her five fingers.

Even in Spanish talk, she knew that meant five minutes. She gave him a thumbs-up sign.

~

Eterio Alonzo had a blistering headache. His long, curling eyelashes hid his lazy eye; black heavy eyebrows dipped in a grimace against the pain. He heard the dishes rattle in the kitchen, his sister's domain. Her voice carried into the back room as she hummed along with the music playing on the radio.

His brother Ruben dropped a plate of *boquerones,* deep-fried anchovies, on the table beside him. The noise made Eterio groan and he held his head in his hands.

"Ruben, for god's sake, stop throwing dishes around."

"We needed your help yesterday. And you were nowhere around here. I know you went to Algodonales. Margarita can't do all the cooking and wait tables too. You know that. Just because she's family doesn't mean you can treat her bad. You know that too." Ruben pulled a chair away from the table and sat down. He placed both hands on the table. "Eterio, tell me what happened today."

"I need an aspirin."

"I mean it. Talk to me."

"I *said* I need an aspirin."

Ruben glared at him.

"Okay. I went to Algodonales to talk some sense into Javier. I thought if I could look into his eyes, he would agree we are right. The money should stay in the family. The Picasso Estate does not need it."

"That's because they know Picasso wanted the money to help poor kids, not because they think we should have it."

FLAMENCO STRINGS UNCORKED

"But, Ruben. It doesn't make sense. That brandy was produced by Alonzo grapes. It was bottled by an Alonzo vineyard. They are rightfully Alonzo bottles and if they are sold, it is our money."

Margarita stood in the doorway. "I can hear you two arguing from the kitchen. That means the customers can too. What's the matter with you two? All you do anymore is fight about something. We have a business to run." She stared meaningfully toward Eterio.

When he rubbed his thumbs against his temple again and didn't answer her, she shook her head and left them again. "*Estupido*."

The music volume immediately increased. The brothers shrugged, knowing their sister was right. She had always used her common sense. Without her, they wouldn't even have the *bodega* bar or restaurant. Dishes clattered in the kitchen to punctuate Margarita's displeasure.

Eterio rubbed a hand across his mouth and scratched at his nose. "We don't need to fight about this, Ruben. You agreed we would work together because families do that. I know I repeat myself all the time about this and I'm getting sick of reminding you. I told Javier that too. He acts like a child about this guitar school. He won't listen to me either. Your arguments do not make sense. Have you been talking to him? Is that why you want me to stop trying to get this money?"

Ruben shook his head. "Did you ever stop and think how those bottles got out of Spain and into France to Picasso in the first place? Remember the Civil War? Maybe Picasso bought those bottles. We know he was partners with Jose Luis Alonzo. We don't know what their business arrangement was."

Eterio slammed both fists on the table and the plate of fish bounced a half inch only to return with a crash. The plate split and crispy *boquerones* sailed onto the floor and across the table top.

"I don't give a damn. This is now and that was then. Don't you think if our grandfather knew how much money those bottles would be worth all these years later, he would keep it in our family?"

Ruben stared at his brother. Without a word, he picked up a wet cloth, threw it at his brother to clean the mess and left the room.

~

Standing near the flamenco guitar shop in Algodonales, Callie slipped the huge key into the lock of the empty building. The front window was dirty, of course it was. The building had been empty several months. Callie rubbed a place in the glass and looked through the Dutch door. She liked the idea of opening the top half and keeping the bottom half closed. Why? She had no idea. But she liked it.

Once Javier pushed the door open so she could walk inside, the first thing she noticed was the wooden floor. When the light switched on, it opened up the space as if the sun just slipped out of the clouds.

The lighting was low and she scanned every inch of the room. It was twenty-six feet wide and forty feet deep. She placed her arms across her chest and spun to look around. The lighting hovered over its bleakness. But she could make it better. She mentally calculated the renovation costs. The floor was scratched but could be cleaned and polished. There were three windows. Once cleaned, it would bring in more light. She could put can lights across the front and above the back area. Her mind was moving faster than her mental pencil could write.

"You like it." Javier stood beside her.

"Yes, I like it. What is the monthly rental fee?" Her mind flew ahead of her thoughts; she was already placing chairs and work tables across the side of the room.

"Rafael told me we could probably negotiate a lease for 700 euros per month. Could the foundation afford that amount?"

FLAMENCO STRINGS UNCORKED

Callie's face swung around toward Javier. "700 euros?" She stared at him. Was it possible to keep the overhead that low? She'd imagined the cost twice that much.

He made a face. "Too much?" He breathed deeply and leaned against the wall. "It needs work, paint, soap and water."

"I am stunned. This place is perfect for the school, but it's so much lower here in Spain than we would pay in France or in America." She turned around and crossed her hands over her chest.

"So, this is good?" Javier watched her point to the walls. He continued, "I can clean the room. Loli can get paint and I have brushes. The bathroom plumbing is good and the toilet flushes. There's parking on the street by the market. The lights may need..." He laughed at her expression. "You want to lease it?"

"*Absolutamente.*" Absolutely. She put both hands to her cheeks and grinned before pointing to him. "Javier. I can see Picasso's dream unfolding before us. But, we need two more things to make this all work."

"What do we need?"

"We need a hostel for the students to live during the school term. And they need small jobs to earn money. The estate will pay for the guitar classes and their lodging. They will need jobs to give them some spending money and feed them."

Sixteen

The next week, Callie and Loli dressed like washer women. Buckets of soapy water splashed across walls, the floor and each other. Their friendship grew and they began to plan for a day in Ronda.

"You're driving, right Loli?"

"I can drive. You don't remember the way to Ronda?"

"Uh...I know the way. But when I drove in the city, my heartbeat was higher than a kite."

"A kite?" Loli looked at her quizzically. When the light dawned, she laughed. "Ah. It was frightening to drive in Ronda?"

"Yes, and I don't want to do it again. You can drive my car, but I refuse to sit behind the steering wheel."

Loli chuckled. "No, my car is more familiar. When should we go? This room is clean and it's easier to see what you need now, right?" Her blue eyes sparkled with excitement. "I love helping on this project, Callie. Thank you for letting me be part of it. There are so many young people who will benefit from this school. How will you do this?"

Callie was thoughtful before answering. "Let's go to Ronda tomorrow morning. As far as a list of students, I do not know how to filter it to find the needy ones. But I think we should keep the group small. We don't have a guitar teacher yet, but Rafael told me he knows a man named Juan Muñoz Galvan who is interested. Of course, I need to know what to pay the man... you know, to make it fair so he will stay with the teaching job. I'm trying to make Picasso's decisions, not just act as his go-between." She stopped scrubbing the floor and squatted down on her haunches.

Loli snickered. "If you were Picasso, you'd be painting in front of an easel. And the room would already be clean. Let's leave about ten, right after first breakfast."

Callie grinned, finished the floor and started on the walls. "Why don't you go home? I have some thinking to do and want to get the light fixtures cleaned up and finish that other wall.

"I can stay."

"Nope. Go home and cook. Can I invite myself to dinner?"

Loli laughed. "Right. About nine? I'll have it ready. I bought some new red wine too."

Callie smiled. "I'll be there, *mi amiga*."

When Loli left, Callie pulled up one of the two chairs they'd brought with them that morning and sat down. The bucket of water was dirty and her hands were swollen. When she rearranged herself on the chair, the small of her back cried out in alarm.

"I haven't worked this hard since I cleaned up the houses to sell and I don't think I like it much." Her voice echoed through the empty room. She glanced up. It was getting dark. She pushed herself out of the chair, finished the floor and scrubbed the far wall with the floor mop. She was ready to paint the walls. She made a mental note to ask Loli about the paint Javier mentioned.

After she put down the heavy bucket, she heard guitar music. She loved hearing the flamenco guitar and wondered who was playing it this late? The guitar shop was closed, so maybe it was a neighbor. The guitar sounds increased in tempo and filtered through the room. Callie laid her head back against the wall and closed her eyes. The music soothed her, but the rhythm made her want to dance. Thinking that young people would learn to play like that filled her with pleasure.

When she heard a different noise, she jumped. She glanced out the darkened window. Was that a shadow lurking out there? Her imagination had moved into overdrive lately after Mateo and Javier had filled her head with warnings. The sounds of flamenco strings were nearby, so she wasn't alone. But, her nerves were still jagged.

She stood back and surveyed the room. After we paint the walls, it will look good. All it needs after that is three long tables, twelve chairs for the students, music stands, and can lights in the ceiling. Six should be good. I want to paint the entrance wall too. No matter how much I scrub it, it still looks like dirty honey.

Another noise caught her attention. Was the door locked? She wandered over to the front of the room, tested the door and felt the doorknob turn in her hand. With a frown, she looked for her purse, pulled out the big key and locked the door. The nearby streetlight sent a feeble glow into the room. Window blinds. She wanted to cover all the glass. Why? The students wouldn't be there at night. Security. Yes, blinds for sure.

When she heard the sound of breaking glass, Callie switched off the light. She inched her way toward the window and she peeked outside. Was she paranoid? Yes. Was someone still in the guitar shop? She grabbed her phone and dialed. No answer.

"Okay, Callie. You're a big girl. It's probably a cat outside pushing over garbage." She was finished anyway. It was time to leave.

She bit the inside of her lip. "Right." Why didn't she bring her little ammonia spray with her? Or a flashlight? Or a gun? She grimaced. God, she was suspicious. She slipped her purse strap over her head and across her chest. Holding the large key between her fingers, she unlocked the door. She opened it slowly and pushed the key back into her jean's pocket. Just as she touched the doorknob, the door crashed into her body. She was thrown about five feet back into the room and then the door slammed shut.

Her hip screamed. Her head hit the floor and bounced twice. She could hear heavy breathing. The meager light from the street showed her nothing. "Who's there?!"

FLAMENCO STRINGS UNCORKED

A deep, alarming voice answered. *"Necesito hablar."*

Callie's Spanish was inadequate, but even she knew the man said 'I need to talk.' And she had no wish to oblige him.

She felt the mop bucket next to her. She was sure the voice was slightly to her right. Her breathing was rough and she started counting in her head to bring it back to normal.

"No." She whispered into the dark. Her fingers curled around the handle of the bucket. Could she throw it? It was heavier than she'd imagined. She was on the floor so she couldn't lift it from that angle to throw it. Why did she let Loli leave? Her body was twisted, but if the man came at her again, she'd kick him.

When she heard movement, she jerked up onto her knees. Pulling upward with all her might, she lifted the bucket full of dirty water. Her muscles screamed. Sloshing the water toward him, she threw it as hard as she could manage. When the man squealed, she ran for the door.

When she reached the doorway, a hand grabbed her foot. She kicked. Hard. Another grunt echoed in the room. She ran outside and remembered she'd walked to the shop. No car. Nowhere to hide. Her feet made slapping noises down the sidewalk as she headed toward the square. Four blocks. Could she make it?

A yell from behind pushed her to run faster. When she rounded the corner that would lead her toward the café, she saw the dark doorway on her left. She threw herself inside and froze.

She heard footsteps run toward her. Crouching into a ball in the darkened alcove, she watched a man run past. It was too dark to see his face but she had an idea who it was. She had the photo of him on her phone, but she couldn't retrieve it in the dark. He would surely see the light. She didn't move from the doorway for a long time.

It was nearly ten o'clock when she pounded on Loli's door. When it swung open, Loli pulled her inside. She slammed it behind her and yelled, "What happened?" Loli's face was aflame with worry.

"He came to the shop."

"Who? Do you mean the Alonzo boy?"

"I th...think so."

Loli wrapped her arms around Callie. She led her to the table where glasses of wine waited beside plates of pork tenderloins and a green salad with sliced tomatoes drenched in olive oil.

When Callie saw the table, she burst into tears. "Oh, I thought I was so smart, nobody was bloody going to scare me. But I lied. He scared the holy shit out of me."

"What happened? Wait, don't answer. Drink this first." Loli handed her the glass of red wine.

Callie looked at Loli and saw the concern on her beautiful face. She'd pulled her bright-colored hair into a bun on top of her head, wisps dropped down over her eyes. The work clothes had been replaced by a turquoise lounge dress that hung in uneven points around her ankles.

Callie lifted the glass to let the red wine trickle down her throat.

Loli sat down, reached for her glass and grinned shakily.

"I hope you gave him a black eye?"

Callie laughed. "I gave him a black something. And it felt good."

"We should call the police."

"And tell them what? I couldn't see him. But, he knows where our school is. I hope he doesn't know where we live."

"Me too. Who told him where the school was located? Nobody in the guitar shop. I am sure of that. Not Javier. Mateo was right to worry. You should call Jules."

"Are you out of your mind? Jules would jump on a plane. Next time, I'll be prepared. I'll carry my ammonia spray bottle, that big flashlight I have upstairs and... I'll start driving my car. No more walking. I'm a big girl. I don't need a man to keep me safe."

"Really?" Loli snickered and took another sip of wine.

~

Across the square, Eterio stumbled to his car. His shoulder was ablaze. She surprised him. He didn't know the small woman would be a warrior. All he'd wanted was to talk with her. He pulled out his mobile phone. "Ruben. I'm going to be gone for a couple days."

"Eterio. Dammit. What are you doing *now*? We need you. Margarita and I can't do it alone. Come home."

"I *said* I will be back in a couple days. Call Ramon to help. We can afford it." Eterio squeezed his eyes shut and lifted his hand to massage his throbbing shoulder. It was aching like a toothache.

"Eterio! What are you doing? Where are you going? Is it the brandy bottles again? Are you in trouble?"

"No, I'm not in trouble."

"Why can't you tell me what you're doing? We are brothers! I have enough to worry about without...."

"Don't worry about me. I will get what's owed to us. Call Ramon. You know he always helps if Margarita needs him." He hung up and groaned. He was glad the woman's bucket hurt his left shoulder instead of his right. At least he could lift that arm to drive the car even though his clothes were drenched with slimy water.

He dialed another number.

A man answered, "*Digame*." Talk to me.

Eterio backed away from the curb. Holding back a groan, he said, "I'm coming to Fuengirola. I know it's late. I'll be there in two hours. It's important."

Before the man could answer, Eterio dropped the phone and spun toward the road leading to Ronda, south toward the Mediterranean Sea.

Seventeen

In Pertuis, France at the manse at Beauvais Vineyards, Janine turned toward Michel and helped him sit down. He'd staggered toward the couch and slipped on the rug. She caught him before he hit the floor, but he was heavy. She couldn't lift him. He'd barely missed cracking his head against a table.

She guided him to the couch. "We have to talk to the children, Michel." They had hidden his illness too long. She knew the children noticed. And she knew that he knew they noticed. How could he not?

"Veronique told me we could call her. I think we should do that."

"And let Aurore be part of this too? Veronique will tell her. *Non.*"

Janine pulled herself up to her full height and looked down at her husband. For the first time in their married lives, she would ignore his wishes. It hurt her, but she had no choice.

"I am going to call Veronique now. She knows a doctor who will look at you. We will go tomorrow."

Her eyes told him she would not change her mind. Michel stared at his wife. When he saw the stubbornness on her face, he smiled wanly.

She reached for the phone.

"Veronique. This is *grandmére.* I am sorry it is late. But you told me to call if I couldn't help *grandpére.* It is time."

"I will drive to the manse right now."

When her granddaughter hung up the phone, Janine turned toward Michel. "It is done. We are not alone. Cendrine has the baby.

Callie is in Spain. Olivier has enough to worry about. Andre will help you too. We are a family and families help each other."

Michel heaved a heavy sigh into the quiet room. He leaned his head back on the dark blue headrest of his easy chair and closed his eyes. The sounds of silence were sometimes better than the worries that filled his head. He had tried to ignore the pains in his stomach for a long time. First, there was Callie returning home. Then, the news that Veronique was Francois's child. A child his son had hidden from them. He couldn't slap his son because his son was dead. And then, Olivier was stolen away from them and found again. And then Callie found out Francois was murdered. And then... He lifted his hand to his heart. Feeling the beating there, he knew he was still alive but he wondered if the events in their lives could stand any more trauma. When his mind flew to Cendrine's tiny girl, Lulu, he smiled.

Janine watched the emotions flit across her husband's face as he sat across from her. They'd been married nearly sixty years and the thought of losing him was too much to endure, to even imagine. Now that they had another grandchild to fit into their lives, they must come together as one. One step at a time. Baby steps.

The doorbell rang.

Michel's eyes popped open.

When Janine opened the door, Veronique hugged her until tears squeezed out of both of their eyes. She turned toward her grandfather. When he held out his arms, she ran toward him and fell on her knees. It was finally time to find answers.

~

Jules tinkered with his laptop, pressed the indentation with the screwdriver and then tossed it aside. He was listless, helpless and worried. Callie hadn't called him and he wondered if calling her would make her feel inadequate. She was insistent on doing this

Picasso thing on her own. But, dammit, he wanted her to turn to him. Was she really so independent that she didn't think she needed him? He tossed the screwdriver across the room and picked up the phone to dial Callie.

Callie picked up on the third ring.

"Hey."

"Jules." She burst into tears.

"What is....?"

"I need you. I really do. I am sorry but..."

Jules started smiling. "What is going on?"

"I wasn't going to call you."

"You didn't."

"Oh. Right." Her voice broke, overwhelmed with tears of relief. "Somebody broke into the school while I was cleaning it tonight. I threw a bucket of water at him. I know I hit him and..."

"What?! Are you alright?"

"Yes, I'm drinking wine."

"Ah, yes you are okay then. And you're not alone?"

They both laughed shakily.

"No, I am with Loli. She told me to call you and I said, no, I can do this on my own. When I saw your face light up the phone, I nearly broke the chair getting to you."

He smiled again and stretched out his legs before he carefully picked up the screwdriver and gently placed it on the table again. "You seem to get yourself into trouble whenever you are away from me. What's up with that?"

He heard the smile across the line. "Right?"

"Who was it? The Alonzo brothers?"

"I have no idea but I imagine so. He said he wanted to talk with me. But I didn't want to talk with him, so I threw the bucket."

He chuckled. "Callie."

"I know. But next time I'll be prepared, Jules."

"Next time?" His voice increased an octave.

She sighed loudly. "Well, you don't think I'm going to just walk away, do you? We have work to do. Loli and I are going to Ronda tomorrow to buy tables, chairs, music stands and…."

Jules blew out a loud breath. "The police need to get involved. I'll call Javier. Please don't go to the school alone. Can you do that for me?"

Callie sagged against the couch without answering.

"Callie?"

"Yes, dear." She winked at Loli, whose laughter rolled across the line from Algodonales, Spain to Pertuis, France. And then she poured more wine into their glasses.

After Jules hung up, Loli turned toward Callie. "You didn't lock the door when you raced out of there, right?"

Callie's eyes opened wide. "Of course not and I don't plan on going back there tonight."

"We'll go in the morning. I doubt the guy is hanging around and besides, I'll be with you. Even though it's unlocked, what is there to steal? The building is empty…unless he took the bucket with him." Loli reached into a drawer by the table and pulled out a hammer. "We won't go unarmed though."

Callie grinned.

The next day, Callie rose before the sun. Later, after locking the school building's door, she and Loli drove down the mountain road toward Ronda. Now that the brandy money was in the bank, she was anxious to get started. She was still unsure how to find Picasso's needy students; people that couldn't afford to learn the arts. She wanted to create a colony that Picasso would be proud of; a school in Algodonales where Jose Luis' legacy could be remembered without the blight of an Alonzo family feud. The village already had a world-renown hang-gliding school; she was determined it would also have flamenco guitar musicians.

The ladies walked into the San Miguel Hotel and walked down the steps past the Botero print. There was an empty couch in front of a window across the wide divide of the historical cliff. They soon had red wine in their hands and green olives on the table. When their fish, called *bacalao,* and vegetables arrived, they ate everything. The night before, they had been too wrought up to finish the meal that Loli had created and today they were famished.

Birds flew past the window above the sun-drenched terrace. The deep abyss dipped down to several waterfalls. Callie shuddered when she thought of the screaming men tossed off the cliff during the war to their death. Forcing the vision from her mind, she pulled out her iPad while she listened to Loli talk about someone named Mari.

Sipping her wine, she watched tourists on the bridge, standing on tip toe to look downward. The scene was surreal, a view from a postcard. She smiled and then jumped when Loli tapped her arm.

"Are you listening to me, Callie? You look like you are in a daydream." Loli's bright hair swished across her face.

Callie put down the iPad. "Sorry. This place is so beautiful and there are so many ideas going around in my head. What were you saying?"

"Mari Sanchez. She can help us with the student list."

"How? Who is she?" Callie picked up the iPad again and typed the woman's name. Fingers poised above the keyboard, she waited for Loli to answer.

Loli laughed at her. "Callie. Do you know how often you use that thing? Why not use pen and paper? Mari works in the human resources department at the college here in Ronda. She and I are childhood friends. I just sent her a text. We are meeting with her in two hours. Good?"

FLAMENCO STRINGS UNCORKED

"*Perfecto.* We can shop for the tables first. I doubt we can find the music stands in the same place?"

"I know where to go. But first, we go to a clothing shop on the main street. They have beautiful tunics like the ones you wear, embroidered with colored threads. We can walk."

~

Mari Sanchez was just over five feet tall, about the same height as Callie. Her hair was dyed ebony and curling strands hung down the sides of her face to swing near her chin. Her makeup was pale except for the bright mauve lipstick. If it hadn't been for her hair and rounder chin, they could've passed as sisters.

Mari broke into a wide smile when Loli and Callie walked into her office. The friends hugged. Spreading her hand toward the chairs, she sat down again and crossed her hands on her desktop. The room was littered with flowering plants and stacks of books haphazardly strewn across the table and shelves.

"So, you need help with your Picasso project?"

Callie's head came up. But of course, the woman knew about the project. Mateo had warned her, but she was still surprised that she never had to explain her presence in Algodonales nor, it seemed, in Ronda. "Loli says you might help whittle down the student applications. I want the ten or twelve people Picasso would have chosen based on their talent and inability to pay for classes.

Mari brought her hands up to her cheeks. "How are you going to advertise for this guitar school?"

Callie and Loli exchanged glances.

"Hadn't thought of that yet? There are a couple of ways you can do that and one is through our college news. Another idea that might work for you are corkboard advertisements. When will your school begin? We'd need time to receive the applications, go through each one and then assign the students to the class.

Callie took a deep breath.

Mari laughed. "Would you like me to do this for you?"

"Would you?! The estate can pay you as our marketing person and it would take a big weight off my mind if you...."

"Of course. You don't have to pay me...but may I ask you to save a spot in the class for my nephew, Miguel? He's eighteen and he's played the flamenco guitar for years, but never learned theory. His parents died when he was young. My brother gave him the guitar. He's been moved between cousins other over the years. He would fit Picasso's criteria just fine."

"It's a deal." Callie's heartbeat sped up. Student number one already in line. "I will be here another two weeks and hope to get the class running by the time I leave. Then, it will be in the hands of the maestro and Javier Alonzo's. They will work together with teaching and overseeing the day-to-day regimen of the classes. Do you know Javier?"

Mari's cheeks turned pink. "Yes. We were high school sweethearts. But we each married someone else. I know he's a widower now and I'm divorced, but..." She closed her eyes a moment and tapped her nails on the desk.

Callie's eyes widened as she looked Mari. It is that old silver lining thing again. Right in the middle of one's life when you are sure nothing will ever be right again, something jumps right into the center of it. She liked Mari and she was happy to hand over the reins on this part of her project.

She couldn't stop grinning. If, in the mix she could add a little romance to the situation? It brought her mind back to Jules and the emotion routed its way from her belly to her heart without a second in between. Everyone needed to be loved, hugged, wanted, and needed. She glanced at Mari and tried to visualize her alongside Javier, but it was difficult to see them together.

"And wouldn't it be nice to work on a project with Javier, Mari?" Loli's voice lingered over his name.

Mari picked up a pencil. She tapped it on top of her desk and she raised a seductive eyebrow. "Too late for us, I'm sure. But it will be fun to be around the man again. He was always so sweet."

Loli snickered.

~

Fuengirola was a seaside city east of Marbella where business happened, tourists lazed under umbrellas in the sand and the sun sparkled off the Mediterranean Sea most of the year. In the springtime, it was perfect because it wasn't too hot and the tourists and locals alike found their way down to the sand. *Chiringuito,* beach cafés, littered the beach, where one could order a coffee and eat breakfast while their toes sifted through the sand beneath the table.

Sun filtered into the apartment window. Eterio woke up and scrunched his body deeper into his friend's couch. His neck was twisted and his raging headache was back. He heard Ricardo in the kitchen and vaguely wondered if he was making coffee. Just as the thought entered his head, Ricardo Galvez brought in a steaming cup of hot water and a jar of Nescafe with a spoon. It clattered down next to Eterio's head on the nearby table. He groaned and pushed his hands through his dark hair, squeezing his temples to ease the pain.

"I can't lose my job, Eterio. Lazing on the beach under an umbrella is the way I like to end each day. What's so important that you drove here in the middle of the night?" Ricardo lifted a toasted slice of bread to his mouth. The freshly-grated tomato tried to slide off the top with the olive oil, but his tongue caught it before it hit the floor.

Eterio sat up slowly, opened the coffee jar and tapped the grounds into his cup. "You had a job the other day with Esteban's friend, an attorney here in Fuengirola named Rosa."

FLAMENCO STRINGS UNCORKED

Ricardo chewed his toast and moved the tomato around inside his mouth to answer him. "Yes, why?"

"Do you want to earn some quick money?"

After swallowing the toast, he washed it down with his coffee. He stared at Eterio for a heartbeat. "You're not pulling me into any of your tricks, are you? That's the reason why I left Trebujena, remember? One of your great ideas? Sometimes you stretch your luck, Eterio."

Eterio chuckled. "No, man. This time, it's something much better and it should be easy. And you can help. Ruben and I found out that our *bisabuelo*, great-grandfather Jose Luis was a partner with Picasso years ago..."

"...*Pablo* Picasso?" Ricardo choked on his coffee.

"Who else? *Bisabuelo* Jose Luis used Alonzo grapes to produce brandy after World War Two ended. Of course, Franco ruled Spain and people were doing a lot of weird things. The brandy bottles were moved from Spain to France where Picasso hid them for years. Someone found them a few months ago."

"Hey. You'll be rich!" Ricardo's eyes lit up.

"That's the problem. Picasso left a letter. He wants the bottles sold....OUR bottles sold to create a guitar school in Algodonales with the money." Eterio's headache eased as he drank the coffee and saw Ricardo's face light up with interest.

"So, what are you going to do?"

"I need to find the bottles and sell them myself. That's the only way we're going to get that money. My attorney is backing out and the woman starting the school is..." Eterio rubbed his shoulder again.

"...Where are the bottles?" Ricardo's voice hitched up a notch.

"That's where I think you can help me, my friend."

"How?"

"Remember the job you and Esteban had the other day?"

Ricardo's forehead creased with confusion.

Eterio rolled his eyes. "The *job*? You told me you guys carried some heavy boxes for the attorney and took them into his cellar?"

"Sure. I remember, but...? Wait! Were Picasso's bottles in those boxes? They were heavy, but we had no idea..."

"That's where you earn your money, Ricardo. Take me to the bottles."

"But, they're in the man's cellar. You'd have to break in and..." Ricardo's eyes rounded. "Hey, man. No way am I going to help you steal those bottles...no, no...not me." He held up his hands.

Eterio squeezed the cup with both of his hands. "I know the man lives alone. His wife died. No kids. He works days and the bottles are in that cellar. It would be quick and easy. The internet gives me everything except his home address."

Ricardo gulped down the last of his coffee and considered Eterio's words. "You say the bottles were from your *bisabuelo's* vineyard and Picasso had them all these years. Did your *bisabuelo* maybe sell them to Picasso? Was that why he had them? And how did they get from Spain to France?"

"Who the hell cares? I think they're here in Fuengirola now and I want them." Eterio's headache was returning. His shoulder still throbbed and he felt rage moving up his spine.

"What does Ruben say about this?"

"He agrees with me, of course."

"Oh. I told you, nothing illegal. I don't want to lose my job. Breaking and entering and stealing..."

Eterio dropped the cup on the table with a thunk.

Ricardo jerked in his chair. "Okay. Okay, but I don't like it. When do you want to do this? I have to be at work in three hours."

The smile on Eterio's face lit up the room like warm sunshine.

Eighteen

That same morning, Veronique and Janine helped Michel into the car after he'd walked slowly across the porch with a cane bearing his weight. Tap. Tap. Tap. Sunshine warmed the property and sparkled off the glazed windows of the manse.

Veronique asked Janine, "Did you call Cendrine?"

Janine sucked in a breath. Rolling her eyes, she nodded toward Michel. "*Non*," she whispered.

Michel settled himself in the back seat and missed the looks between the women. He laid his head back on the headrest and let out a big sigh. Closing his eyes, he tinkered with the seat belt. When he slid it across his belly, he let out a yip and tossed it aside.

Veronique's eyes clouded and she patted her grandmother's arm after she slid into the passenger seat beside her. Although she saw Janine's body quaking, Veronique knew that she was relieved to get Michel to a doctor. She knew her grandmother had been worried about him for months. He'd asked her not to speak about it to the family. And Janine had been frustrated and frightened.

When Veronique questioned her grandmother, she'd admitted he was ill. "Each morning is worse than the day before and he is weakening before my eyes." Janine had burst into tears and the rest of her fears had stumbled out. "When he agreed to see a doctor, I ran to the bathroom, sat on the toilet seat and let the tears come." She said she hoped it wasn't too late.

Veronique drove them through the streets of Pertuis and turned at the big roundabout that led to Aix en Provence. She'd contacted Doctor Paul Havre that morning. He was waiting for them at the hospital. It hadn't been easy, but he was her best friend's

FLAMENCO STRINGS UNCORKED

father; she'd known him for years. He recognized the Beauvais name. When Veronique had explained Janine's worries, he'd juggled his calendar to see him. Now, she glanced in the rear-view mirror. Her grandfather grimaced when her car bumped over a rough patch in the road.

It was springtime and everything shone like new. Fields of poppies guided them south and then mustard flowers clotted the landscape sending a shimmering, yellow panorama for miles.

Janine was quiet and she kept turning around to watch her husband as he rested with his eyes closed. He'd been in so much pain the day before, she knew it was time to find out what was going on with his belly. And she wouldn't stop fighting him until they had answers.

She glanced at her granddaughter, a young woman whom she'd only met two months earlier. She smiled and shook her head. Francois' daughter was such a blessing that even thinking about the day Callie introduced her to them brought tears to her throat. A granddaughter who'd lived only a couple miles from them for twenty years. They'd missed her growing up years. They'd missed her laughter, her smiles, and her life. Now her father was gone. He'd voluntarily missed it too. Her son hadn't trusted anyone with the knowledge and she wished she could spank him like a child. She chuckled silently. And she wished for the hundredth time that he wasn't dead.

Veronique turned toward Janine and patted her arm, thinking the sound of her mirth was something else. Janine covered the young woman's hand with her own.

Janine's thoughts turned to the girls again. Cendrine was her daughter Chloe's child; Chloe died. Veronique was her son Francois' child; Francois died. Now she was a great-grandmother to three children; the twins and baby Lulu. And then there was Francois' widow, Callie, who'd just given them new information; Francois had been murdered. Janine's breath caught on the word and she held the tears tightly against her eyelids. She couldn't lose Michel too. She wouldn't. Her fingers tightened in the folds of her skirt. She pulled down the sun visor to watch Michel in its mirror. He appeared to be sleeping and the creases on his face were smooth. So, not so much pain today. She looked at her watch. They were nearly there. She took a page from his book, laid her head back and closed her eyes.

~

When Jules called Javier Alonzo that morning, the Spaniard shook his head. "How should I proceed? My cousin is serious about stopping the guitar school and it makes my brain scream with anger. I do not want to believe he would have hurt Callie last night."

"This can't happen again, Javier." Jules knuckles were nearly white as he hugged the phone to his ear.

"I will talk with the police when we hang up, Jules. I saw Callie and Loli go inside the school this morning, but only for a few moments. They planned to drive to Ronda today, so Callie is not alone."

Jules made a sound in his throat. "I can't get away from my business for a few days, Javier. Please let me know what the police say about Callie's attack. Everyone should be thrilled to have that school in the village with Picasso's..."

"We *are* proud, Jules. This young man is just one of a few who think the money should go to his family."

"*One of a few*? There other people who might try to stop Callie?" His voice was agitated as he leaned his forehead down on his hand.

"Well...I've been told most people are glad about Picasso's wish to open the school. However, others think the money from those bottles should go to the Alonzo family… at least half of it, since Jose Luis and Picasso were partners. There is that."

"Oh, God. I didn't know. Did you tell Callie?"

"No. I didn't want to upset her. She is working very hard to bring this project together. Her smile lights up everything around her. She is delightful and I love hearing her laughter…"

Jules sighed heavily. "Yes, she is all those things, Javier. But she must be prepared. If others try to stop her or…"

"I know. As soon as the ladies return, I will talk with her. For now, I'll go see the police."

When he hung up, Jules was filled with uneasiness. He was massaging his eyes with his fingers when Claude walked in with more computer problems. Since his return, they'd had issues come up that precluded his leaving France any time soon. Maybe next week. Callie would have to manage this one on her own. She thinks she can anyway, so why worry? He laughed, knowing the worry wasn't going to leave him anytime soon.

~

In Aix en Provence, Veronique drove into the circular drive at the Doctor's Institute where Dr. Paul, worked. There was a wheel chair at the entrance and she hoped her grandfather would use it.

Michel inched out of the back seat, using Janine's arm as a crutch. Veronique wheeled the chair toward him, but the look on his face told her that he wasn't going to sit in it. She shrugged, pushed it aside and held the door open for her grandparents.

Once inside the brightly-lit lobby, she whispered to the girl at the desk and then led her grandparents to a loveseat in the lounge. "I'll park the car and be back in a moment. I've already told them you are going to see Dr. Paul, *oui*?"

Janine and Michel nodded and made themselves comfortable. At least Janine did. Michel's face was ashen and he sat as if a broom held up his spine.

One hour later, Michel was laying on a bed with medication flowing into his bloodstream through an IV. Dr. Paul Havre was congenial, but serious. When he had touched Michel's belly with the tips of his fingers, the old man nearly jumped off the bed.

The doctor had given him an examination followed by pain medication. "I ordered a CT scan of the abdominal area. That will rule out appendicitis or tumors. I'll order an upper and lower gastric intestinal X-ray if the scan doesn't show anything unusual. Since Michel has suffered so long, his condition isn't going away soon."

Janine squeezed her husband's hand and stared at the doctor. Veronique stood quietly beside his bed as the doctor continued.

"I want you to stay overnight, Michel. There are tests that should tell me what is going on inside there. I don't like it that your pain has increased so rapidly." The doctor's grey eyebrows arched upward and he touched Michel's hand on the bed.

Michel nodded and closed his eyes. "I do not care where I sleep. I just want the pain to go away."

Veronique and Janine looked worried, but not surprised. Veronique hugged the doctor before guiding her grandmother to a couch in the waiting area near Michel's room. "Once he's put into his own room, shall we drive home or do you want to stay here?"

Janine's eyes filled with tears. She reached for her granddaughter's hand and said slowly, "I really don't know." She struggled to swallow, willing herself not to cry. But in the next minute, she'd lost the battle.

"We should call Cendrine, *grandmére*. Please."

Janine closed her eyes and nodded. "I have already pushed Michel into getting help. I might as well go the rest of the way."

~

Jules was conflicted. He noticed Mateo's voice changed over the phone the last time he mentioned Callie's name. The man sounded enamored with her. He shook himself to be rid of the thought and lifted the phone to dial the attorney's number.

He pulled the files toward him, thinking of Callie far away and wishing it wasn't so. The computer business was in full swing and he was needed here. He knew that and wished that wasn't so either. But he couldn't be taking off every time Callie needed him. Really? He chuckled. It's exactly what he wanted to do.

When Mateo answered, Jules' files were stacked and placed inside the box to haul to his car. The presentation wouldn't take long, but it would take all of his concentration.

"*Hola,* Jules."

"Mateo. Thanks for returning my call. Things are happening in Algodonales. Someone attacked Callie last night at the school building. We think it was Eterio, but she didn't see his face because it was dark."

"What?!"

"She hit him when she threw a bucket of dirty mop water and then ran like hell. Who knows if he will try to hurt her next time? Javier is talking with the police. I wanted you to know…" Jules words came to a whispered halt.

"Thanks for calling me about this." Mateo sighed loudly. "The good news is that the bottles will be collected tomorrow. I don't want to open my bottle of brandy yet, but I'm anxious to taste the stuff."

Jules made a sound in his throat. "It is very smooth. If you go to Algodonales, please call me?"

"Yes. I will drive there tomorrow after the bottles are gone. It will be nice to see Callie again. She is spirited, huh?"

Jules closed his eyes and heaved a sigh. "Yes, she is."

Nineteen

Ricardo pointed to the house across the street with an enclosed courtyard. "That's it. The boxes we carried into his house are in his cellar. I don't want to do this, Eterio. We don't even know if those boxes have the brandy bottles inside them. If we get caught stealing them, you might go to jail this time and I don't want to be your cell mate."

Eterio snorted and thought a moment before opening the car door. "You wait here. I'm going to have a look around before we do anything..."

"You mean before *you* do anything..." Ricardo whispered.

Eterio slammed the door and readjusted something inside his pants pocket. He looked back toward Ricardo with a disgusted look on his face and walked across the street.

~

Michel was resting quietly in his hospital bed when Janine walked in the next morning with Cendrine beside her. When she saw her grandfather, she rushed to his side and picked up his hand where it lay on the bed covers. He opened his eyes and gave her a wan smile. His white hair was disheveled, but his face was devoid of the pain she'd seen on his face for weeks.

"*Ma petite.*" His grip was firm.

She smiled at him and lifted his fingers to intertwine them with hers. "*Grandpére.*" Her long hair fell across her face and she lifted it with a swipe of her hand to twist it behind her neck.

"Where are the children?"

"Olivier is with them. He sends you a hug and tells you to hurry up and get home again." Her eyes glossed over and she squeezed them closed with a sniff. When she had her voice under control again, she whispered, "You know that…"

Dr. Havre walked into the room and tapped Michel on the foot. "You, sir, have had all the tests that I need to learn what has been keeping you down for the past few months." His stethoscope dangled across his white jacket. One hand held it from swinging across Michel as he bent over to feel Michel's wrist. When he saw Janine and Cendrine near Michel, he asked, "Veronique?"

"Bringing coffee," Cendrine murmured as her cousin walked into the room balancing a tray with three coffees and chocolate croissants amid napkins and cream pots.

The doctor nodded and pulled up a chair, urging the ladies to sit down on the small couch and chair across the room. Veronique pulled them closer. They huddled in a circle around Michel, who watched the grouping with a sigh.

"Dr. Havre glanced toward Michel. "You have Ulcerative Colitis, Michel. Treatment can help you, but this condition cannot be cured."

The women all responded as one, "What?"

He raised his hand toward them before he continued in a raspy voice. "It is an autoimmune disease where T-cells have infiltrated the colon. The imaging and test results show that it is confined to the colon and ileum. The innermost lining of the large intestine in the colon and the rectum are inflamed. It is a chronic condition that can last for several years or lifelong."

"What caused this condition?" Janine's hand clasped her throat to still the shaking.

"Nobody knows. One possible cause is an immune system malfunction. There are other causes but nothing definitive."

"His bloody diarrhea and abdominal cramps along with rectal bleeding should have been addressed long before this," he said and shook his head toward Michel.

When Michel tried to push himself up on an elbow to argue, the doctor pressed a hand to his leg through the covers. "I understand you didn't want to worry anyone, my friend, but we're here now and I'm glad of it." He gave a meaningful glance toward Veronique who was fighting tears.

"Michel, you have a toxic megacolon which is a potentially life threatening complication of ulcerative colitis. That's the pain that has kept you so low the past few months, I think. This is where a portion of the large intestine becomes paralyzed, stops working, and swells to many times its natural size."

Janine's intake of breath was loud in the room as she moved her chair closer to squeeze his hand. He breathed loudly and rubbed the top of her hand with his fingers in mute acknowledgement.

"You said you can treat it. What are you going to do?" Cendrine's fierce whisper was met by Veronique's worried face.

"It needs immediate attention."

"Does alcohol make it worse? Certain foods? Cheese? Citrus? Bread?" Janine's voice wavered.

The doctor again held up a hand and smiled tiredly at her. "Carbonated drinks also cause distress. They frequently produce gas and trigger the flare ups, but alcohol? Not necessarily."

Cendrine's face turned pale and she stood up quickly. "Carbonated? Such as sparkling wine?"

"Why yes. Sparkling wine would be a trigger to this condition. I believe that when sparkling wine is uncorked, the yeast ferments sugars and form carbon dioxide gas making it fizzy."

"Oh. My. God. *Chloe Rosé.*" Cendrine's breath stilled and she stared at her grandparents. She felt Veronique's hand slide into hers.

"*Chloe Rosé?*" The doctor's eyebrows met above his nose and his deep gray eyes looked confused.

"My sparkling wine," Cendrine whispered. "I may have caused *grandpére* this pain from his drinking my sparkling wine." Everyone stared at her. "At Beauvais Vineyard. We began a new label for my sparkling wine and..." Her voice broke.

The doctor's eyes swung toward Michel. "Wait. I'm just saying it could have been the culprit but let's not put the burden on you, my dear. Let's decide what we're going to do about it, instead, shall we?"

Cendrine's shoulders sagged and Janine reached over to squeeze her knee. Michel shook his white head against the pillow and touched his wife's hand. "Cendrine. *Non, ma petite*. Please..."

"What is the treatment? Is there a special diet?" Janine put on her no-nonsense face to stare at the doctor. It eased the tenseness in the room.

"There is no actual diet for this condition, Madame Beauvais."

"Janine please."

He smiled at her. "Some people recommend avoiding a high fiber diet such as raw fruits, vegetables, seeds, and nuts in addition to other foods that would aggravate Michel's symptoms. It may be reasonable to keep a food journal to track the foods that do and do not aggravate his symptoms.

She stared at him fixedly as if she mentally typed the words on her brain. Her fingers caressed Michel's and she turned to give him a worried smile. "I can do that."

The doctor nodded. For example, bananas, white rice, white bread, applesauce, bland soft foods. Those foods are probably the best for him."

Veronique spoke up as her eyes wandered across her new family, one that she'd been introduced to a few weeks earlier. Her heart expanded until it was hard to breathe, but she was anxious to learn everything she could about her grandfather's illness. "Why does this cause bleeding from the rectum, Dr. Paul?"

He smiled at the endearment she'd used for him during the years he'd known her since a child and winked at her. The colon is the part of the digestive system where the water is removed from undigested material and the remaining waste material is stored. The rectum is the end of the colon adjacent to the anus. So, when it isn't working, it leads to the symptoms Michel has been experiencing. Now that he's here, his quality of life should dramatically improve."

All eyes turned toward Michel. When he closed his eyes and smiled, Janine gripped his fingers and didn't let go.

~

In Fuengirola, Ricardo tapped his fingers on his thigh as he watched Eterio walk toward the house on the quiet street. And then he lost sight of Eterio when a white van drove past and obliterated the vision of the attorney's house. When it stopped, his eyes rounded and he whispered, "We have problems." When the van drove into the attorney's driveway, Ricardo read the sign on the side of the vehicle.

Vinos que encarnan sueños. Wines that embody dreams
Jiménez Bodega y Vino
Arcos de la Frontera, Cádiz, España

Eterio walked leisurely to his car while his eyes darted between Ricardo and the van. He slipped into the seat beside Ricardo. He snarled and tapped his fingers on the steering wheel. "We wait."

"Wait for what? They are...." He stopped mid-sentence when he saw Mateo Rosa open the courtyard door to greet the driver. Another young man walked up to shake his hand. And then they were inside the house.

When Mateo shut the door, Eterio groaned. "We *wait,* I said."

"What are you going to do, Eterio, rob the van after these men store the bottles?" He sneered at the suggestion.

Eterio turned toward Ricardo and stared at him through hooded eyes. "*Sí, exactamente.*" Yes, exactly.

Ricardo raised both of his hands to cover his face. "No, man. I told you..."

Eterio grabbed both of Ricardo's hands and shoved them downward with an oath. He stared into his friend's face. "We are going to do this. Before that van returns to Arcos de la Frontera, that brandy will be in my trunk." His dark eyes seemed to drill a hole into Ricardo.

Ricardo looked away first. He squeezed his eyes to a squint and slammed his fist into Eterio's car door. The window shook and his anger permeated the inside of the car.

And then they saw the two men materialize beside the van with the pine boxes that Ricardo and Esteban had taken into the house only a few days earlier.

Twenty

Callie huffed out a jagged breath when she walked up the last three steps to the rocky viewpoint above Algodonales. She glanced between the antique chapel high on the hill and the white village below. Leaning against the stone wall that was just high enough for her to boost herself onto, she sat and stared across the way. As her breathing returned to normal, jasmine-scented air filled her nostrils. She glanced into the crevices around her to spy the white flowering vines she knew must be nearby. The fragrance mingled with the view of the village and her heart gave a lurch.

She felt like crying. Nobody had left her alone since the man surprised her two nights earlier. She'd needed to be alone to decompress. Callie had cradled the small ammonia spray bottle in her pocket, along with mild apprehension, when she escaped that morning. The lure of the old church and the view of Algodonales and the hills beyond were calming.

Algodonales seemed a town frozen in a time warp. The twelve water fountains in the village fascinated her. She had passed a few when she walked up the winding street at the edge of town moments earlier. Callie tried to grasp the concept of residents filling bottles from the fountains situated throughout the village as they'd done for centuries. The old cistern where the women had rubbed their laundry clean next to the fountain now sat unused, a testament to the old days.

Callie tilted her head to stare at the sky, closed her eyes and caught the whiff of the illusive Jasmine again. "Mmmmmmmm." She inhaled deeply and spun around. She enjoyed the silence, but it was time to return to the village, so she retraced her steps. As she walked down the deeply inclined walkway, she was alert for anyone lurking nearby.

She mused about the possible maestro teacher that Rafael said was an excellent flamenco guitar player. Could the man teach his musical secrets to children? She hoped so. Options were limited and she hoped that Juan Muñoz Galvan would be the man for the job.

She laughed aloud as she hit the bottom of the uneven street and bobbed between narrow buildings littered with tightly parked cars and flower pots. She would be an audience of one for a flamenco guitar concert. Hopefully by the end of the day, the José Luis Alonso Foundation would have its guitar teacher. She tapped her feet along the cobblestones, suddenly anxious to return to the shop.

Two hours later, she shook Juan's hand. He kissed both of her cheeks. The deal was set. Now he needed music students and a start date for his first semester of classes.

Callie could still hear his flamenco guitar music dancing through her head. She wanted to celebrate the occasion with a chilled *tinto verano con limón* at the café in the square. However, when she turned around to reenter the school, she lost her train of thought.

Mateo Rosa was leaning against his silver car. When he began walking toward Callie, her face filled with confusion. Her eyes blinked against the sun while Juan loaded his guitar case in a small Fiat, waved to her and then drove away.

"What are you doing here?"

"Jules called."

"And?"

"We've decided you need a body guard."

"You're joking." Anger spurted upward into her chest. She squeezed the top button on her blouse and nearly ripped it off.

"No joke."

Callie rolled her eyes and stared at him. She could see her reflection in his sunglasses where they sat on his long nose. His hair was windblown and he was dressed casually in jeans with a light pullover shirt. She shook her head and wanted to stomp her foot. He wasn't going away.

"Well, Mateo, make yourself useful then. The furniture delivery truck is coming around the corner right now. You can help unload and put the tables together for me." She ignored the look on his face and turned on her heel to reenter the school again.

The large truck from Ronda lumbered to a stop. She lifted an arm to point where she stood between Mateo and the driver. When she saw Mateo's eyebrows raise in astonishment, she turned to hide her twitching lips.

He placed both hands on his hips and looked between Callie and the truck. It was obvious that unloading furniture and assembling it was not what he signed up for.

He walked inside the school.

They stared at one another.

"Since I can't take care of myself, how on earth can I possibly screw tables and chairs together?" Her eyes sparked.

He shook his head with resignation and headed toward the truck without a word.

Callie marched inside hard enough to pound nails into the floor. She kicked the broom out of her way before pushing the infamous bucket against the door. He'd need room to haul in everything she bought in Ronda. And Callie had no intention of helping him. Men.

Javier walked in the door, scratching his head after he passed Mateo on the sidewalk. When he saw Callie's face, he asked timidly, "Callie, Mari Sanchez will be here this afternoon and asked if you could join us for dinner? Loli is going to meet us and…" he stretched his head outside again. "Maybe we should ask Mateo too?"

She closed her eyes, defeated. "Yes, Javier. Of course." She reached down to pick up the broom and concentrated on sweeping the floor instead of throwing it across the room. She had no idea why she was so agitated. He was only trying to keep her safe. And Jules had been worried or he would never have called the man. She couldn't put her finger on why she felt so frustrated. She needed to get her mind right, but wished she was still on the hill overlooking the beautiful village next to the tranquil chapel, inhaling Jasmine.

During a normal evening in Algodonales, the community honored the traditions of sharing a meal and conversation. At nine thirty that night, lights twinkled from the trees and the church bell gonged, masking their conversation in the sleepy main plaza. Callie and Loli sat across from Mari and Javier. All four held a glass of red wine and shared green olives perched on a plate with bits of bread. When a menu was placed into their hands, Loli and Javier barely looked at it. They obviously knew what they planned to order.

Callie enjoyed the savory Spanish cuisine, always looking for something new to try. So far, her favorites was *salmorejo*, a thick, cold tomato based soup which was a cousin to *gazpacho*. The tiny pieces of serrano ham and boiled eggs on top were delicious. She liked *paella* but it was usually for two people because of the intricacy of creating the dish. She also liked *solomillo,* a pork tenderloin she'd eaten in Ronda. Here in Algodonales, she had played it safe. Tonight was different.

Mateo had worked nonstop. All the tables were in place and chairs lined the back wall at the school. The music stands stood up next to the chairs like soldiers. He hadn't complained. In fact, he hadn't said one word to her. She felt chagrined. She knew she was wrong and had worked herself into a tizzy trying to make up for it.

When he tapped her hand as it was splayed across the menu in front of her, he rolled his eyes toward the server who waited patiently for her order. She pointed the *carrillada*.

FLAMENCO STRINGS UNCORKED

After ordering a second glass of wine, she gradually unwound. She'd felt like a tightly coiled spring. Laughter filled the night air from the tables around them and she guiltily looked at Mateo.

His eyes met hers. "Friends again?"

She chuckled and raised her right hand, which he shook with a grin on his face. While the others discussed the student list and complemented Mateo on his work earlier in the day, she lifted her wine again. "I'm sorry I was snarky today. I just want to...well, I'm just so motivated to get the school going and... you and Jules are making me feel inadequate. I could let someone else do it, I suppose, and go back to France...but..."

"Well, you cannot start the school if you are incapacitated before the first students walk into your door."

She rolled her eyes and raised her glass. "Touché."

"Ah, what does snarky mean?" His forehead creased.

Callie laughed. The night air was cool but comfortable. The church bell gonged again and birds settled in the branches of the huge tree above them. Tables were scattered across the stone patio. Muffled conversation rose and fell in tandem with the alcohol intake. Callie was comfortable and the wine had calmed her down. In fact, she found herself enjoying herself so much that she'd nearly forgotten why Mateo had arrived in the first place. *Okay, I'm glad he's here.*

She shot him a look, hoping she hadn't spoken the words aloud. His eyes met hers and held a moment longer than was comfortable. She clutched the arm of her chair and lifted her head to enjoy the soft breeze in her hair. Threads of her silver bangs lifted and then fell across her forehead.

"That silver hair doesn't fit with the rest of you, Callie. Did you have it done on purpose or is it natural?" Mari's fingers lifted her own black strands, pulling several down to look for frayed ends.

Javier laughed. "Yours used to be that ebony color, Mari. Are you coloring your hair because you don't want your silver to show? You don't want to look old like the rest of us?"

"Javier!" Loli scolded.

Callie noticed Mari's shoulders shrug inside the bright blue tunic she wore.

Mari lifted her glass and stared at Javier over the rim. "Javi, my perception of old is a moving target depending on how many candles I've managed to collect on the birthday cake. And I color my hair because I like it that way. Silver is fine. Just not on me." She gave his salt and pepper hair a knowing look and sipped her wine.

Javier laughed at her and lifted his glass in a toast. "Here's to stretching the passages from spring to winter then." He sipped his wine and watched her face change from a lion to a kitten.

Callie lowered her eyelashes and measured her words. "Mari, attitude is the Fountain of Youth. If you have a zest for life, an interest in the world and the pursuit of a passion with a desire to learn, youth follows you. It doesn't matter the color of your hair, the shape of your body or the people around you. And I for one refuse to age quietly." She took a sip of her wine.

"Amen! Mari and Loli raised their glasses in camaraderie.

The men laughed at the women.

"Well said, Callie. Your words make music." Mateo's voice was warm, almost intimate.

The server delivered several hot, steaming plates of food and then disappeared. Callie saw large, brown lumps of meat slathered in dark gravy. Bits of crispy, grilled potatoes sat alongside a variety of vegetables. With cautious interest, she took the first bite of her meat and groaned with pleasure as her tongue curled around her fork.

"You like it then." Mateo whispered.

"Yes. Delicious. What is it?" She stabbed another piece and plopped it into her mouth, liberally doused with the dark gravy.

"Pig's cheeks."

She stopped chewing and snapped her head toward him. "Pig's cheeks?" She swallowed the meat and studiously wiped her lips on the napkin.

Everyone laughed at the look of surprise that swamped her face. She held up her fork before stabbing the meat for another bite. She'd never tasted anything as good as this. *Pig cheeks. Oh my.*

When Mateo's phone buzzed, he ignored it. "I don't recognize the number and I'm hungry." He slipped his fork into the food on his plate, snagged a large prawn and said, "*Gambas,* my favorite. I don't like to answer my phone when I eat." He chewed thoughtfully and swallowed some of his wine.

Everyone ate while they listened to the musician who sat on the low stone wall beside the church. His guitar was in his arms and flamenco music filled the square. The music was steady and mesmerizing. His open guitar case lay at his feet. When two women walked over and dropped some coins inside, he strummed his guitar in a quick cadence in response and nodded his thanks.

Mateo's phone rang. And again, he ignored it.

Callie dabbed her bread into the gravy with her fork and ate every bite of food on her plate. "The food in Spain is very different from America; I want to taste everything." The fish she'd eaten at *La Casa Redonda* with Elvira had been exquisite. In fact, everything she'd eaten at the B & B was delicious except that nasty Marmite Elvira spread onto toast. She made a face at the memory.

When Mateo's phone rang a third time, she wasn't surprised when he clicked it open. Within seconds, the look on his face had everyone's attention.

"What the hell? You don't think I had anything to do with this, do you, Pedro? I will return to Fuengirola tomorrow. I am so sorry. There must be something we can do..." He picked up his wine glass,

FLAMENCO STRINGS UNCORKED

emptied the last drop and lifted it into the air to get the server's attention for another.

Everyone was thoroughly mystified as they waited to learn what the conversation was about. All eyes watched Mateo as he sighed deeply.

Mateo closed his eyes a moment before he whispered through another deep sigh that sounded like a groan, "The Jiménez Bodega van was high jacked and all the *Sueño España* bottles were stolen. The driver was knocked unconscious."

Time stood still.

Twenty One

Stunned silence enveloped the table. Javier and the women stared at Mateo as if he had two heads.

Callie was the first to speak in a voice sounding like gravel. "Stolen? During delivery to their winery, all the bottles…stolen?" Her white knuckles pressed against the table top and her stomach knotted.

The group stared at Mateo and fingered the stems of their wine glasses while a breeze lifted the edge of their table cloth. Music broke the ominous silence as the guitarist strolled by their chairs.

Mateo looked weary and rubbed both hands across his face trying to make sense of it. When he looked at the others, he chose his words carefully. "This theft makes me look complicit. Pedro Jiménez is angry, obviously. It's too much of a coincidence. They were delivered to me for storage. His delivery van was only known within our immediate circle." He leaned back in the wrought-iron chair and slumped his shoulders.

"How could this happen, Mateo? It must be the Alonzo brothers, but how could they…? Who else could it be?" Callie ran shaking fingers through her hair. She braced her head up with both hands and her elbows leaned on the table as she looked at him beseechingly.

Mateo reached for his phone and dialed a number. When the man on the other end answered, he met Callie's eyes. "Cristóbal. We have a problem. The brandy bottles were stolen from the Jiménez delivery van this evening. Have you heard from either of the Alonzo brothers? I have a very bad feeling about this. Pedro Jiménez just called me. I think we may need your help." He made a sound in his throat and hung up after saying, "*Vale.*" Okay.

He stared at Callie, took an audible breath and nodded. "He doesn't think it's a coincidence. He's making some phone calls and will get back to me. When Pedro calls me again, I don't know what the hell I can tell him. His driver and helper met me this morning. They loaded the bottles and drove away. The driver had strict instructions to deliver the bottles directly to his vineyard."

"Mateo," said Callie in measured tones. "It was that newspaper article. There must be others who knew about those bottles. Picasso's name is known everywhere. We need to start backtracking. Who knew about the delivery and pickup?" Her glance showed she had her own doubts.

Mateo's mouth opened a fraction of an inch, but nothing came out because his face was parched for understanding.

Callie took a gulp of wine and swallowed, but the knot didn't disappear. She laughed shakily. "The bottles were everything. We might lose the school, return the money, and cancel the dream..."

Mateo frowned and touched Callie gently on the shoulder. "Callie, let's take one step at a time. The police are talking to the driver right now at the hospital. Pedro will call me back after he talks to the other man."

Callie took another sip, more determined than ever to find answers.

~

Across the miles in Aix en Provence, France, Janine stared at the doctor. Open mouthed, she said, "Surgery?" She was dumbfounded into silence as the doctor's kind, brown eyes looked at her.

Dr. Havre took off his glasses. "If rapid widening is allowed to continue, an opening or rupture can form in the colon. Therefore, most cases of toxic megacolon need surgery to remove part of or the entire colon. Michel will receive antibiotics to prevent sepsis, a severe infection. And we should do this soon." He turned toward Michel. "Surgery is never easy for a man your age, Michel, but without it, you will not see another birthday."

The old man's eyes bored into the doctor's and then he looked at his wife who'd slipped her veined hand into his. When he saw her nod, he tried to ignore the tears forming in her eyes. "Yes, we must do this. I have a new granddaughter and great grandchildren; I want to see them age. I'll soon see a daughter get married. When can you operate?"

Dr. Havre patted Michel's leg and snapped the top on his pen. When he stood up, he nodded to the women and smiled at Michel. "I will look at the operating schedule now, my friend." He left the room.

Veronique and Cendrine stood to embrace their grandmother and then turned to their grandfather with watery smiles. The sounds of the clinic echoed around them; the seriousness of the situation kept them quiet. Janine's mouth quivered.

Cendrine looked at her watch and motioned to Veronique to follow her out of the room. Whispering in the hallway, she said, "Let's find food and let them have a few minutes?"

Veronique nodded and followed her cousin toward the elevator past potted plants and children playing on a padded rug. Things appeared normal outside but their stomachs had definitely taken a nosedive. As they slipped into the elevator, Cendrine's voice wobbled. "We should call Callie."

Veronique couldn't speak, but nodded in agreement.

Inside the hospital room, Janine smoothed back her husband's white mane of hair and leaned down to kiss his forehead. "Michel, I love you." She sat in the chair and laid her head on the bed beside him, enjoying the feel of his hand as he gently ruffled her silver hair.

"And I love you too, *ma chère.* But, we must face reality. I am old and the doctor said surgery will be difficult. I may not come out of the operating room alive." He felt Janine's body shake under his hand.

"Please, we must be strong for the children. We've had a long, wonderful life together and..."

Janine lifted her head suddenly. "And I want more of it!" They stared at one another. "You and I both know we could die any day. It isn't so much the dying as the one left behind. Please, Michel. You must think positively. I can't even think about that," she told him as her voice strained against her throat. Among all of the alarming events that had happened in their lives, this was one she didn't want to discuss at all.

Michel slowly opened his eyes and then lowered them shut again. He dropped his head onto the pillow and his fingers felt for her hand. When her fingers slipped into his, he smiled and stopped talking altogether.

That is how the girls found them when they entered the room thirty minutes later laden with warm croissants filled with ham and cheese. The aroma brought Michel's eyes awake and Janine's head lifted. Food always made them feel better and today they needed that and more.

~

In Algodonales, Spain the dreaded phone call arrived not long after the dinner plates had been removed from the table. Their wine glasses had been replaced with new ones, each filled with Rioja and accompanied by small dessert plates of *flan*, a golden custard.

Mateo's face filled with trepidation. A hush fell upon the table as Javier, Mari, Loli and Callie all leaned toward him to listen to his conversation. Nobody had to ask who was calling. They could see Mateo's face as he lifted the phone to his ear and heard his apprehensive intake of breath.

Mateo listened for a full minute without saying another word. When he responded, his voice was quiet. "Pedro, I am not involved with the theft. I am as shocked as you are. Yes, I know it's not my money sitting in the bank without the bottles to show for your purchase." He listened a few seconds more and answered, "We will get answers and it will be my mission to find your bottles. No, I do not know. I am glad your driver will recover. Hopefully, he will give the police a clue...What? *Madre de Dios. Vale. Vale."* Mother of God. Okay.

Callie's face mirrored the others when their foreheads creased with questions. Their *flan* hadn't been touched. Mari tapped the caramel topping with her spoon. Javier held his breath and Loli stared at Callie when she lifted the wine for a quick sip and saw it wobble in its glass. They waited for Mateo to speak again.

Mateo lifted his own glass, took a large swallow and tapped his fingers on the table after he dropped it down again. "The driver heard one of the men yell at the other, distinctly hearing the name Eterio. We don't have to look any farther to know who stole the bottles. I have three questions. Was his brother, Ruben, with him? How in hell did they know where I stashed the bottles? Who knew the date for Pedro's pick up?"

Everyone at the table stared at him. Javier picked up his spoon to stab into his *flan*. He lifted a bite to his mouth. Mari had eaten nearly half of hers in one trip toward her lips and Loli tapped hers with a finger to watch it lob around her plate like jelly.

Callie didn't move toward her *flan* or her wine. "Eterio again. How the hell could he know...? Did you tell anyone else about the bottles besides the boys who carried them from the boat and took them inside your house? Did you know these boys? You said they didn't know the bottles were inside the boxes. Now I wonder...?" One hand curled toward her chest, the other lay limp on the table.

Mateo raised one eyebrow and drank his wine slowly, tapping his teeth against the glass. He hadn't really noticed the headache before, but now felt it throb against his temple. "I will go straight to the *chiringuito* when I get back to Fuengirola in the morning. Esteban and Ricardo arrive at the restaurant in the sand about nine for first breakfast. I'll be sitting at one of the tables ordering the first glass of *café con leche*."

When Mateo finished speaking, a fresh commitment to Picasso's dream bloomed in Callie and spread like a flare in the night sky. When the bottles had been transported and later the money was in the bank, she had accepted it as a given. Now the bottles were missing and there was a possibility her job was over before it began. She dug in her heels. She would not stop. It was too important to the village and to children with their hearts set on learning to play flamenco guitar.

The guitarist walked by again, his haunting notes weaving through the night crowd like a butterfly flitting through flowers. The lilting sounds resonated with Callie. Although sitting among friends, she felt as alone as if she was on the hill above the village. She closed her eyes, inhaled the night air and sipped more wine.

Flamenco music was now in her blood since she'd toured the shop. The people she'd met with equal interest in Picasso's school were important and she couldn't let them down either. Sip. Sip. Sip. "I'm stomping both feet down. Hoodlums are not going to stop this project." She tapped her *flan* with the back of her spoon as a thumping end to her statement.

Loli and Mari tapped their wine glasses down onto the table at the same time. "So there!"

Both ladies, friends since childhood, laughed at the kindred spirit that had invaded the group. Javier watched Mari finish her *flan* and didn't take his eyes off her for a time. Mari was unaware of his perusal, but Loli noticed and smiled into her wine glass.

Twenty Two

Earlier in the evening, Ricardo stood beside Eterio's car. His fist banged into the car door as he said, "I told you I didn't want to get involved in this, Eterio. One minute you say it will be easy and then the next minute you're jerking the guy out of the van. When you attacked him afterward, I couldn't..." A deep red flush climbed up Ricardo's neck.

"Hey, man." Eterio shook his head at him.

"You didn't have to hit the man. He was a good guy. He stopped to help us when you waved your arms from the middle of the road. And the other guy? Why did you have to hurt them?" He was fighting tears.

Eterio glared at his friend. "That's why you refused to help me unload the damn boxes? Because I hit the guy? We couldn't let him see us. You're just like Ruben." Eterio's face turned stony with anger.

"Ruben? You told me he wanted to do this as much as you did. I should have known you lied. Just like when we were kids, you lied to get your way. I'm surprised you didn't go to prison after your last adventure." He pounded the car with his fist again and made a deep dent in the hood this time."

"Stop beating on my car!" Eterio took a step toward him. The sun had gone down behind the mountain long ago. They were parked on a side road not far from the village roundabout and it was dark as coal outside. Eterio ignored Ricardo's ranting and skimmed the wooden boxes in his back seat with a flashlight.

Ricardo stumbled in the dark where he was pacing alongside the car, narrowly missing the ditch. His mumbling grew into a storm of invectives and he kicked the tire on his last trip along the road.

"Ricardo! Stop. Listen to me. We can do this. We'll take the bottles back to Trebujena and hide them up at the windmill. There's a small hut there. And then…"

"…And then? Who do you think is going to buy these *señorita* bottles, Eterio? Do you think the Jiménez people are going to just walk away from this brandy? My God, you are delusional. Nobody will touch them because it will be all over the news that they were stolen. There will be police crawling over every inch of Fuengirola. After all the noise you and Ruben made about wanting the money for these bottles, do you really think they'll ignore you in Trebujena?" Ricardo spit onto the ground.

"I have a man who will find me a buyer. Don't worry. Trust me." Eterio stood beside the car, his hand poised to open the driver's door.

"You have a man who can sell stolen goods? The same guy who got you in trouble last time? You're a fool, Eterio." Ricardo stomped toward the edge of the road and stared toward the stars with his back to the car. He pulled out a cigarette, lit it and inhaled deeply. The red tip was the only light on the dark road.

Eterio watched him and slipped his hand into his pocket. He slumped against the car door and lifted his head toward the sky. Rotating his head around on his shoulders, he stood up and stretched his back, pushing out the sore muscles from lugging the heavy boxes from the van to the car.

"Take me back home," Ricardo rasped out. "I'm not part of this and if the police ask me, I'll tell them it was your idea. I was just along for the ride. You forced me to do this. You better pray to God that you didn't kill those men." Ricardo hunched over the car's hood with both hands splayed in front of him, arms stiff as rods.

Eterio turned angrily toward him.

Ricardo lifted his head at the sounds of stones crunching beneath Eterio's feet. He saw only a shadow moving toward him. An instant afterward, fear slipped into his consciousness as a pine-box lid was bashed into his head.

~

The next morning, Cristóbal Navas García struggled with indecision about whether to call Ruben or visit him at the *bodega*. He was the weak link, so it was the obvious choice to contact the younger Alonzo brother. His fingers hovered over the keyboard on his mobile phone. A moment later, he laid it on the kitchen counter of his small house in Jerez and fumbled through the file beside the toaster. Flipping through the papers, he found what he was looking for.

He pulled the *bocadilla* bread roll from the toaster and slathered it with freshly-grated tomato. He carried his cup of hot coffee and small plate of breakfast to the table and fingered the paper in his hand. He would drive. He wanted to see the young man's face when he questioned him.

Two hours later, in Fuengirola, Mateo maneuvered his silver Mercedes off the ramp at the exit leading him down *Calle Santa Amalia.* He followed the signs to the Bioparc, swung around the roundabout and passed the *Plaza de Toros*. His favorite *chiringuito* was on the *Paseo Marítimo Rey de España* where the sand met the boardwalk. His car seemed to know the way and within minutes, he parked next to a Volkswagen one block from the beach bar.

He'd told Callie he'd find answers. Now he wasn't so sure. He shook his head as if to push her out of his thoughts. She seemed to be lodged there when he woke up in the morning, off and on during the day and just before he fell asleep at night. He liked her sassiness, her bold look at life and her laughter. When she turned those soft brown eyes toward him, he sometimes lost his train of thought. She was the first woman, since Elisa died, who'd tangled up his thoughts. He allowed himself a soft smile and then jumped out of the Mercedes. A cup of *café con leche*, a strip of sand and two boys needed his attention. He couldn't let the woman's face slow him down this morning.

He walked toward the small bar, where he saw Esteban stabbing umbrella posts into the sand. There were several tables beneath the pergola and three of them were empty. He'd hoped to talk with the young men alone, but it wasn't going to happen.

Esteban saw Mateo and waved a tanned arm. "*Hola, que tal?*" Hello, how are you?

Mateo returned his wave and slid into a plastic chair sunk into the sand. Esteban made a motion with his hands mimicking a sip of coffee and Mateo gave him a thumbs up sign. He looked around the sandy beach looking for Ricardo. He wasn't putting up the umbrellas like he usually did this time of the morning.

Mateo looked at the surrounding area and saw the *Mediterráneo* Statue. He felt the freedom her stance evoked in him. He'd always liked the massive statue and never tired of looking at her. She was a slim woman who stood inside a boat, wearing a sari-type skirt barely covering her lower body, clasped at one hip by a seashell. Her arms were stretched outward in supplication as if thanking God for the sun, the sea and her freedom. Naked breasts lifted and a dove was perched on her sculpted streaming, wet hair.

As Mateo mused over her, a woman wearing a bright-colored strapless top with black stretchy pants, stepped up onto the bricks that surrounded the statue. When he saw her spread her arms and position herself to mimic the statue, he laughed aloud, seeing her wild abandon. When her companion photographed her, he heard her laughter dance across the sea breeze. He wished the world could feel the freedom her body portrayed.

When Esteban sat a glass of *café con leche* in front of him, Mateo touched his hand. "Esteban. I need to talk with you for a few minutes. And Ricardo too."

Esteban's face changed. "I can join you in a few minutes. But that bum, Ricardo, didn't show up for work today. He's never late, loves this job, but he must have had a hard night, maybe met a girl, maybe..." He grinned, held up three fingers and moved to the next table.

Mateo was thoughtful as he lifted the hot coffee by the rim of the glass. Staring into the sea, his mind churned like the waves splashing across the sand and rocks. "A hard night? A girl? Or something else?" He sunk his chin onto one hand and turned on his attorney's brain. The boys did not know the bottles were in those boxes. My name wasn't in the Olive Press newspaper article about the brandy, so they couldn't have connected me with the bottles. Was there a connection he was missing?

A shadow crossed his line of sight and Esteban sat down, munching on a *churro*. He washed it down with orange juice instead of the usual cup of thick, dark chocolate. "Ivan's working this morning since Ricardo didn't show up. He's just arrived and I've put him to work. I have about five minutes. What is happening, Mateo? You need me for another job?" The young man grinned and stuffed a piece of hot, crusty *churro* into his mouth.

"Esteban, I'm here about that *last* job."

The young man stopped chewing. "Oh."

"The boxes you and Ricardo put into my cellar. Do you know what was in the boxes?" Mateo studied the boy's eyes and saw honesty.

"No. But, I know they were heavy. Why?" His dark head dropped a notch as the waves crashed behind him. The sea breeze increased and Mateo's words were brushed into the wind.

"Those pine boxes were filled with bottles. Very old brandy bottles. I stored them for a client. These bottles were from Picasso's stash from France."

Esteban's eyes rounded. "Picasso. You mean *Pablo* Picasso?" He was clearly interested, but his forehead still creased with confusion.

"The one and only. The buyer picked up the brandy bottles from my house yesterday morning."

Esteban smiled. "Sounds like your job is done. Since they were Picasso's, he must have paid lots of money for them."

Mateo's face turned serious. "That's the good news. The bad news is someone hijacked the delivery van, knocked out the driver and his helper. They stole the brandy when it was on its way back to Arcos de la Frontera." He gulped the last of his coffee and stared at Esteban.

"So...what are you asking me, Mateo? You don't think I had anything to do with that, do you? I didn't know what was in those boxes and I'd never steal from you. I wouldn't steal at all." His color spiked and his eyes turned toward Mateo with disbelief.

"I'm only trying to find answers. Tell me about Ricardo. I know he's a new guy in town. I like him. But it seems coincidental that he's gone missing the morning after the heist. I don't want to believe he was involved, but I need to follow every clue."

"*No lo creo.*" I don't believe it. Esteban gulped his orange juice in one long swallow and pushed back his chair, spraying sand in every direction. His fingers gripped the empty glass and he shook his head at the notion that his friend was part of the theft.

"I don't want to jump to conclusions, Esteban, but I needed to..."

Esteban stood up. "I'll find Ricardo when I leave work today and prove it to you, Mateo. He is honest and sensitive. He wouldn't steal anything, I'm sure of it." He nodded to Mateo and left to work his tables.

Two hours later in Jerez, northwest of Fuengirola, Cristóbal parked next to the Alonzo Bodega. The patio tables were filled with customers where bougainvillea blossoms crawled along the side of the white building. Colorful pots were lined up on the half-wall that surrounded the patio. Conversations stopped when the attorney walked up the steps.

He nodded to several men at the nearest table. *"Buen día."* Good day. He must have passed inspection because their conversation resumed after the men returned his greeting. Once Cristóbal stepped inside the bar, he saw the man he'd come to see.

Ruben wiped off the counter, lifted a tray filled with several glasses of coffee and wove his way around the bar. When he saw Cristóbal, he sat the tray down and gazed across the room at the attorney. When the sounds of outside chatter commenced, he picked up the tray after holding up a finger, assuring Cristóbal he'd return in a minute.

The attorney glanced around the comfortable bar and thought how welcoming the men had made it for patrons. It was clean and decorated as if a woman's hand had touched the walls and the doorways. The paint smelled fresh and the place hummed with activity.

When Ruben slid onto the stool beside him, his face was alight with curiosity. "You have news for us?" He waved toward his sister Margarita, whose face he could see peeping out of the pass-through window. He shrugged his shoulders in response to her unasked question.

Cristóbal ran the tip of his finger across an eyebrow, pausing to word his response carefully. He stared at Ruben. "You tell me."

Ruben pulled his head back to look into Cristóbal's lined face. The attorney's suit was a little rumpled and it looked as if he'd forgotten to shave that morning. His fingers were tapping against the table top and his mouth worked against his teeth.

"What does *that* mean? What news could *I* tell *you*? You're the *abogado*." He stared at the attorney, his fingers tapped the top of the bar to match Cristóbal's in a duet. One. Two. Three. One. Two. Three.

Cristóbal watched the man's agitated response and pursed his lips. "Where is Eterio? I think he's stepped into a bee's nest this time. And I hope you aren't part of it."

Ruben stared at him and swallowed. Hard.

The attorney's shaggy eyebrows came together in a frown before he placed his hand over the younger man's rat-a-tat drill on the bar. He knew the boy was hiding something. He glanced up toward Margarita and felt the same thing there. One or both of them had answers and he needed to know what they were.

When Ruben took a deep breath, the attorney knew he'd come to the right conclusion. The younger brother had no idea what his older brother had done. How could these boys be children of the same mother? One was honest and good and the other always made bad choices. He glanced at the woman again, the boys' sister. He saw goodness there too. So, it was only Eterio Alonzo then. Why hadn't he noticed the marked difference between the men when they'd first come to him with the scheme to ignore Picasso's letter? He'd been an attorney for many years. One would think...

When he saw Ruben lift his head to look at his sister again, the truth was on his face. Yes, the young man definitely had a story to tell and he hoped he would share it with him.

Ruben gripped the older man's hand.

"We can talk privately in the back room, Cristóbal.

Twenty Three

The surgery lasted much longer than Janine expected. Her granddaughters had not left her side. Luckily, Cendrine had filled bottles for Lulu with the breast pump for Olivier. He called while caring for the baby and twins, disappointed because there were still no answers. The girls whispered to one another, treating their grandmother like a piece of glass.

When Janine heard Callie's name in their conversation, her head came up. "No. We won't call Callie yet. She has enough to worry about, especially with the men getting in her way in that village. Sometimes I wish she and Jules had never found those dusty old bottles." She traced a scratch along the arm of the chair with her fingernail. When her silver head dropped and her chin crimped against her chest, she heard both young women approach her.

Cendrine pulled one of her hands to her lips. "*Grandmére.* You don't believe that for a minute." She kissed the freckled hand and held it next to her lips a moment longer and gazed into her grandmother's eyes. Janine nodded and squeezed her eyes tightly against the ready tears. When she opened them again, she saw Cendrine's throat tighten.

Before Veronique could say a word, the door opened and Doctor Havre walked in. His green surgical mask hung limply around his neck and he looked tired. Without a word, he sat next to Janine.

Veronique's eyes leaked with tears.

The look on his face wasn't hopeful. "Janine. I had to remove more of the intestine than I'd originally proposed. His belly is very inflamed. He may have waited too long. The anesthetic will keep him asleep for a while and we are monitoring him closely. I've stopped the worst of it and his pain should diminish, but…"

"But, he will live?" Her voice was so low, the girls had to stoop close to hear her. Cendrine had not let go of her hand and Veronique hovered close. The three women seemed as linked as a fine gold chain.

Doctor Havre twisted his lips in a semblance of a smile. "I can't promise you that at this point, Janine. Even though the surgery was a success, sometimes the patient can't live through the trauma. And with his age..."

"I don't want to hear about his age. I know we are both old. We've had a long life together. I'm not made of porcelain, doctor. Please tell me exactly what we can expect." She sat up primly and rolled her lips together to moisten them and let out a soft breath.

The doctor looked at her gravely. "He will sleep until the anesthetic gets out of his system. Then, he will be in pain from the surgery, but hopefully not from the colitis that brought him to me. I want to keep him here for at least a week. And then, if there's no sign of sepsis, you can take him home. I can't promise anything further. As I told you and Michel, there is no cure. But I can keep him comfortable if his body allows me the time to do so. Palliative care is better than no care at all."

He heard the young women's intake of breath. When they started to approach their grandmother as if she was already grieving, he gave them a look and shook his head. When they backed up and sat on chairs beside her, he smiled tiredly.

"Someone will tell you when Michel is out of the recovery room so that you can sit with him. For now, we wait." He touched Janine's shoulder and got up with a creaking sound as if the chair moaned behind him.

Janine stood up and walked around the room to stretch her limbs. She fought the quaking she felt inside her chest and the agitated butterflies that flit within her stomach. Her life was turning upside down and she had been unprepared for it. Despite seeing

Michel turn paler over the past few weeks, she couldn't imagine living in that great manse without him. She shook her head to knock out the cobwebs. When she turned toward her granddaughters, she gave them a moist smile. Waiting wasn't one of her best virtues, but today, that is exactly what she would do. Wait for Michel to wake up. Wait for him to live. Wait for a miracle.

~

In Algodonales, Callie paced back and forth in her apartment as the morning sun streamed through white voile curtains. The shadowy outline of the mountains behind the house drew her eye and she opened the back door to step onto the small balcony. Pots of bright flowers lined the long walkway and it reminded her of the boat pier she'd left behind in Oregon. Leaning both hands on the railing, she inhaled the scent of jasmine and then wandered toward the back of the house to the table and chairs. She placed her coffee on the table and wrapped both arms around her body. Raising her face to the morning sunshine, she wondered if she was fighting a losing battle.

"*Buenos días*, Callie." Loli was beside her with a steaming cup of coffee in her hand. She wore a loose, flowing gown and her naked toes peeked out from beneath its hem. The grass was soft and dry.

Callie's moroseness eased and she swung around to face her new friend. Sometimes being alone wasn't always the best thing and sharing her worries might be the medicine she needed. She grinned at Loli. "Good morning, back at you. I'm a mess." She lifted her cup and sat down.

Loli brushed off the chair seat with a hand and joined her. "We can't do anything until we hear from Mateo or..."

Callie smiled. "You like him, don't you?" Her right eyebrow lifted as she asked the question. A romantic at heart, she didn't miss the looks Loli had given Mateo. When she saw a slight blush rise on Loli's face, she knew she wasn't far from the mark.

"Of course. He's a nice man and he certainly wants to help get the guitar school started. I felt sorry for him last night when the vintner accused him. He took it personally. But how could he have stopped it? I wanted to shake him."

"Oh? I think you just wanted to touch him."

"Stop it, Callie. You know what I mean."

Callie laughed. "And you know what *I* mean."

Neither woman commented further while they sipped their coffee. And while both worried about the theft and Picasso's wishes, their minds wandered in different directions.

The days had been filled with fast-paced work and this morning the slow meandering of the minutes bred uncertainty. The school was newly painted and furnished. Mari had six students already registered, including her nephew. Juan had accepted the teaching position. Javier had the bookkeeping situation under control. And now the bottles were missing. Callie leaned back to let the sun warm her face.

"Maybe we should join them." She pointed her finger across the back yard above the mountain. Paragliders hung in the sky like small butterflies from that distance. It was a paraglider's paradise in Algodonales and people came from afar to enjoy the perfect wind above the mountain.

Callie laughed. "Nope. Not for me. I'd rather parasail, so if I fell I'd hit water and not smash into those beastly rocks and trees."

Loli snorted. "And I thought you were open to new adventures." She drained her coffee cup and started to get up when Callie's phone rang to disturb the silence of the beautiful morning.

"Good morning, Jules." Callie's eyes smiled.

Loli returned to the house behind her.

"I thought of you the minute I woke up this morning. How's your day so far?" Music played in the background. His voice was warm, inviting.

"Oh, you haven't heard. Of course, you haven't. I should have called you last night, but I was too angry." She took a deep breath.

Instantly alert, Jules' voice changed to worry. "What happened?"

"Pedro Jiménez's delivery van was robbed last night. All the bottles were stolen and the driver and his helper were attacked. They heard someone call out Eterio's name, so the police are looking for him. Mateo is trying to figure out how he knew where the bottles were stashed and the delivery timeline. He said Cristóbal is looking for Ruben Alonzo. And I'm sitting on my butt waiting to hear news so I don't have to return all the money and close the school before it opens."

"Oh, that's all that's going on in your world?" He asked dryly.

Callie chuckled. "Yes. How's your morning going so far?" She sipped her now-cold coffee and made a face as she plopped the cup down again.

"Do you need me?" His voice sounded far away.

Callie closed her eyes.

"Callie, did you hear me?" Jules wasn't letting go of it.

"I think adding you to the mix is a bad idea, Jules. Let the police work on it and hope they find Eterio and the bottles. I hate to give up on this venture. It's just not fair." She knew she'd avoided answering his question, but she wasn't sure if she needed him or not. *Damn.*

"You'll let me know when you hear anything then." His quiet voice told her he hadn't missed her uncertainty. Call me next time something this serious happens, so I'm not the last one to hear about it? I worry. I know you're a big girl, but dammit...I want..." He took a breath.

"Jules. I will call you the minute I know anything. Promise." That would have to do for now. She had enough irons in the fire and his probing didn't ease up on the flames.

Loli arrived with a small European coffee pot and a pitcher of milk on a tray. When she placed it on the table, Callie's voice was muted. The tray also held marmalade and toast. The sun warmed the patio and the women as they ate and drank more coffee. They sat there on the patio without speaking for several minutes as they watched the distant paragliders glide over the *Sierra de Lí-jar* mountain range.

Sipping her hot coffee, Callie wondered if her relationship with Jules was sliding away like the distant panorama. The coffee burned her tongue. The thought burned her heart. And the conflict continued.

She would call her best friend, Olivia. They hadn't had a good video call since she was in Barcelona after her car was trashed. She missed her terribly, one of the big sacrifices she faced by leaving America. Maybe she could help Callie think straight. She'd always been able to see through the fuzz and get to the point. No. Callie knew it wouldn't help since she couldn't put her misgivings into words anyway.

Smiling across the table at Loli, she was glad she wasn't alone.

Twenty Four

Eterio Alonzo swiped at the sweat running down his face and into the neck of his shirt. He'd pushed Ricardo off the road the night before and pulled down thick forest branches to cover his body. Still shaking, his mind had screamed over and over, *I had no choice*. The man was going to tell the police about the bottles and give them his name. Of course, he had to stop him, didn't he?

He'd waited until morning to hide the bottles; he knew the hidey hole would be illusive in the dark. The sun was now shining through the windshield even though he had parked sideways next to a big tree for shade not far from his bar. When he'd recognized Cristóbal's car near the steps of their *bodega*, his heartbeat sped up so fast, it nearly knocked him down. He stayed inside his car and counted the minutes. How long had the man been inside? Ruben couldn't tell him anything, he was sure of that. And it was Ruben he was talking to; he was also sure of that.

But it was Eterio the attorney was looking for. He bit his lip until he felt a trickle of blood. Wiping his lip and smearing sweat with a dirty hand, his mind worked. What to do first? He'd wanted Ruben to help him store the bottles. Now, he could forget that plan. He drove toward his sanctuary above the hill. He knew he was on his own now.

And then he would call Manolo. The man would not scare him this time; he had a bargaining chip. He needed a buyer. Eterio would sell the bottles and pay Manolo the money he owed him. And this time, after that was done, he would stop breaking the law. He would mind his own business, work in the *bodega* with his family. Pretend he hadn't killed his friend.

FLAMENCO STRINGS UNCORKED

He pulled into the abandoned area high on the hill to a place that had always taken his mind away from problems and given him peace. When he opened the back door of his car to reveal the boxes inside, he ruefully acknowledged that he'd brought the problems with him. No amount of meditation would erase the fact that he killed Ricardo to cover up the mess.

Huffing back and forth between the car and the hidey hole, he stashed the last box. Lifting two bottles out, he held one in each hand, and studied the label. The Spanish *señorita* looked happy as she rode the bottle as if she was at a party. Eterio's eyes suddenly turned hard, the black orbs staring at the label but seeing something beyond the laughter and her pretty face.

"If the woman hadn't tried to sell these bottles, I wouldn't have had to steal them. And I wouldn't have killed my friend. It's her fault I'm running from the police and that attorney." The words ricocheted off the bottles as he replaced them inside the box. His mind worked again. His face changed. A decision had been made. Eterio closed the small gate. After he padlocked it, he stomped back to his car. Rubbing his grimy hands down his jeans, he got in the car, checked his gas gauge and headed east. Nobody would push the Alonzo family around again.

He dialed Manolo's phone number and left a voicemail message. And then he drove away from Trebujena; away from his brother, the attorney inside with him and the brandy bottles that started him on this road to hell.

~

"I can't find Ricardo, Mateo. I looked inside the window at his apartment and it looks like someone slept on his couch last night. He doesn't answer his phone. His motorbike is propped up next to the house with the lock still on the wheel. He isn't home. Something is wrong."

Mateo took a moment to answer and pushed the file away from him when his secretary placed it near the phone. He nodded for her to leave it and spoke quietly, "Esteban. I have a bad feeling about this too. I'm going to the police station. What is Ricardo's address? I know he's your friend and I'm sorry for this, but I think he's involved in this theft."

"But, Mateo, I don't think…"

"Esteban, *escúchame!* (Listen to me.) If he isn't involved, it will make me happy. I like him too. But the police need to have this information. Those brandy bottles are worth a lot of money and the vintner has already paid for them. A lot of people will be hurt unless we return those bottles to their owner. What is Ricardo's address?" Mateo felt heat rise inside of him like a storm cloud.

"*Claro.* He lives at 67 Fernandez Flores, number four."

"*Gracias.* Do you want to go with me to the police station now or wait until they call you?" Mateo was sorry he'd put the young man in this position, but the bottles were his only priority now. And Callie, of course. He fought a tired smile.

"Oh, God. You're right. I'll meet you at the police station in a few minutes. I'm closer than you are, so I'll wait outside for you."

"*Perfecto.*" Mateo replaced the phone and stared grimly out of his office window where palm fronds rustled against the white building. He wondered idly if he should call Callie with the news, but decided against it. He didn't have answers, just the beginning of clues and she was already posed to take this personally. That was just one of the reasons he found her so attractive. He rolled his eyes. After he locked his desk, he spoke to his secretary and left his office.

Fifteen minutes later, he saw Esteban leaning against the white wall outside the police station on *Condes San Isidro and Mar*. His dark head was bent and his chin lay on his chest. He was kicking a stone against the building and didn't hear Mateo walk up the steps.

"Esteban." The young man's head jerked upward and a profound look of relief crossed his face. Mateo's heart clenched. He'd come to care for this boy and hated to see the sorrow etched on his features. He gave him a swift squeeze on the shoulder and they walked into the building.

~

Near Jerez, in the town of Arcos de la Frontera, Pedro Jiménez held his head in his hands. He was a short man with a bald head and a hearty laugh. Today, he wasn't laughing. Losing 140,000 euros made him angry, but losing those Picasso brandy bottles made him livid. How could this have happened? Nobody knew when he was picking up those bottles except the attorney. He'd carefully made contact with only the man, not the woman in charge of the estate, not the journalist that hounded him and certainly not Salvador Trujillo Ruiz who wanted them for himself.

He stared at Mateo Rosa Trascasas' business card and pounded a fist on his desk. It came down to the attorney. It was the only answer and that's why he'd given the man such grief the night before. Pedro clucked his tongue against his top lip. He lifted the color photograph of the brandy bottle and smiled sadly at the beautiful *señorita*. He traced his pointer finger across her luscious, long black hair. She was a beauty. "Where are you now, *señorita*?" He pursed his lips. "Where are you now?"

Inside the Fuengirola police station, Esteban's fingers nervously tapped his bare knees. Mateo sat next to him and listened to the conversation between the young man and Agent Ángel Campos. There didn't seem anything more that Esteban could add and Mateo was getting frustrated. He tapped his foot against the floor and nearly missed the policeman's last question.

"Do you know where Ricardo lived before coming to Fuengirola?" The agent jotted down Ricardo's answers in a small notebook. He glanced up at Ricardo, ready to pencil in his response.

"Trebujena. It's a village between Jerez and Algodonales."

Mateo's head lifted quickly. "Trebujena? Did he know the Alonzo brothers? They have a bodega bar there."

Esteban shrugged his shoulders.

The policeman stared at Mateo. "*Eterio* Alonzo? That's the man we're looking for." Agent Campos looked at the clock on the wall behind Mateo. "We have contacted the police in Trebujena at the *Plaza de España* station. Where's the *bodega* bar?" His voice lifted with a tinge of hope.

In Trebujena, Ruben slumped at the table. Margarita gave both men glasses of steaming coffee with toasted bread, tomato slush, olive oil and a jar of marmalade. Her eyes darted between them. She listened, but kept her silence.

"I am sure Eterio has done something bad. He's been nervous and gets angry every time we talk to him." Ruben glanced at his sister, who nodded in agreement. Her apron was twisted on her short body and her fingers moved in and out of the pockets like a yoyo.

"Do you know where he is?" Cristóbal put his hand around the steaming coffee, but pulled his fingers back quickly as it burned him.

Margarita gave him several napkins with a worried look on her face. When a man stood in the doorway and motioned to her agitatedly, she returned with the server to her kitchen.

"I don't know where he is. He's been gone two days. Tell me what he's done." Ruben drank his steaming brew and licked his lips. His dark curling hair touched his collar, but his white shirt was clean and smelled of laundry soap. He breathed deeply and didn't take his eyes off the attorney.

Cristóbal explained about the theft. "The driver heard someone yell Eterio's name before he was hit from behind."

Ruben shook his head angrily and slammed his hand on the table. "I knew it! I told him to forget it, but I knew he wouldn't. Is the driver all right or did he...?"

"He has a concussion and a very bad headache. His helper is fine. But, he was able to tell the police the story. A man, probably Eterio, was standing in the road half way between Fuengirola and Arcos de la Frontera waving his shirt in the air for help. The driver stopped and pulled to the side of the road. Eterio or another man pulled him out of the van. Just before everything went black, he heard someone yell out the name, 'Eterio'."

Ruben listened with wide eyes. "Oh, dear God."

"I don't think God can save him this time. Those bottles belong to Pedro Jiménez. He's already paid for them. I know you think the money belongs to your family, but Ruben...think about it. You don't need that money; this *bodega* bar is a beautiful place."

He swung a hand to encompass the room and the patio beyond the beaded *cortina* curtain at the front door. "The money from those *señorita* bottles is important to many people. Picasso wasn't normally a philanthropist, but he must have loved Jose Luis Alonzo to want a school in his name. I love the idea. We can't let Eterio's bullheadedness and scoundrel activities stop the project."

Ruben rubbed a hand across his chest as if to slow down his heartbeat. When he lifted his eyes toward Cristóbal, the attorney knew he'd touched the man's conscience.

"I know why Eterio is so focused on those bottles. I think he's been gambling again and that slime ball, Manolo, is part of this story."

Cristóbal lifted a hand to his mouth. "Not again, Ruben." He let out a long disgusted breath. "That man is part of the mob from Marbella. The police have tried to arrest him for gambling racketeering and prostitution activities. So far, nothing has sent

FLAMENCO STRINGS UNCORKED

Manolo into prison. If he's part of Eterio's life now, I cannot help him. You may be right about the reasons because Eterio hasn't looked me in the eye for a while. Now I know why."

Margarita had quietly joined them and she heard the last part of their conversation. When she caught her breath, the men looked up questioningly. Her hands covered her mouth and her eyes filled with tears. She tried to speak, but her lips quivered. She was the older sister, who took care of her little brothers; she had been twenty when they were ten and eight years old.

Ruben got up and pulled out a chair for his sister and then he motioned to Alberto, the server. "It's all yours out there for a while. Margarita is taking a break."

Alberto nodded reluctantly and carried another tray of coffee to the front patio. The noisy conversation blocked out his mumbling as he joined the crowd and resumed a job meant for two.

Margarita caught her breath and then pulled Ruben's hand into her own. She stared at the attorney a minute before she began to speak. Her dark hair was riddled with silver, its thick strands held back with a silver, jeweled comb. Red and silver earrings dangled from her earlobes. They swung jerkily when she said, "It is Manolo Chacon. He threatened me. He said he would kill me if I talked. It is much more than Eterio's gambling, Ruben. He finds girls from our village... There are men in Marbella who use them...and Eterio takes..."

"...What are you saying, Margarita? Eterio is part of that prostitution ring?" Ruben jumped up from the table and paced the floor as he ran his hands through the black curls at the nape of his neck. "How could this happen and why haven't I heard of it before? Why didn't you tell me this?" He stopped to stare at his sister and then resumed pacing again.

Margarita bent her head down. Her posture told the men she was ashamed for not saying anything sooner. She looked at her brother tiredly. Her lips quivered and she touched one of her earrings as she gathered words together.

Ruben stopped to pound his head against the wall several times and groaned. "How do you know this?" He returned to the table and looked deeply into his sister's brown eyes.

"Manolo and I..." Her breath caught again and then she broke into gulping cries. She wrapped her arms around herself and swayed back and forth, closing her eyes and turning her face to the ceiling.

"Oh. God. No, Margarita." Ruben's eyes swam and he wiped away tears before they could race down his cheek. "Don't tell me..."

Speechless, Cristóbal's head swiveled back and forth between them. He wondered if he should leave, but he was too fascinated to hear what she'd been hiding from the brothers. And then she knocked them off balance.

"That was when I was much younger, Ruben. I was slim and pretty. It was just after Paco died. I was alone. Vulnerable. We needed money for the *bodega*..."

"...But, Manolo?" Ruben's voice was choked. He reached for his sister's hands and hugged them with his own. She was like a mother to him and Eterio; seeing her devastation knocked him crooked.

"You see, Ruben, I didn't know that *I* was the interest he expected while we paid off our loan. And when I tried to stop the relationship and begged him to leave Eterio alone, he cut me on my body where you could not see.

Ruben's eyes shot sparks and his fingers tightened on hers. His breath came out in gasps. Cristóbal was sure that if Manolo was in the room, he would have been fighting for his life.

When Margarita stopped to catch her breath, she continued. "Manolo told me the next time I got in his way, he would kill me." She paused a moment and then whispered, "And you and Eterio too."

Twenty Five

Marina Lopez Romero opened her door when Eterio banged on her window. He nearly fell into the room; his face was smeared with smut and his clothes smelled like he'd crawled out of a cave. He rushed toward the bathroom and left her staring after him.

"Take a shower while you're in there, Eterio!" She shouted at the closed door and snorted when she heard his mumbled reply. The smell of burned toast wafted in from her kitchen. Snapping the towel she was holding across her thigh, she glanced at her watch. It wasn't yet noon and her work day began at one o'clock. When she heard the shower running, she smiled. Marina finished cleaning her kitchen, and tossed the corners of uneaten toast into the garbage bin, spreading crumbs onto the floor.

Ten minutes later, Eterio's black hair was dripping in rivulets down his temple to slide off his chin. He swiped at it and ruffled the remaining drops from his hair before tossing the towel onto the tub. He stared at himself in the mirror, swiping the condensation away with an impatient hand. One dark eye stared back at him, the other hovering off to the side. His thick eyebrows shifted upward in defiance. Blowing out a deep breath, he unlatched the door and went to face Marina, hopeful that she wouldn't see the story behind his eyes.

"What now?" She stood with hands on her hips when he entered the living room again. This time, he was clean and smelled much better than when he'd walked into the house.

He looked at her with a look of surprise. "Since when do I have to answer to you, Marina? You said I am always welcome, so here I am." His eyes challenged her. When she didn't drop her hands off her hips, but instead began walking slowly toward him, he grinned.

When she slapped him hard across the face, he sobered instantly. "Something has happened, Eterio. I see it in your face. Is this still about those bottles?"

He didn't have time to compose his face before she glared at him. "Are you still fighting the woman? I spoke with Rafael yesterday and he says the school starts next week. They have several students and two are from Algodonales. I wanted you and Ruben and Margarita to get some of that money, but... It's a good thing for the village. What is driving you to this lunacy? The bottles must have been sold already because the French woman is spending money." She flopped down on the couch beside him.

He laughed. "That's why I'm here, Marina. The bottles were sold and she probably has the money. But Jiménez doesn't have the brandy." A sly smile crossed his face and he put both feet onto the table in front of the couch.

Marina slapped at his legs and his feet dropped onto the floor again. "What do you mean, Eterio? Is Jiménez the man who bought the brandy? And how do you know he doesn't have the bottles? You are talking in riddles." She smoothed her thick hair back and pulled it into a clip. His silence brought her head back to him to stare into his face.

"Because I have the bottles," he said smugly.

"You. Have. The. Bottles." She snapped out the words like pistol shots. She shook her head in disbelief. "Don't tell me Ruben and Margarita agree to this. She told me she was frightened because you've been acting crazy. Is this why?" Marina dug her fingers into Eterio's upper arm.

He yanked out of her grasp and stood up. Looking down at her, he said, "Of course they agree with me. It's Alonzo money."

"And how did you get them? Have you thought about who will buy them when they belong to someone else? This isn't a quiet matter, Eterio. The whole of Spain is talking about Pablo Picasso and

Algodonales." She stood up to glare at him nose to nose. "Tell me the rest of the story."

Eterio struggled to keep his face straight, but he swallowed instead and looked away. His heart was beating loudly in his ears and holding the truth inside of him made him stagger.

Marina pushed him and he nearly fell down. When he twisted his head to look at her and braced himself on the edge of the couch, he snarled, "I killed someone to get those bottles. So, I am deadly serious about getting that money. Manolo is going to help me." His dark eyes bored into hers.

She sat down again with a shocked face and made a deep sound in the back of her throat. "Manolo again. You don't learn, do you, Eterio?" She glanced at the clock behind him and got up very slowly. "You k...k...killed someone."

He stared at her as he fought for control of the conversation, but her glare kept him speechless. She moved like a robot when she picked up her purse and walked to the front door. He was unsure what to do next.

She turned toward him with one hand on the doorknob. "When I get home from work, I want you gone." And with a soft cry, she said, "And don't come back again. I don't want to see you. You're too much trouble for me. I don't need a man so much that I'd share my bed with a killer. That's done too." She slammed the door behind her.

The silver Mercedes climbed the mountain road toward Ronda. Mateo's knuckles gripped the steering wheel. He wanted to talk with Callie, tell her about Esteban's surprising information and tell her they would soon have more answers. He glanced at the clock on his dashboard. The police should find Eterio in Trebujena soon. His blood pressure jumped up a notch. And the *señorita* bottles? Where were they? He hoped they'd find them too.

Too many clues pointed toward Eterio Alonzo and now he was missing. Ricardo was missing. The brandy bottles were missing. He turned up the volume on the radio and thumped his fingers in time with the music streaming through the speakers. It reminded him of the flamenco guitar school. He barely avoided a crazy driver passing on a blind curve. He honked his horn and followed the road upward. When he turned toward Algodonales after passing the outskirts of Ronda, he smiled, imagining Callie's surprise when she saw him.

~

Callie laced up her tennis shoes and jogged down the long stairwell to the metal door of her apartment, *Casa Baraka*. She tugged the long steel bar repeatedly before it swung to her left and the door opened to warm sunlight onto the quiet street. She couldn't sit and wait for news and she was powerless to do anything about the stolen bottles. Several cats wove around her legs and a dog yapped in the bright blue doorway to her left. The cats flew by her with the dog close on their tails. She laughed. If life could be so simple. When she thought about the dog barking and the cats running for their lives, she snorted. Simple? She'd been running for months.

First it was Nate Leander who showed her there was a place in her heart after Francois died. She'd run away when she knew it wasn't love she felt for him at all, but gratitude. She broke his heart and then a Scot chased her into a corner and she found Picasso's brandy bottles, with Jules' help of course. Jules.

She stumbled a little as she rounded the corner, waved at the server at the café next to the *Iglesia de Santa Ana* church and turned north. The sidewalk narrowed after she left the square. She dipped onto a side street, anxious to feel cobblestones under her feet. Jules. When she'd realized she was falling in love with him, she'd felt pressure again, like the cats with the dog nipping at their heels.

When she'd learned that Francois had a daughter he'd kept from her for twenty years, the pressure turned to anger. But when she instantly connected with the young woman, her anger changed to sadness. The fact that the girl was also Jules' niece sweetened the pot. No amount of pressure kept her from loving both of them.

She saw the spring fountains at the edge of the village and began the upward hike where the peaceful chapel waited. Why was she pushing Jules away? She'd sold everything in America to make her home in France. With him. It seemed as if she'd come full circle. People loved her in Pertuis and she adored them. A family. Her family. She felt frustrated tears coming, but she sluffed them away.

Now the brandy bottles were missing. Another dog at her heels. As she made the abrupt turn at the end of the road, she thought she heard someone behind her. When she dipped her head to see who was on the road with her, the cobblestones were empty. She thought she heard a noise, but being fanciful was her middle name. Callie shrugged off her unease. The village was quiet in this part of town.

When Javier had first shown her the vista from atop the hill behind the village, she'd been awed with its beauty. Since then, she'd chosen the spot to meditate several times. Today, she felt the promised peace invade her when she reached the top. She saw the stone bench beside the alcove where the saint's statue stood behind the steel grill. The arch-shaped door was padlocked below a colorful tile with the words, *Ave Maria*. She walked down the steps toward the *mirador*, a lookout. The view of Algodonales with its white-painted houses fit together like a crossword puzzle. A nearby sign led serious hikers into the hills above.

A noise broke the silence of the surrounding courtyard. Embedded gray stones made footsteps indistinguishable from the wind that coursed between the grasses and trees nearby. She turned around and clutched her chest, but there was nobody there. More cats? Had they followed her? She didn't hear a dog, so probably not a cat.

Holding her hand against her throat, she urged her heart rate to slow down and looked downward. The cars weaving along the streets looked like black crickets. She sighed loudly, trying to get her paranoia under control. Callie lifted her knee to rest on the stone wall and reached toward the iron railing to stare into the distance. But when she turned to sit on the wall, she knew she hadn't been imagining it; someone was nearby. She felt inside her pocket for the ammonia bottle. Empty. Glancing around, she saw nothing to defend herself. Oh, God. If someone didn't mean her harm, why didn't they show themselves?

"*Quién está allí?*" Who is there? Nobody answered. She pushed her back against the iron railing, poised her feet against the stone patio to push herself off if she needed to run. A hundred stone steps led back to the village, but she had to pass the blind gateway to get there. The wind blew softly through her hair. She yanked the strands out of her face and called out again.

"*Hola?*" Hello? She struggled to gather her wits and move. When she reached the first stone step that led off the patio, she felt a hand on her arm. She screamed and tried to twist around, but the man's strong arm pulled her back against his chest. In a heartbeat, she heard her policeman friend's words telling her to drop to the ground in a fake swoon. She'd fainted once before in the real world and remembered her bruises when she'd come awake. That time it had been pain induced. This time it was stark-raving fear.

When her world turned black a moment later and the stone-patio came up to kiss her, she realized she wasn't faking at all.

Twenty Six

Spring flowers flourished in pots along the white-washed buildings of Trebujena. Steel stanchions lined the street and the clock tower chimed the hour. Bees lazily buzzed and dipped into the nearest bougainvillea when police sirens broke the peacefulness. When two red-striped white cars cruised toward the Alonzo Bodega with its lights flashing, everyone stared. The men and women on the patio stopped eating, some grabbed their purses and others did not move at all. Alberto lost his balance and dropped the tray on a table.

When the policemen from the *Policía Local de Trebujena* stepped onto the porch in their heavy black boots, everyone watched them walk directly over to Alberto. Their black trousers and lime-green and black shirts were a mainstay in the village. When their heads bent toward Alberto with their black-visor hats trimmed in a black and white hound's-tooth, all conversation hushed.

Calle Cabildo hadn't seen that much activity since the last patron saint's day. Alberto picked up the tray with shaking fingers.

"*Donde está Eterio Alonzo?*" Where is Eterio Alonzo?

"*No lo sé.*" I don't know. He led them to the back of the *bodega* where Ruben and Margarita talked with the attorney. He knew they must have been alerted by the police sirens.

When the uniformed men stood in the doorway, Margarita covered her heart with both hands. Ruben pulled out chairs. He nodded toward Cristóbal and the group sat down.

Ten minutes later, the policemen appeared on the patio again and their feet pounded down the steps of the *bodega*. Everyone resumed talking, clearly excited for the resulting gossip they were anxious to share.

Inside the *bodega*, Margarita was crying against Ruben's chest.

Cristóbal lifted his phone to his ear and waited for Mateo to answer. He saw fear scamper across the woman's face as a heavy stone-like pressure built up beneath his breast bone. He looked at Margarita and said, "Adding Manolo's name to this-complicated set of events will move this chaos to top-priority for the police. You were right to tell us about this. It might save Eterio's life."

Margarita's wailing increased and Cristóbal knew it was time to leave. He left Mateo a voicemail message. He gave Ruben a long look, shook his head and left them. He'd done everything he could for the situation. Now he would wait, hopeful for good news before he settled into bed that night.

~

Callie wasn't moving. Eterio had caught her head before it hit the stones to lower her to the courtyard stones. He was frightened. Had he killed her too? His eyes darted around the patio, down the steps and up into the hills. He could hear hikers on the trail above him. He tried to lift Callie into his arms, but he struggled with the burden. Despite being a small woman, his muscles strained against the dead weight.

"Oh, God. Oh, God. Oh, God." He was suddenly whimpering. Making a snap decision, he turned toward the stone steps and jogged back down into the village, leaving her there alone. His feet skimmed the cobblestones and he braced his hand on a white-washed building as he sped around the first corner. He was sweating again, wondering what to do. Marina wasn't going to help him again. Javier was angry at him. Ruben wasn't speaking to him. And Ricardo was dead. As he jogged around the last corner onto the main street, he mingled with the crowded villagers in the common area.

Javier sat at the corner café as the church bell gonged above him. Waiting for Mari to join him, he idly stirred his glass of coffee and blinked with surprise when Eterio pulled up a chair next to him.

He scowled at his cousin. "You! Did you do it?"

Eterio's face turned pale. "Did I do WHAT?" He looked around and lowered his voice. Lifting a hand to his cousin's arm, he said, "Javi, I need…"

Javier Alonzo pushed the hand back toward Eterio. "Do you know that the police are looking for you? Did you think you could steal…?"

Eterio's eyes widened and he pushed back his chair, knocking it to the stone floor. And then he turned toward the church and ran blindly up the street.

Javier yelled behind him.

"Javier?" Mari's voice questioned. He turned toward her and felt the warmth of…what? He'd known Mari all his life. Why all of a sudden did her proximity make him smile? He reached out a hand, righted the chair and invited her to sit. Raising a finger to order another *café con leche*, he smiled at her. Black tendrils of hair escaped from the clip perched on her head and she nodded toward the area he'd yelled as she joined him.

"It was Eterio."

"Did he steal them?" Her eyes held his.

"He didn't answer me. He looked shocked to hear the police want to find him. When I told him, he jumped up and started running. With only 5,600 people living in Algodonales, he shouldn't be too hard to find now that we know he's here."

Mari accepted her *café con leche*, glad he'd ordered it in a cup for her to stave off burned fingers. "Where's Callie? I don't like that man running around when he's already tried to hurt her once."

Javier picked up his phone and dialed Callie's number. When there was no answer, he called Loli.

"Is Callie there?"

"Callie was in her apartment earlier. We had coffee on the terrace. Why? Do you have new information about the bottles?" Loli's voice sounded urgent. "Did you call her?"

"Yes, no answer."

"I'll go upstairs to see if she's there. Maybe she just didn't hear the phone. I'll call you back. Where are you?"

"At the café with Mari."

Javier heard a chuckle. "Oh? With Mari, huh?"

"Don't start, Loli." He heard her laughter as he punched the phone off. When Mari looked at him quizzically, he rolled his eyes toward the large tree beside them. Birds sang in the branches and landed at their feet, zipping around looking for fallen crumbs.

When a silver Mercedes drove slowly by the café, Javier looked at the license number and waved. Mateo? He hadn't realized he was returning after he'd left at dawn that morning. He saw the car drive around the square and turn off on a side street as Mateo looked for a parking spot. In the main area of the village, they weren't easy to find.

Javier waved his fingers again to order Mateo a coffee.

When Mateo walked swiftly toward them a few moments later, his coffee was waiting. He pulled out a chair and nodded his thanks at the same time that Loli returned Javier's call.

"She's not here. She's not answering her phone. I called Rafael and he hasn't seen her at the school. Maybe she took a walk. She does that sometimes when she wants to be alone." Loli was breathless. "I'm walking down toward the café now. I don't like this."

Mateo raised his eyebrows at Javier and saw Mari's fingers tapping the tabletop, beating out a chord in triple time. When he turned toward her, he saw her eyes swing back toward Javier. He stared at them over the rim of his coffee cup and then he glanced around as if he was missing something.

"We can't find Callie."

When coffee spewed from his mouth, he grabbed a napkin to dab his chin. Choking on the hot brew, he put down the glass and stared at them. Before he could say anything, Loli pulled out a metal chair and sat down with a thud.

"Did you find her?" She'd been running; her face was pale.

"No."

"I just arrived. She promised not to go out alone." His eyes swung between the three people and he started to get up from the chair. "Where did she park her car? Maybe she went somewhere."

"She wouldn't go anywhere, Mateo, unless one of us knows about it. Maybe she hiked up to the chapel. That's where she goes when she's thinking. This theft has her mind in a quandary."

Before anyone could say another word, Mateo was running down the street. When Javier and the women followed him, they saw him jump into his silver car and swing it into the street that would lead up to the chapel.

Callie groaned and gently arched her back. Without opening her eyes, she said, "It feels like I'm lying on bricks." When memory returned, her eyes blinked open and she saw blue sky. Two doves landed on the patio beside her. She groaned again. When she tried to get up, it seemed like too much work, so she lay there spread eagled and listened to the birds tapping across the stones.

It worked. Fainting, I mean. But where was the man? Ever so slowly, she turned her head. The chapel was to her right. The stone wall was to her left. She was lying at the top of the stone steps. She was alone as far as she could tell. Pulling her feet to her butt with her knees in the air, she braced her feet. When she reached for the low stone wall, her elbow stung. Callie saw blood oozing from a tear in the skin where pebbles had riddled it raw.

She gulped and closed her eyes a moment before she twisted onto her side to get into a sitting position. The squeal of car tires pushed her into action. She sat up and moved as fast as she could in order to grab several large stones in her hand. Her body screamed as she stood up again. Crouching beside the wall, she heard pounding footsteps. She pulled back her arm like a baseball player and threw the rocks with all her strength.

Mateo's voice yelled into the breeze. "Dammit! Callie?!"

Callie popped her head from behind the low stone wall. "Mateo?" She whispered his name, clearly surprised to see him standing above her. "What are you doing here?"

He squatted next to her and pulled her up the step and into his arms. "When you asked me that the last time, I spent the day unloading your furniture and putting together tables and chairs. This time, I had to dodge stone missiles."

She started shaking and he held her still, rubbing his hands over her back. He saw blood dripping from her arm and a bruise turning purple on her arm above the elbow.

"Oh, Callie. What happened up here? Did you fall down?"

"Not exactly," she said and pushed her face into his shirt. Her legs didn't want to hold her upright, so she held onto him.

"Dammit. You went off alone." His anger made the statement sound like he was ready for war. He brushed the leaves from her hair and kicked loose stones off the patio.

When she pulled away to look into his face, he grabbed her and kissed her so hard that she nearly fell down. She was stunned into silence. Feeling his arms around her felt good because she'd been frightened and alone. And she was angry because they were Mateo's arms around her, not Jules. She admitted he was very attractive, but not...

"What are you doing?" She sputtered.

Her deep brown eyes told him she was caught off guard. They also told him he'd made a tactical error. She pulled away from him and rubbed her lips with a hand to erase his warm kiss. Shaking her head, she was just gathering a mouthful of steam when Javier, Mari and Loli ran up the stone walkway toward them.

Everyone started talking at once. Callie's chest heaved as if she'd been walking at a fast trot. When she sat down on the chapel bench a few feet away from where she fell, she exhaled brokenly.

Loli grabbed a handkerchief from her purse and wiped the blood off Callie's elbow. Mari massaged her shoulder and then sat down beside her. "You okay?" She lifted her chin to stare into her eyes.

Javier and Mateo stood below the women and felt completely lost. Neither man could voice their relief at seeing Callie alive.

"Did she fall down?" Javier whispered, afraid to question Callie while she was obviously in distress. His thumb rubbed against his fingers like a drum beat.

"No. I don't think so. I was so glad to see her safe that I didn't get a chance to find out. But from what she did say, I have an idea it was just as we feared." His lips pursed. He couldn't take his eyes off of her. When Loli touched Callie as if she was a lost child, he smiled at the gentleness he saw there.

Callie held the handkerchief against her elbow. The blood had stopped dripping, but the pain she felt when Loli rubbed it told her some of the pebbles had found their way under her skin. Wobbling just a little, she turned her body toward the men.

"A man attacked me. I felt a scratchy beard against my neck and smelled onions. I went into self-defense mode and pretended to faint. I was told that would stop an attacker because they wouldn't waste time lifting an unconscious woman off the ground. But, I must have really fainted because I just woke up a few minutes ago. That's why I threw the stones at you, Mateo. I thought my attacker had come back. And then you…" Her eyes reflected a pinch of anger.

He grimaced. She could see that he knew what she was thinking. The kiss had been impulsive and she knew he wasn't sorry.

Javier groaned and all eyes turned toward him. He raised his face toward the sky and covered his eyes with a fist..

Mari walked over to stand beside him.

Mateo looked away from Callie to question Javier. "What is it?"

Javier mumbled, "I saw Eterio at the café this morning and I asked him if he stole the brandy. He started running toward the edge of town, the bus station…"

Twenty Seven

Eterio Alonzo walked into the café across the street from the bus stop on the main road into Algodonales. He was afraid to go back to his car. Since the police were looking for him, they'd be checking license plates and probably knew the model of his car by now too. The day had turned from rocks to shit since he'd left Trebujena. He had to lose himself. And fast.

He ordered a beer from his childhood friend, Paco, who didn't question his being in town. So, not everyone knew the police were looking for him. His mobile phone vibrated in his pocket and he dug it out with his fingers. Looking at the screen, he glanced out the window to make sure he was not being followed by anyone in the village.

"Manolo."

"Hey, man. Where are you?" The scruffy voice scraped across Eterio's ear like sandpaper. Heavy breathing followed the question.

"Why?"

"Because you left me a phone message, *estupido*. I found someone. He wants them fast. The man said the brandy bottles are too hot to wait any longer. So, where *are* you?"

Eterio saw a bus pull off the main road and drive beneath the portico across the street. He gulped his beer and said, "I'm getting on a bus in Algodonales now. Meet me in Trebujena, but be careful because police are everywhere." He dropped the empty beer glass on the counter, waved to Paco and started walking across the street.

"As if that's stopped me before, man? I'll drive over there now. Meet me at the old yellow building near the train tracks when your bus arrives in Trebujena. You can give me the bottles and I will take them to the buyer." When Manolo outlined the plan, Eterio knew he was ready to implement it.

"No." Eterio's answer was swift and firm.

"What do you mean, *no*? You said you had the bottles and needed a buyer. I have one. And you owe me that money, Eterio. You think I forget?" His rough voice turned meaner.

"*I* will meet the buyer, Manolo. When *he* pays me, *I* will give him the bottles. And *then*, I will pay *you*. That's how it's going to work. I did all the hard work of getting the brandy and then I had to k..." Eterio's voice stalled.

"You had to what? What stupid ass thing did you do, Eterio, besides stealing the bottles?" He waited and spit out an oath when his questions were met with silence.

"I'm getting on the bus. I'll see you when I get there. Don't expect me to hand over the bottles, Manolo. Get the buyer to me." Eterio hissed out the last sentence, closed off his phone and jumped on the bus. After dropping the coins into the meter box, he sat in the farthest seat from the door. As the bus made the sharp U-turn to drive back out of the village, Eterio saw a police car driving into Algodonales from the other direction. He burrowed down in the seat, thankful he'd already gotten on the bus.

~

That afternoon in Aix en Provence, France, Michel Beauvais sat hunched over in the back seat, still refusing to gather the seat belt around his belly. Doctor Havre released him with a promise to call him if he started bleeding again. Janine had agreed.

He was happy to see the smile on his wife's face, even though they both knew this would be a slow healing process. Or he might not heal at all. Gripping the soft blanket that covered his legs, he flipped it off and onto the back seat beside him. He wasn't dead yet and didn't want to be treated like an invalid. He gasped out a shaky laugh because he knew that was exactly what he was, an invalid.

An hour later, back in the old manse again, he brushed crumbs from his trousers. When he returned the empty plate to Janine, his eyes thanked her and he watched her walk away.

He looked out the tall windows beside his chair and marveled at the colors. Michel hadn't realized how much he'd taken all the little things for granted. Bright, blue birds. A yellow pillow threaded with blue silk flowers. A red cushion on the footstool beneath his feet. Green trees lined up along his driveway all the way to the stone pillars like soldiers marching toward the Beauvais Vineyard sign slung across the entrance. Blue sky amid clouds that looked like puffy cotton. He stared at them, watched them slide across the sky. Windy. Red poppies. Yellow mustard flowers. The turquoise dress that Janine wore like a princess. Colors. And sounds. The laughter in his wife's voice. The tinkle of baby voices. The cry from Lulu. The music from the speakers across the big room. The Three Tenors. The Vienna Orchestra. Vivaldi. Puccini's *La Boheme.*

He smiled. Puccini wasn't exactly French, but his brilliantly bohemian opera captured the gritty atmosphere of Paris in the 1840s. It also happened to be one of the greatest operatic love stories ever written. Michel lay his head back on the pillow that Janine had squeezed between his head and the back of his easy chair. A love story that resounded of his life with Janine. He wasn't ready to die and leave her behind, but he knew he wouldn't have a choice.

When he heard her beside him, he opened one eye and saw the glass of cold lemonade, one of his favorite cool drinks. He grinned, feeling as if he could drink it without pain. He lifted one hand for the glass and the other toward his wife.

She slid onto the arm of his easy chair and leaned over to kiss the top of his silver head. They both groaned with emotion that no words could describe. He reached up and pulled her hand into his and they sat there like that, still as statues, as he sipped his lemonade.

Colors. Sounds. Tastes. And Janine. If he went away from there that moment, he would die a happy man.

~

Callie stopped Mateo when he started down the steps to open the door to her apartment. Instead, she gave him a look and walked down, albeit slowly, to open the metal door herself. They'd been expecting the visitors, so Mateo had brought her back to her apartment and he refused to leave.

The *Guardia Civil* police followed Callie up the deep stairs to the apartment above them. She moved slowly, painfully, and muttered under her breath. She wore a bandage on her elbow and another on her upper arm. A purpling bruise covered several inches of her shoulder that peeked out from beneath a red blouse.

Mateo Rosa guided her as she limped toward a stuffed chair. After Mateo and Callie shared an uneasy look, he pulled up a kitchen chair from the table and sat across from the officers. The policeman was busy with his notebook, leaving the observations to his partner.

"You didn't see the man who attacked you?"

"No. He was big. I did not see his face, but it was unshaven."

"Did he say anything to you? Could you recognize his voice?" The policeman held a pencil poised above his notebook.

Callie's head throbbed. She glanced at Mateo and wished he was gone. She didn't want to be reminded of the kiss they'd shared. Well, not shared exactly, she rearranged her thoughts discriminately, drawing the fine distinction in her head.

"Ms. Beauvais? *Como está?*" How are you?

"Oh. Sorry. What did you ask me?" Her brown eyes concentrated on the woman's face and then she glanced at Mateo.

"I asked if you thought the man could have been Eterio Alonzo." The policeman's voice was brisk, but his voice carried a note of warmth.

"That would be my first guess. The man has tried to stop me before." Callie pulled hair away from her mouth.

"Stop you?" The policeman's pencil was poised midair.

"Yes, from our opening Picasso's flamenco guitar school. The bottles. The money." She looked from one to the other. They didn't know anything about why she was in Algodonales?

Several minutes later, the policewoman pushed a stray curl underneath her uniform's hat. "Eterio Alonzo. Several police stations are looking for the man. When we heard you were attacked in his home village, we assumed it might be the same man. A woman named Marina reported seeing him earlier this morning. She said he was angry with you. There are others searching the village. If he is the man who attacked you, he may try again."

Mateo sat up straight and let out an agitated breath.

The policeman's phone rang and he dropped his pencil. When he hung up, he smiled at Callie. "We've just been told Eterio Alonzo boarded a bus from here headed toward Trebujena, so you should be safe until we pick him up."

Mateo visibly relaxed and he raised an eyebrow toward Callie. She, in turn, gave him a look before letting the police out of her apartment. This time, she let him walk them to the door. When he returned, he put a pot of water on to boil and fixed hot tea.

She accepted the cup and he sat across from her with one of his own. It felt warm in her hands. She felt safe again. When she looked at him over the rim of her cup, he smiled.

"I won't apologize for kissing you, Callie."

She caught her breath and stared into her tea cup.

"But I will explain a little about me. And then you can… Well, my wife died five years ago. Since that time, I have not been attracted to a woman until you walked into my door." His fingers inched around the cup to get a better hold on it. When he saw her face study him without a response, he continued.

"First, I thought it was because you were different. Exotic. Not Spanish. And then I thought it was because you were a bit feisty when I told you what to do."

She laughed and took another sip of her tea.

"And then I realized it was because you had a good heart. When I saw you laying on that stone floor, I felt like someone kicked me in the stomach. When I admitted I have wanted to hold you for some time, it surprised me. After rejecting a sexy woman in Jerez dancing flamenco, I didn't think I was interested in romance. I was wrong. I just needed to be with the right woman. When I held you in my arms, I couldn't help myself. I guess I'm not against romance again after all."

Her eyes filled with tears and she put down her cup. She reached for a tissue and blew her nose. "Would you believe me if I told you that I know *exactly* how you feel? Not just a little, but exactly." She pushed the tissue into her pocket. Her story came out slowly at first and then in a rush. She told him about Francois, her desire to separate herself from men. Her romance and Nate three years later. "So, I believe your wife would want you to love again."

"I hear a *but* in your voice. His eyes were kind and his voice was soft. He crossed his legs, swallowed more tea and watched her.

She gave him a slow smile. "Yes, there is. I am in love with Jules Armand. We've had issues since I left America and I came to Spain with Picasso's project. I find you attractive. And that upset me because I love Jules. I'm trying to resolve concerns with our relationship, and this Picasso project and the missing bottles aren't helping me. The good news is you are charming, romantic and sweet. Just not for me." Her eyes smiled at him. "But I think I know just the person for you to practice on."

He chuckled. "I guess I'll add sassiness to the list, Callie."

Twenty Eight

After promising to meet him for dinner later at the café in the square, Callie called Cendrine. When she didn't answer the phone, she dialed Janine. When both numbers led her directly into voicemail, she was disturbed. She dialed Olivier and he picked up on the first ring.

"*Halo*, Callie." His voice sounded strange, almost disoriented.

"Olivier? Neither Cendrine nor Janine are answering their phones. Is everything okay?" She heard him catch his breath.

When he answered, he sounded wary. "Yes, everything is fine here. Tell me about the project and the missing bottles. I couldn't call you back after you left the message."

"What, too many children, Olivier?" she asked teasingly.

When he didn't laugh, she knew something was wrong. "Olivier? What is happening there?"

"Callie, I'm just a little tired. Nothing new since yesterday? Maybe we should cancel the guitar school. It makes me sad to say it. But, it is too close to payment and delivery for us not to be worried about whose responsibility it is. If Eterio Alonzo is the thief, he'll be caught, but in the meantime, where are the bottles? Are they lying properly to keep the cork wet? Are they getting hot and spoiling the brandy? Maybe you should come home?" His voice held an edge to it that Callie hadn't heard since he'd been abducted weeks before.

When she heard him suggest they give it up, her mind started spinning with solutions. And then, without hesitation, she responded, "Olivier, we will not give up. If we have to return the money, I will use my own. I have the money from one house and the second house should sell soon. This is too important to these young people and to the village. I've come to love it so much and..." Her voice broke and she sniffed loudly.

"Use your money, Callie? That's too much to ask."

"You didn't ask."

He laughed shakily. "There's the dragon again. We can talk about it soon. Now, you said the police are looking for the man. Let's wait until we get more information. Mateo told me that Pedro Jiménez practically accused him of stealing. It's unfair after all the work Mateo did for us. But, I can't blame the man. God, 140,000 euros and nothing to show for it."

"Where's Cendrine?" Callie wanted answers.

"She's...she's at the market." His stuttering words didn't help.

"Really? And since when does she leave you with Lulu and not answer her phone when it rings? What *aren't* you telling me, Oliver?"

"Callie. Please. I will ask her to call you the minute she arrives home, *oui*? I must get back to the children. Be careful. They are only bottles, after all...not people."

"But, Olivier, their value is going to help people. Please don't try to stop me. And don't tell me to talk with Jules or Mateo. I'm serious. And don't forget to tell Cendrine to call me."

When Olivier hung up the phone, he saw his wife raise her eyebrows. "You can't put her off, Cendrine. You must tell her."

~

Just before Eterio's bus reached the outskirts of Trebujena, a farmer's truck pulled to the side of the road miles away near Arcos de la Frontera. The driver had seen something red in the bushes not far from the ditch and he stopped to investigate. When he removed the brush to explore the red object, Ricardo Galvez Santos' eyes were staring up at the sky. His head was caved in and he'd been dead for some time. Flies were feasting on the man and the smell nearly knocked the farmer off his feet. He was shaking so hard, he had difficulty pulling his mobile phone from his pocket.

~

FLAMENCO STRINGS UNCORKED

That night at dusk, a large wooden table was set up beneath the massive tree in the square next to *Iglesia de Santa Ana* church at the café. Loli and Mari were already there when Callie and Mateo walked down *Calle Beatas*. Javier was crossing the street and walking across the neatly-lined ceramic tiles when they sat down. Rafael had closed the guitar shop earlier than usual to join them.

Callie's mobile phone's volume was set on high. With the loud conversations of five Spaniards, she also kept it on her lap. If it vibrated when it rang, Callie would not miss Cendrine's call.

Everyone was nervously awaiting word about Eterio's capture. A tangle of conversation also trailed to the flamenco guitar school.

Javier turned toward Rafael. "The school is in jeopardy if the estate must return the money to Pedro Jiménez." He sipped a glass of deep, red Rioja wine and twirled the stem on the table afterward.

"No, it is not." Callie's voice rose above all the others.

"What?" Loli and Javier responded as one.

"No. If we return the money, we don't lose the school. I told Olivier Benoit today that I will finance the school. I have more money than I need and I'm selling a second house in America. That should fund it for a while until we can find people to donate to the project. I planned to look for donors after the school got started." She lifted her glass in a silent salute toward the sky.

Everyone lifted theirs in slow motion, their faces etched with disbelief. Rafael couldn't speak. Javier reached for Mari's hand, happy that her list of students wouldn't be left in the cold. Loli noticed he didn't let her fingers go anytime too soon. Mateo stared at Callie and shook his head as if to say, see? I said you had a good heart.

She grinned across the table at him.

"Loli, I'd like you to work with Mateo on the paperwork if you have time?" She lifted the wineglass to her lips again and saw the surprised look on her friend's face. When she glanced toward Mateo, his eyebrow went up meaningfully. Callie realized they both recognized her intentions. She reeled in Cupid, who was alive and well.

When Mateo walked Loli and Callie back to *Casa Baraka*, the stars were shining in the night sky. A soft breeze blew down the narrow street. It was shadowed, but lively, as neighbors chatted nearby. .

Callie's phone rang the minute she put her foot on the top step into her apartment. She nearly tripped over her feet to answer the phone call from Cendrine.

"Callie?"

"Oh dear heart, thank you for calling. Before you tell me there's nothing wrong, don't bother."

Cendrine laughed. "Well, there is something going on, Auntie."

Callie flopped onto the couch. Cendrine never called her that unless her heart was so full, she couldn't get words out. She waited.

"It's *grandpére*. We took him to the hospital four days ago and he's had surgery. He has a health condition that cannot be cured, but it is treatable."

Struggling with a landslide of emotions, she held a hand to her throat and listened to her niece as heat crawled up her body. "I knew something was wrong with him when I saw him. Please tell me everything."

Thirty minutes later, Callie hung up and laid her head back on the gray couch, pushing the bright colored cushion beneath her head. She closed her eyes but her eyelids couldn't stop the flow of tears leaking out and rolling down her cheeks.

Early the next morning, Callie heard pounding on her metal door, clanging as if a group of kids were trick-or-treating. She leaped out of bed and pulled on her robe. When she pattered down the steps, her arm and shoulder throbbed from the fall to the stones.

"Who is it?" Her heartbeat sped up.

"Mateo."

She pulled back the steel bar and opened the door only an inch before unlatching it fully.

Mateo stood there with a look of shock on his pale face. "I need to come in." He had difficulty speaking further.

Callie opened the door and let him pull her up the steps. When they walked into the kitchen she automatically plugged in the water pot so they could have coffee. Twisting the tie of her robe into a knot, she turned toward him.

He sat down. His hands were shaking as he squeezed his knees.

"What in God's name has happened now?" She had to force her mouth closed as it gaped open like a wounded fish. Standing in front of him, she pulled his chin up with her hand. "What, Mateo?"

"They found him."

"Eterio?"

"No, Ricardo." He slumped his head forward and she automatically put her arms around his head, pulling it toward her belly. She felt him shaking and then he cried, wetting the front of her robe. She was horrified.

"You mean...?"

He lifted his head and tears filled his eyes. "Yes. He's dead. A man found him beside a ditch not far from Pedro's vineyard. While we were meeting with the police earlier today, a farmer was pulling this beautiful young man out of the bushes."

She gave him a box of tissue and poured two cups of coffee. She eased a cup into his hand. "When will this nightmare end?"

"If I hadn't asked the boys to carry those bottles into my cellar..." His voice was broken. "I killed him even if it wasn't by my own hand."

"Oh, Mateo. No. You're not thinking straight. Ricardo must have helped Eterio. Please..." She urged him to drink the coffee and sat across from him on the couch. Her chest hurt so badly she thought it was going to rupture.

"He was a good, happy kid. All he wanted was to work in the *chiringuito* on the beach, drink a cold beer and play in the sand and sea after his shift. He and Esteban were good friends. I don't think I can..." Mateo's lips trembled. "I needed to tell you before I left this morning."

"You're driving down that monster mountain in this condition? No. Please wait awhile. Surely, your secretary...?"

"Maria Angela has made so many apologies for me over the past few days, I'm going to lose clients. She's a jewel at the office, but I can't expect her to fill in for me or make more excuses." He rubbed both hands over his face, pulling at the skin until it turned red.

"Let's talk about this. I wonder if another person can help with brainstorming. Something more is going on that we know nothing about. Let me call Loli over."

He laughed brokenly. "I know what you're doing."

"Of course you do."

Loli knocked at her back door within two minutes. When she walked in and saw Mateo's face, she went to him and sat on the bench between him and Callie. When she reached for his hand, he let her hold it tightly. Callie managed a small smile, even though the horror of his news shocked her to the core. She poured more coffee.

Callie left Mateo and Loli alone while he told her the story. She entered her bedroom, closed the door softly and tapped her phone awake. And then she dialed Pertuis.

"Jules. Would you mind terribly catching a plane to Malaga as soon as you can? I was wrong. I need you madly."

Twenty Nine

Salvador Alejandro Trujillo Ruiz rolled back his chair and steepled his fingers beneath his chin. He'd just listened to a man in Marbella telling him the *Sueño España* brandy was available for sale again. The vineyard owner curled the ends of his white mustache and shook his head in wonderment. His contact was a dependable character who typically kept Salvador in tune with the workings in the Marbella syndicate. Today, he'd delivered the startling offer.

He'd heard a few days earlier that the brandy had been stolen from his competitor, Pedro Jiménez. He'd laughed at the time, but now he wasn't laughing. The man won the bid fairly even though Salvador had been livid when he didn't get the bottles.

There was a time when Salvador walked the thin line between Spanish law and Salvador's law. But he was getting old and the game wasn't much fun anymore. He'd watched Manolo Chacon Ortega over the years turn Marbella into a swamp of nastiness. When one of his friends mentioned Manolo's name in passing a few weeks earlier, Salvador's ears had perked up. He knew the police were continually thwarted by the scoundrel because they couldn't pin anything on him. The man used others to do his dirty work. But, this time, Salvador thought he might have the key to the man's demise.

"Salvador, Manolo Chacon just called a friend of mine in Marbella. He tells me those stolen brandy bottles are now in his hands. He needs a buyer. I tried not to laugh when he told me, since nobody we know would touch those stolen bottles and get away with selling them. How dumb can this guy be?"

Salvador joined in his friend's laughter. "You mean, Pedro's bottles are now in Manolo's clutches and he wants to find someone to take them off his hands? He is a stupid, stupid man. The prostitute ring he runs in Marbella should give him all the money he needs. Now, he's opening himself up at last. The police will love this. How do I reach out to his agent and tell him I'm interested?"

"I hoped you would say that, Salvador. Do you want me to call the police or do you want to do that?"

"No, my friend. Let me handle it. Keep quiet. Do not discuss it with anyone. Let me think about it and I will call you with a plan. In the meantime, those bottles are mine." Salvador chuckled and hung up the phone.

~

Late the previous day, when Eterio was near Trebujena, he walked to the front of the bus. When the driver stopped at the outskirts of town to make his right turn into the village, he said, "I want to get off the bus now."

"This isn't a regular stop." The driver pulled his hat down over his forehead and gave his rider a look that would stop most people.

"I want off. Here. And now." Eterio moved toward the man.

The driver snapped open the door and Eterio saluted him with a saucy grin. The bus drove off. Dust billowed behind him. Eterio coughed and sputtered. He straightened up his clothes and started walking toward the buildings a mile in the distance. Manolo better be there, he thought. And he didn't want any surprises from the police, who would surely be watching the bus arrive just a few miles up the road.

When Eterio reached the train tracks, he followed the rails toward the old buildings on the left. He saw the yellow building Manolo owned and walked toward it. As he neared the area, he kept glancing over his shoulder. He wondered if the police knew about the decrepit building. So far, nobody was around. Dust blew toward the building stirring up enough debris to cause Eterio to sneeze.

The stucco building had long been in need of fresh paint. Now, the faded yellow of yesteryear peeled and fell off in clumps. The inside, however, was fresh and clean. He'd been there many times since it was the usual meeting place with Manolo. There were small cubicles along one wall where the girls slept until Manolo found housing for them in Marbella. Eterio had never liked that part of his job. Instead, he'd tried to dissuade Manolo from taking any of the village girls. But he got a clout alongside his head when he tried to keep them home. He'd learned at an early age not to argue with the man, but this time, despite owing him money for gambling debts, he was in charge.

Until he walked through the door.

The smell of smoke and something more filled his nostrils. When his eyes adjusted from the bright sun to the dim room, he couldn't believe the vision before him. His sister Margarita was tied to a chair, her hands were bound, a gag in her mouth. Her hair stood out in various directions and her eyes darted behind Eterio with fear.

"What the hell?" Eterio didn't get another word out before he was clobbered from behind. He fell forward, dumbfounded. His sister's frightened groan filled him with fear. He moved his head to see that Margarita's eyes leaked with tears. Her chest heaved with sobs.

"So, little man. You want to be in charge? This is what happens when you tell me what to do." Manolo kicked Eterio in the ribs. The man's heavy boot sent him into a paroxysm of pain. When he tried to curl into a fetal position, Manolo kicked him and the loud, crunching sound echoed in the empty room.

Margarita's sobs were louder now and Manolo walked over to her and pinched her cheek hard. "Shut up."

She quieted instantly, but her loud, jagged breathing made Eterio want to kill the man who stood above him. His ribs wouldn't allow him to make a move in either direction; he couldn't help his sister and he couldn't kill Manolo. Instead, he writhed on the floor waiting for the moment when he *could* do something.

He heard Manolo drag a chair over beside him. When the big man yanked him off the floor and shoved him into the seat, he held a hand to his ribs. He was sure one or more were cracked or broken. His wrist throbbed, but he knew it was his ribs that would slow him down.

"Now, little man. Where did you put the bottles?" The spiky scar on Manolo's chin stood out like a welt and his dark eyes sparkled eerily from the wall light.

Eterio's good eye glared at Manolo stupidly.

Manolo slugged him in the face with a meaty hand. "I said, where are the bottles? Do you want me to use Margarita as my punching bag instead of you?" His voice sounded like a growl. When he walked toward Margarita, Eterio whimpered.

"Okay, you *bastardo*. I will tell you, but first let my sister go. Untie her. When she is gone, I will take you to the bottles." Eterio's ribs howled against his chest like a wounded animal.

"Oh, you still want to tell me what to do?"

Eterio spit in Manolo's face.

Manolo laughed and kicked the chair out from under him. And then he walked toward Margarita, who flinched away brokenly. He untied her gag and pulled a small sharp knife from his pants pocket. When he sliced through the yellow rope that bound her, he pulled her out of the chair and pushed her toward the door. "You better run and hide because if your little brother tries to cheat me, I'll come after you."

Margarita took one last look at Eterio sprawled on the floor behind her and ran out the door, crying.

Despite the injured wrist and the crunched ribs, Manolo simply pulled Eterio out the door. Once he'd pushed him into his large car, a Spanish SEAT, he asked Eterio, "Where?"

Eterio looked around the deserted area to assure himself that his sister was gone. When he turned back to look at Manolo, he wanted to kill a second time. Nodding his head east, Manolo drove outside the village and up the hill toward the broken outbuildings and old windmill. Once they parked, Manolo pulled him out of the car and stared at Eterio.

When Eterio knew he had no other choice, he pointed to the gated hut behind the windmill and dug out the key to his padlock with his good hand. Manolo grunted, took the key and within fifteen minutes, all the pine boxes were in the back of his vehicle. Grunting from the exertion, he leaned against the SEAT to catch his breath.

Manolo looked at Eterio, pushed a hand into his pocket and fingered the knife. When he pulled it out, he hesitated and spit on the ground. Pocketing it again, he pulled out his car key, pushed Eterio to the ground and drove away.

~

One hour's drive to the west, in a vineyard office, Salvador Trujillo stared at the fledgling shoots in his vineyard and made up his mind. His veined hands played with the pocket watch on his desk. He didn't want to run the risk of being questioned by either the police or Mateo Rosa Trascasas. He wasn't overly fond of solicitors and he hated the police. If he wanted Manolo Chacon stopped, he had only one choice.

When Callie's mobile phone rang, she assumed it was a marketing call and ignored it. On the fourth ring, she changed her mind and answered it with a tinge of impatience. "Hello?"

"Callinda Beauvais?" The accented voice sounded grim.

"Yes, this is she. Who is this?" She tapped her finger on the table.

She heard a startled chuckle. "Salvador Trujillo Ruiz. And I am the answer to your prayers."

FLAMENCO STRINGS UNCORKED

"Salvador...? The answer to my prayers? The man who wanted to buy the brandy bottles?" She was astonished and fascinated, nearly undone with curiosity.

His voice rattled in the back of his throat. "The same."

"And you're calling me because...?"

"Because, young woman. You are going to help me get back Pedro's brandy bottles, throw a criminal into prison, save many young women from prostitution and give the *Guardia Civil* a rare gift."

"You definitely have my attention, *señor*. How do I...?"

"First and most important, you don't tell anyone. This is between you and me only. If you cannot promise me that, the deal is off. There are people in Algodonales who would help Eterio Alonzo. You cannot trust anyone, but you'll have to trust me. I wanted those damn bottles and I threw a tantrum. Today I want to make a difference. I want the good people to win and the bad people to get their asses thrown in prison. We have the key to do this and this is what I want you to do."

Callie held the phone to her ear and listened for fifteen minutes. She didn't interrupt, but several times nodded her head and made purring sounds in her throat. When he was finished, she couldn't stop the smile that spread across her face.

Worry for her father-in-law would have to be put on pause. She just hoped the sting would be put into play before Jules arrived so she could keep her promise to the old Spaniard. She liked his voice and his idea. For now, she had to be happy with that.

She would follow his instructions and keep her mouth shut. She hated keeping secrets from her new friends, but she also knew if the wrong person heard about the plan, all bets were off. Trying to quell her excitement, she lifted the phone to put their plot into gear.

Thirty

Manolo Chacon Ortega backed away from the deserted windmill and took a short cut behind the village to avoid police. The last street behind the *bodega* was noisy. It was past five, time for *merienda*, a time that usually brought villagers out for hot chocolate and *churros*. Today was no different; the narrow street was abuzz with people standing in clumps or leaning against the colored walls. Several outside cafés were busily attending to their customers as umbrellas swung gently in the breeze. A man with a fedora lifted a cold beer to his lips while a woman sipped on red wine beside him.

He drove slowly past the second street, closer to the *bodega* and scanned the crowd. Margarita must be inside by now. He knew he'd scared her and she wouldn't talk. Manolo chuckled when he remembered her face, the sounds of her voice echoing panic and fear. Too bad, she kept his bed warm and he'd miss her, but he must take care of her. She knew too much. Maybe he should stop by the bar now.

The sounds of an approaching car caught his attention. *Policia.* No, not today then. He pulled his big car into the market's parking lot and lay down on the front seat. The cruiser passed him and turned into the next street. Sweat ran down Manolo's face. Inching himself up again, he put his car into gear and followed the road to the last roundabout and left Trebujena.

He'd be in Marbella in two hours. Plenty of time to do his business. Getting the brandy out of his car and into the buyer's hands was first on his agenda. Prostitution and gambling had always been his main business, but today he felt giddy. Picasso's brandy. He rolled down the window to let his laughter follow the breeze. His powerful car rolled past smaller cars like a demon. His radar scanner beeped periodically and all he could think about was putting those beauties into the hands of... His head came up. Who was the buyer? Manolo didn't do business with strangers and didn't want to make an exception this time. Antonio said it was a winemaker, but who was he?

Manolo's forehead creased as he drew closer to the Mediterranean where Marbella perched on the Costa del Sol. He loved the city with its shining buildings, international connections, rich marks and rolling waves. His thoughts returned to Antonio and the buyer. Pursing his lips, he changed lanes and drove onto the AP-7 highway. Traffic grew thicker, faster.

And he was starving. Paella. Yes, that's what he needed. He'd eat first and then call Antonio. He wasn't going to give up these bottles until he knew who he was dealing with. He turned onto the N-340 and headed toward *Paellas y Más*, his favorite restaurant on the beach.

When he parked his SEAT, he studied the pine boxes in the back area of his car. He glanced around and decided it was safe. Who would steal pine boxes? He laughed as the thought slid into his mind. Yes, who indeed? He was still smiling when he pushed open the door.

Since Manolo was well known in Marbella, he never needed a reservation, especially at this restaurant. The hostess smiled at him and he followed her skin-tight dress, the fabric caressing her like a lover. He marveled at the way she was able to walk on the stiletto heels without falling on her butt. She knew his favorite table. She also knew he didn't need a menu. Two servers materialized, both anxious to please.

Manolo unwrapped the linen napkin from around the utensils and laid it across his lap. When he raised his eyebrow to one man, his *paella* was ordered. When he lifted a finger to the other server and pointed to the third row from the left in the wine cupboard, a bottle of

Ribera del Duero red was brought to his table. He never did business on an empty stomach and today was going to be big. Very big.

While he sipped his wine, he casually lifted his phone and dusted off his pants to remove a piece of lint that clung to his knee. He stretched his shoulders to ease the ache from the heavy work of packing the wine and his two-hour drive south. Groaning softly, he waited for Antonio to answer the phone. Stiffening his spine, he prepared himself for an argument.

"Antonio. How are you, my friend?" Manolo's voice carried the lazy insolence he wore like a shadow. He heard the man's recoil over the phone. Why is that?

"Manolo." The noises of the restaurant were muted when he pushed the phone closer to his ear. Seagulls perched on the chair outside the window near the sea and hopped from the railing to the boardwalk.

"I want to tie up a few loose strings." He drew a breath and blew it out slowly, considering his next words. "You know I never do business with strangers. And you neglected to tell me the buyer's name. I will not hand over those bottles to strangers without knowing who I am dealing with. You realize that, don't you?"

His contact was a man he'd known for over ten years. He trusted Antonio like he trusted everyone; not at all. The man was secretive and often held his own counsel. This time, Manolo was uneasy. Something was off and he didn't like it.

Antonio responded carefully neutral. "Manolo. The man wants to remain anonymous. You know some business arrangements are sensitive and these Picasso bottles aren't something to advertise. The buyer told me his name was not to be shared. You can understand that, can't you? My God, once these bottles are on the black market, all hell could break loose and my guy isn't stupid."

Manolo clenched a fist on the table. "The brandy goes nowhere unless I am comfortable with the exchange. Maybe we're moving too fast. Maybe I should store these bottles until..."

"Do you really think you can sit on these bottles and wait around for a better offer? Is that what you want? You asked me to find a buyer and I got one. I have a pick-up site tonight at nine. There's a small, dark area behind *Abuelita's Restaurant* at the back of the boardwalk. You know the place?" Antonio rushed through his words.

Manolo's eyes turned shrewdly toward the window again and gazed at the rolling sea. He bit the inside of his mouth and sipped more of his red wine. "I don't like it, but you're right. These bottles are burning a hole in my car. Nine. *Abuelita's*," he said in a low-voice, jerking his chin toward the window and squirming in his chair.

"*Perfecto*, Manolo. You are a smart man, *amigo*."

"*Por supuesto*, he murmured. Of course.

The *paella* arrived, overflowing with *gambas, clams and chorizo* sausage, steaming hot just as he liked it. The jumbo-sized prawns were plump and delicious. Manolo scooped the rice and clams into his mouth with the meat as if he hadn't eaten in a week. His mind still rumbled quietly in the background, but the food and wine kept it at a low purr.

Thirty One

Callie arrived in Marbella at the same time Manolo was munching his *paella*. She'd told the others in Algodonales that she was driving to pick up Jules from the airport. It was only half a lie. Jules was coming later. Her mind had been jumping through hoops all the way down the curving mountain below Ronda.

She tried to veer away from the young man's death, but could still feel Mateo's shaking body beneath her hands. Ricardo had been young and had so much life to live. Unable to keep her mind from churning, she focused on Eterio and the fright he'd given to her. Where was he now? Had the police found him yet? And the pimp in Marbella? She shuddered, changed lanes and looked at her GPS. She certainly didn't want to get lost. Not today when the clock ticked with each mile she covered toward the sea.

She took a deep breath and thought of Jules. He always told her to ease panic or fear, she should go slow and easy. "Slow and easy," she repeated out loud. "Slow and easy." Squeezing the steering wheel, she saw the speedometer reach 120 and she eased her foot off the gas pedal. She wanted to see the police on her terms, not theirs. "Slow and easy," she said again. And then she saw police cars. She parked and took a deep breath. Show time.

They were waiting for her. When she introduced herself to the policewoman at the front desk, Callie was ushered into a room where three men and two women sat around a large, round table. All eyes turned toward her. She nodded, sat down and pulled out her iPad where every note she'd listed after speaking with Salvador gave her the steps to follow.

"How did you learn who had the bottles?"

"Where is Eterio Alonzo?"

"Here in Marbella, we have certain protocols to follow and there is no precedent for a private citizen to..."

Callie held up her hand to stop the questions. Barely understanding them, she also said, "*Despacio, por favor.*" Slow please. She tapped the keyboard on her iPad and then spread her hands on the burnished, wooden table.

In halting Spanish, she said "I cannot tell you who gave me this information. The man told me to trust no one."

"I speak English," a woman across from her said. Her eyebrows were plucked high on her brow bone. Her smile reached her eyes.

Callie felt herself relax. "Oh, good. My Spanish is new. The man who called me said that Manolo Chacon was a person of questionable character here in Marbella."

The group snickered and eyed one another.

"That's true," the woman said. "My name is Louisa."

Callie nodded and continued, "My contact told me about the man's history with prostitution and gambling and that you want to put him into prison. This time, I can help you arrest the scoundrel and put him in jail." Callie's confidence level rose when she saw the interest on everyone's faces. She had their complete attention after the woman translated her words to them.

"Tell us what you know and we will prepare our strategy." Louisa turned to translate Callie's statements and they nodded again. "We have tried to catch this man several times without results. What makes you think you can help us get this man and do our job?"

Callie bit the inside of her lip. So, she'd ruffled their feathers. She took a deep breath. Slow and easy, Jules told her. She swallowed. "This man, Manolo, has been kidnapping girls from Trebujena with the help of Eterio Alonzo. Maybe you all know that? And he has been terrorizing a woman who lives there...the sister of Eterio, named

Margarita. She and her brother Ruben called her cousin in Algodonales to relate what happened to her today."

Once Louisa told the group this latest news, they leaned forward and stared at her with new respect. The fan barely moved the air and it felt stuffy and overly warm. Callie loosened her blouse and toed off her sandals. She hadn't gotten used to the hot climate and their air conditioning seemed sluggish.

Louisa gave her a look and Callie began again. "When Eterio needed a buyer for the brandy bottles he stole from Pedro Jiménez's driver the other night, he called Manolo Chacon. He wanted the bottles for himself. When Eterio arrived at their meeting place in Trebujena, Manolo had Margarita tied and gagged in a chair. When her brother Eterio arrived, Manolo beat him and then he let Margarita leave the building." Callie lifted the pitcher on the table and poured herself a glass of water. Others did the same.

She waited patiently until Louisa finished translating Margarita's story. Brushing her hands through her hair, Callie stared at each of them. "Margarita does not know where Eterio is now, but she said Manolo must have the bottles because he was seen driving from Trebujena shortly afterward." She sipped more water. "And my contact said the man setting up the sale just talked with Manolo and a place and time has been set for the exchange."

The tension in the room changed from interest to excitement. They spoke at once after Louisa told them this information.

"*Abuelita's*. Nine o'clock." She held up nine fingers and pointed to the clock. They understood her immediately. Callie felt the hair raise on her arms when she watched everyone jump up and gesticulate to one another, speaking with their hands.

"*Quiero ir.*" I want to go. They ignored her. She raised her voice several octaves and repeated, "*Quiero ir!*"

FLAMENCO STRINGS UNCORKED

The group stared at her. She placed both hands on her hips and heard them chatter to Louisa. The woman turned to Callie. "You have their attention. They don't like it. You ride with me."

Everyone disbursed to set the sting in motion. Within thirty minutes, Callie was sitting in a police car riding along the Mediterranean Sea. She'd promised to stay in the car because she wanted the man in handcuffs and Pedro's bottles. Salvador and Pedro would be nearby. She hadn't shared that with the police. Another one of Salvador's instructions.

At *Paella y Más,* Manolo pushed the *paella* pan away from him and laid down his fork. The plate looked as if he had licked it clean. The wine bottle was mostly empty and he wiped his lips with the linen napkin. The servers were standing in the corner watching him, but not approaching his table without his invitation. Everyone knew Manolo's idiosyncrasies. None wanted to feel his wrath. Others had and were no longer working at the restaurant.

He saw lights blink along the boardwalk. Watching people wander by for their nightly walk, the *paseo*, he poured the remaining wine into his glass. Lifting his wrist, he looked at his watch. Eight fifteen. Plenty of time to finish his wine and go pick up his money. He had a good view of his SEAT. Nobody dared go near it. The lights shone brightly over the vehicle, so nobody would steal the bottles. He laughed at the irony and sipped his wine.

When his phone rang, he silenced it. He didn't like being interrupted when he was feeling peaceful. The wine went down like honey. He burped into his napkin and wiggled his finger at a server to clear away the dishes. He had plenty of time. If he was late, the buyer could wait for him. He stared into the glass and smiled at the wine inside. Life was sweet.

Thirty Two

Salvador Trujillo and Pedro Jiménez greeted one another with a firm handshake and the cultural kiss on each cheek. They were both respected vintners from the old, proud Spanish lines that went back generations. Their vineyards were both successful, the best in the south of Spain.

"Pedro. I lost. You won. And you will get your brandy." Salvador's eyes were dark and expressive. His swarthy complexion and youthful smile belied his age. He'd just passed his eightieth birthday, but he hadn't slowed down yet. And he didn't plan to do that until they put him in a box and took him away feet first.

"You're a good man, Salvador. I don't know how you found my brandy and I won't ask, but you know I am relieved. Where are we going?" Excitement warred with the seriousness of their venture.

Salvador held a finger to his lips and grinned at the look on the Pedro's face. "I can't tell you that, Pedro. But the woman in charge of Picasso's flamenco guitar school will be there and she's bringing her party along with her."

"Salvador. You old rascal. If what you say is true, you will be my hero. And I will give you six bottles of my *Sueño España* brandy if tonight goes well. I want to get my hands on the thief. I hope he rots in jail...he hurt my driver and I've been told he probably killed the young man who helped him steal them from my van." His shaggy eyebrows rose during his fervent speech.

The men raised their right hands to one another and tapped them together. Salvador started his car and drove toward the boardwalk. He eased the large Mercedes into the spot behind *Abuelita's Restaurant* and turned off the key.

"Now we wait, Pedro."

Pedro looked around the area, dark and a little forbidding. He didn't answer but instead removed his seat belt and chewed on his lip. Lights lit up the far alley and several cars drove slowly toward them.

A group of teenagers inched by with their windows open. Music blared loudly and the old men's eyes widened. The ground shook beneath them and they exhaled deeply when it passed and the music drifted away.

Salvador pointed across the alley where four cars sat in the dark. Callie had sent a text to him before he'd met Pedro and he knew she was inside one of them. She had followed his instructions perfectly.

When the large, dark SEAT pulled into the street, Salvador pulled Pedro down beside him. It drove slowly past the tall palms. Then they saw it slow down and park beside ghostly bougainvillea pots where the blooms climbed to the roof of the house behind them.

Salvador tapped out a text on his phone.

Immediately, one of the car's headlights at the far end of the darkened area popped on and it made a slow pass along the alley.

Manolo waited, anxious for his money. He vaguely wondered why Antonio hadn't met the buyer with him, but he snorted. The man was afraid of his own shadow and Manolo liked it that way.

The car parked to the right of Manolo's SEAT, turned off its lights and sat a minute before the driver's door opened. A big man in a dark suit stood between the cars. He adjusted his suit coat and walked slowly around the SEAT to tap on Manolo's window.

"You Manolo Chacon Ortega?" The stranger asked in a voice that sounded like steel. His hat was pulled low over his forehead. His suit jacket bulged with a gun holstered beneath his armpit.

Manolo rolled down the window and stared at the man. He looked into his rear-view mirror. Silence and darkness pervaded the area. Manolo was surprised because *Abuelita's* usually had a crowd parked at the back. He guessed it was his lucky night all the way around then. No spectators.

"I am Manolo Chacon Ortega if you have a pocket filled with money. Show me the money before I get out of this car." His voice wasn't as strong as he hoped it would be; the man was intimidating and that surprised him.

The stranger reached into his suit coat.

Manolo said, "Hold it."

The man's hand stopped mid-air and he stared at Manolo.

Manolo rolled down his window and beckoned the man toward him. He saw the other man pause with indecision for a heartbeat before he leaned forward. "Let me take out the money. I know you have a gun and I don't like surprises."

The man chuckled and leaned toward the window. As soon as Manolo had the envelope in his hand, the man spoke into Manolo's ear. "My turn. Where's my bottles of Spanish brandy?"

Manolo saw the packet of money stuffed inside the envelope and didn't bother counting it. He could do that later. The heft of the packet told him all he needed to know. He opened his door and popped his trunk open. And then all hell broke loose. He was blinded by several sets of headlights that lit up the parking area.

Manolo swung around in shock. An adrenaline dump dropped him into a brain pattern of fight or flight. He chose flight and bumped the stranger away from the car as he jerked open the car door to run.

Before he got far, several cars revved their engines and swerved across the lot to form a circle around him. The officers swarmed out of the cars and knocked Manolo to the ground. He fought and squealed, but his wrists were pulled behind him and manacles locked with a loud click. Dirt filled his mouth.

While the police yanked him to his feet, another car drove slowly forward and blocked the alley. Pedro Jiménez and Salvador

FLAMENCO STRINGS UNCORKED

Trujillo walked toward the assemblage with smirks on their faces. Manolo stared at the old men and tried to make sense of the situation.

The policemen pulled Manolo toward the closest police car.

Callie's breath hitched as she watched the man being led away. Thoughts of her own childhood abuse and Lily, the young girl in Portland made her reach for the door handle. Her mind flew to the women this man had forced into prostitution and her throat filled with tears. She jumped out of the car, intent on looking Manolo in the face.

Louisa yelled at Callie, "Stop!" She tried to catch Callie's arm, but she slid out of her grasp because Callie could not stop running forward any more than she could stop the sun from rising each morning. Her vision went blurry. Stopping in front of the man, she whispered, "You hateful, disgusting devil. Those girls deserve a life and you've given them nothing but shame and sadness. You make me sick to my stomach and I'm glad you're going where you can't touch them anymore."

Manolo twisted and jerked when she hissed at him. He tried to pull away from the policeman, but he was held firmly in his grasp. He stared at Callie with loathing. And in that split second when chaos charged the air around them, Manolo head butted the policeman and rushed toward Callie.

The policeman held his head with both hands and wiped blood from his nose as he lunged toward Manolo again. Louisa pulled Callie out of the way and pushed her behind her.

Manolo yelled, "You bitch. They love it. Every minute they pleasure a man, they learn to love it. Do you have any idea how much they crave a man's touch?"

And then Manolo was running, plainly hindered by his hands tightly clasped behind his back. The alley was dark except for the dim street lamp on the corner and the cars' headlights.

The police screamed at him, pushed Callie out of their way and ran after him like spurned bulldogs. Louisa caught Callie around the waist and pushed her toward the old men standing with shocked faces beside her.

Callie's brain started functioning again. She saw a shadow in the far corner of the lot and realized the police had run by Manolo headed in the wrong direction. When the thought clicked into her head, she started running and panting out the words, "Slow and easy."

When she reached the shadows, she stopped to twist around the corner of the cement block building. The police were running toward the boardwalk, away from them. Something shifted inside of her and she knew it was her one chance to make a difference for those abused girls.

He was crouched behind a rain barrel. His hands were on the ground as he fought to step through the manacles. They were now in front of his belly. She heard his heavy breathing and she noticed, in the faint light, the rocks behind him. He'd hear her. Stooping low, she duck-walked around the other side of the tall bushes that hid him from the boardwalk. When she calculated she was in front of him, she jumped through the opening in the shrubbery and kicked upward with all her strength. Her right foot met his chest. When she heard the wind go out of him with a loud woof sound, she twisted around to the left and gave him a strong back kick to his crotch. When he went down, she heard the yelling close by.

Four policemen and Louisa rounded the building. Startled at seeing Callie on her feet and Manolo on the ground gripping his privates, they stared at her, clearly dumbfounded.

Her heart was beating hard. She had so much difficulty swallowing her fear, that she didn't say anything at all. As she tried to catch her breath, Manolo was yanked from the ground and frog stepped toward the police car by three policemen.

Louisa let out a harsh breath. "I told you to stay in the car. What was that all about?

"*Lo siento mucho.*" I am very sorry.

The policewoman shook her head. The remaining policeman looked between Callie and a screaming Manolo and scratched his head.

The enormity of the event struck her suddenly. "Well," she said. "I am a white belt in Tae Kwon Do." She raised both eyebrows toward the officers and rubbed her hands together. She hoped they didn't notice her legs shaking as she walked away..

"Callinda Beauvais?"

"Yes?" She turned around and the two old men were looking at her in awe. She knew they must be the vintners. When she reached toward Salvador Trujillo, he pulled her into a soft hug and kissed her on both cheeks. She turned toward Pedro Jiménez and shook her head with a toothy smile, sure he was the owner of the *Sueño España* bottles. After more kisses and a long hug later, the three of them stood beside Manolo's vehicle.

The remaining policeman told them, "This SEAT is being appropriated along with everything in it."

Callie's stubbornness emanated from her body like the thorns on a rose. "Oh, really? After our plan helped you put that nasty man into your jail, you think you are going to keep this brandy?" She was so furious, she wasn't sure if she'd be in jail beside the thug or not. And she didn't care.

"This is Pedro Jiménez. He owns these bottles and he will take them home *now*." Wild with impatience, she stood nose to nose with the officer. They stared at one another. He adjusted the black cap on his head, nodded toward the gentlemen and bowed toward the pine boxes as if he was asking her to dance.

"And who are you?" The officer was looking curiously at Salvador Trujillo Ruiz. The other officers had driven away and taken

Manolo with them. He looked like he wished a couple had stayed behind. He stared at Salvador with a raised eyebrow."

Salvador grinned and pointed toward Callie and Pedro. "I'm with them."

The policeman gave him the side eye and wound tape around the front of the car. When he shrugged his shoulders, the men opened the pine boxes and counted the bottles.

Pedro lifted one into the air and handed it to Salvador. "There's number one. Do you have room for five more?" The men laughed.

When Callie saw them lift the boxes from the back of the SEAT, she offered to help them. The men snickered and carried each box to Pedro's trunk as if they were filled with cotton. Neither man stumbled nor groaned under the weight.

Louisa stood nearby, fascinated with the wine label after Pedro pulled out the bottle. "I've never seen that label." Her hushed tone indicated a reverence that made Callie smile again. The policewoman shook her head before she joined the remaining officer.

When the brandy was loaded, the vintners opened the back door of the Mercedes to drive her back to the police station. She held a hand over her heart and grinned at the men.

"You are a good man, Salvador."

"Pedro, we must stay true to ourselves and our vineyards. Without respect, who are we?"

The men chuckled.

"Thank you for the brandy. You didn't have to give them to me. I didn't expect any payment. I just wanted you to have your bottles and if we can throw Manolo into prison at the same time, that is good."

"But do you think he hired Eterio to steal the bottles?" Callie was struggling to understand the connection. Mateo told me that Ricardo, the young man who was killed, used to live in Trebujena. So, they were all linked to Manolo Chacon?" She continued to brainstorm aloud.

Salvador made a sound with his mouth. "I think Eterio owed Manolo money. I think Eterio and Ruben hired an attorney to get some of the money. And then I imagine Eterio stole the bottles when he knew he couldn't get the money. So, he had to find a buyer. And who better to go underground with stolen brandy than Manolo? And then Manolo wanted all of it. Just my personal opinion."

Pedro chuckled. "Your *personal* opinion, Salvador, or someone told you who was connected to the whole thing?"

Salvador whispered, "My lips are sealed."

When Salvador parked near Callie's car, both men got out with her. After more kisses and hugs, she promised to share news of the flamenco school as it progressed.

"You are returning to Algodonales very late."

She felt a frisson of excitement and exhaled deeply. "No, I am driving to Malaga. My fiancé arrives in two hours."

Both men nodded and grinned at her.

She waved goodbye and threw a kiss toward the brandy bottles. Driving eastward, the clear sky shone with a thousand twinkling stars. A soft breeze caressed her with whispered promises. She had two less worries; the brandy bottles were with their rightful owner and her heart had spoken.

Jules.

Thirty Three

Olivia called Callie as she was driving east toward the airport on the A-7. It was two o'clock in the afternoon at Larkspur Insurance Company in Portland, Oregon, nine hours earlier than Spain time.

When she saw her friend's face light up her phone, she tapped the speaker mode on her iPhone. "Livvy."

"I didn't wake you, Callie? The time difference is still confusing but I know people eat late in Spain, so here I am. I needed to hear your voice."

"Livvy, I am definitely awake. In fact, I'm driving to the airport."

Olivia mumbled.

"What? You aren't coming in very clear."

"I said I hope you are getting Jules. You've probably been lonely for him in that quiet, little village getting the school started?"

Callie laughed. She had a lot to tell Livvy, but not tonight. "I am indeed on my way to pick up Jules. We're going to that bed and breakfast I told you about near Malaga for a couple of days."

Olivia laughed delightedly. "Oh…the round house?"

"Yes, ma'am. Elvira Smiffy made it into a bed and breakfast. It's the house that Darla's father built high on a hill. It overlooks a beautiful valley filled with vineyards and orange groves."

"Ah. Well, I'm calling to find out the date of the wedding. Bram and I need to make reservations. The last time we spoke, you put me off and then told me you were going to Spain alone. Do we have a date yet?"

Callie's face turned soft. "First, I need to see Francois' parents and then I'll let you know. It's complicated."

"Why? They're happy you're marrying Jules, aren't they?"

"Yes, but *Peré* just had surgery and Cendrine tells me it's not good. I'm worried sick."

"Well, you need to get on with it then."

Callie grimaced at her logic. "I'll call you soon. This might also delay Lily's arrival to stay with Cendrine for the school year. Michel has been looking pale, so I'm not surprised. I hope a wedding will be just the thing to put the color back into his cheeks."

"Well, I know it will put color back in yours...among other things," Olivia whispered.

Callie laughed because she visualized the smirk on her friend's face. "I'm coming into Malaga traffic, my friend, and it's not an easy thing."

"Right. Call me. I want to hear more about Lulu too."

Callie felt butterflies flit around inside her stomach. Traffic was still heavy at midnight. She was unsure if it was the cars weaving next to her or imagining Jules' arms around her that woke them up.

Twenty minutes later, she parked near the tobacco shop across from the Malaga Airport's entrance. Grimacing at the crush of humanity around her, she opened the door and laced both hands on the top of her car. She scanned the travelers streaming out the doors. She glanced at her watch. He should arrive any minute. She thumped her fingers and leaned against the door.

"Are you going my way?" The deep voice purred into Callie's ear.

She spun around and threw herself into his arms. They circled around her to draw her close. Both moaned satisfied groans of pleasure. It felt like warm honey and they didn't want to let go.

When Elvira saw the headlights at her grilled gate, she unlatched the Dutch door and walked into the dark passageway. After hugging Callie, she led them to the large bedroom and smiled at the good-looking man. When Jules spoke to her in English with his French accent, she nearly swooned. She could tell they were away with the fairies when they closed the bedroom door. Elvira smiled all the way back upstairs to her bedroom.

The lights down the hill toward the village glittered through the window. Pesky, Scalli and Scamp readjusted themselves inside their dog beds in the room near the garage after being woken by their arrival. Callie grinned in the dark as Jules wrapped his arms around her and swung her off her feet.

"Jules, it's so good...."

"Oh, yes. You can show me just how good it is as soon as I get my shoes off." He made a deep sound in his throat.

She chuckled and kissed his naked shoulder as he sat down beside her. When she heard the second shoe drop to the floor, that's exactly what she did.

The next morning, Callie wasn't sure what woke her. The sound of a rooster crowing, the braying of the neighbor's burro or the sound of Elvira calling the dogs to get into her car for their morning walk. But then again, it could have been the warm fingers that danced along her spine.

They spent another hour deliciously getting to know one another again and then she slipped out of bed to make coffee. Elvira had other guests this time, so they didn't have the house to themselves. However, when the couple walked into the kitchen a few moments later, it was obvious they were joggers. They left the house after filling two water bottles.

Callie filled two cups with steaming coffee and returned to Jules. The day stretched ahead of them. She had nothing to do and all the time to do it. And she wouldn't be doing it alone.

When she pushed open the door with her foot and balanced both cups in her hands, she nearly dropped them when she saw Jules. He was standing on the bed in his bare feet, meticulously working the gauzy mosquito netting with his fingers to untangle it and reattach the flowing fabric to the ceiling again.

"Huh. Not sure how that came loose." She said knowingly.

He looked at her with a grin and reached for the coffee. "Really?"

That afternoon, after a long talk on the phone with Janine, she turned to Jules and fought tears. She thought she would be prepared for it, but one never is. "She's demented with worry. The flamenco guitar school starts on Monday. There are now nine students. Mari and Javier are pretty much in charge and I know they'll do a good job. Loli has agreed to work with Mateo on the estate's paperwork. And I'm hoping it might be the beginning of romance for all of them."

Jules rolled his eyes. "Callie."

"No. Seriously, I saw sparks."

He laughed.

"And that means I can go back home early." She sipped her coffee and met his eyes.

"And?"

"And that means we have a wedding to plan."

Jules put her cup on the table and picked her up to swing her around like a top. When he put her down, he kissed her deeply and pulled her face nose to nose with his. "Then why is your face so sad?"

"Because," she said. She reached for a tissue beside the chair. "I'm not sure how much longer *Père* is going to be with us."

Jules sat down in the chair and air whooshed out of the cushion. "Tell me about Michel." He reached for her hand and pulled her onto his lap lacing her fingers with his.

~

Three days later, Olivia and Bram Carle arrived in Aix en Provence, rented a car and drove to Pertuis. Olivia hadn't wanted to pull Callie or Jules away from the family to pick them up from the airport. Michel Beauvais' health was weakening daily. In two days, there would be a wedding ceremony. Everyone was sure the old gentleman was waiting to see Callie, who he called Callinda, marry Jules. It was no secret he loved her like a daughter since she'd married his now-deceased son. He wanted to see her happy again. It would be a bittersweet beginning for her friend.

"You have the dress?" Bram steered the rental car northward.

"Mmmmm."

"Shoes? Earrings? Callie's gift?"

Olivia tapped Bram's arm. "Who are you, my valet?"

He chuckled and pulled her hand into his. "It will be nice to be back inside the manse again since we were married there. We can celebrate our six-monthiversary." The rented BMW glistened in the sun when the clouds lifted to welcome them to French soil.

Olivia smiled. The memories of their wedding wove through her mind like beautiful ribbons. She hoped she could give Callie the support that her friend had given to her. It would also be her friend's second marriage, only different. Olivia had been a divorcee. Callie was a widow. Different but the same; they'd both found magic again.

~

Janine clapped her hands together. "*Non. Non.* You must not, Callie. This will be a forever memory for you and Jules. Just because Michel is ill, doesn't mean you should do this."

"*Maman.* We don't need all the flowers and fancy music. We just need each other." She pulled her mother-in-law down onto the couch beside her. "Please, I know this is a sad time and I am having difficulty getting in a celebratory mood."

Janine Beauvais put her face close to Callie's and whispered, "It is too special to me and Michel. Do it for us if not for yourself." She kissed both of Callie's cheeks, blew her nose into a lace handkerchief and left the cottage.

Callie's breath held a moment before she exhaled. Janine was right. It wasn't fair to anyone if she had a stark wedding when the day would be a family celebration. It might be the last time all the family was together. Her heart was breaking and she caught a sob with her handkerchief. "I must get my head straight," she whispered.

She glanced into the kitchen and saw the lone bottle of brandy with its unique label on the front. The *señorita* was still riding across the label and seemed to be singing Callie's wedding song. If it hadn't been for that woman, she would not be marrying Jules in two days.

Walking toward the kitchen, she lifted the bottle with both hands. "You, my darling, will be one of the guests at our wedding." She chuckled with the thoughts in her head and reached for her iPad. She still had several items to buy and the caterers were waiting for a number count. Andre was bringing two large bouquets of grapevines to thread among the poppies. It's all she wanted, except maybe her mother's favorite flower, Lilies of the Valley.

Her heart hurt. She imagined her mother walking through the vineyard and along the stone pathway by the mill house, where Callie and Francois had made it into a beautiful home. She lifted a flower to her nose, and smiled at the scent. Later, she lifted a piece of fabric for Callie's approval, touched the toe of a fancy shoe, sure it would match her daughter's wedding dress. She tasted the wedding cake sample before her daughter ordered it. She made Callie's day perfect.

Callie burst into tears. It never got easier. She missed her mother like it was yesterday when she died. She cried because her mother died too young, because she missed her and because she would never know Jules. After she cried herself out, she picked up her iPad again.

Thirty Four

Olivia and Bram drove up to the mill house and parked under a tree near the cottage. Callie didn't hear them arrive. She was on her knees in the bedroom pulling her mother's pearls out of the jewel box. She'd tried to dry her tears but when she'd held the natural pearls in the palm of her hand, she'd sunk to the floor.

A noise brought her head up. And before she could get up, she saw her best friend's face beaming from her bedroom doorway.

Short blonde hair framed Olivia Carle's face and her bright green eyes sparkled. "Good grief, just because I'm coming to visit doesn't mean you have to get on your hands and knees to clean the floor," she said with a wide grin.

And then Callie started crying all over again.

Cendrine knocked on the front door and then opened it when Callie didn't answer or call out to her. Lulu was tethered to her chest and Bernadette shadowed her. When they found the women both on the floor with tears flowing, she said, "Hey. This is supposed to be a happy time, you two."

Olivia jumped up and opened her arms wide. First, Cendrine kissed both of her cheeks and then she unwrapped Lulu and pushed her into her Aunt Livvy's waiting arms.

Olivia kissed the baby's soft cheek and cooed over her. Running her hand over the little butt bump, she grinned at Cendrine. "I knew she was a girl."

"Uh-huh. Me too. Sorry to barge in, but when I saw you arrive, I couldn't wait. Bram went to find Papa in the vines and Olivier went with him. If they find him in the cave, they'll probably spend the afternoon tasting the new wine we put up last week." She winked. "It is wonderful. A new blend. Maybe we should…" She looked at Callie.

"…No, dear. I want *Chloe Rosé* Sparkling Wine."

"You are reading my mind, auntie."

Callie laughed and struggled to get up. "Veronique is coming by with the dress. But we need to go shopping for shoes. I want new ones to match."

"Pink?" Livvy teased, knowing it was Callie's favorite color.

"No," Callie answered with a huff. "My dress is cream colored with a frothy sash around the shoulders and it ties at the bust to flow down to the hem. I want cream colored shoes."

"Is there pink in the sash?"

"Yes, and blue and lavender."

"The shoes must be pink then."

Callie and Olivia gave each other a look.

"You win. Pink it is. Let's go. Maybe we can meet Veronique at the shop and save her the trip. The reception will be held there and she's working madly getting it perfect for Saturday."

Cendrine put out her hands to gather Lulu up again, slipped her into the wrapper and kissed the top of her downy-soft head. When Callie saw the loving gesture, her heart filled up again.

When Veronique Beauvais saw her step-mother and Olivia walk down the sidewalk toward Hybrid Designs, she ran to open the door. The chimes sang when they entered and she was pulled into an embrace by both women.

The shop was stunning. Tables overflowed with upholstery fabric in muted colors. Scented candles filled the shelves behind the work counter and the aroma tickled Callie's nose. Sharing her interior design expertise with her step-daughter had been only one of the delights over the past months. She pointed to the three-shelf unit near the door where she'd suggested Veronique place small hand-painted figurines called *santons*. "Ah, you ordered the Deniau Santons."

"But of course, Bertrand and Christianne contacted their son in Aix and we made a very good trade. He makes me the *santons* and I…"

Callie's forehead creased. "…And you what?"

Veronique grinned and her cheeks blushed. "I'm seeing him." The young woman clapped her hands like a child. "I sell his *santons* in my shop. He takes me to dinner when he visits his parents once a week."

"Oh? He drives all the way from Aix once a week to visit his parents. What a good son he is. It was my understanding he didn't visit them much at all. That's why they were so attached to Olivier when he had amnesia and they took care of him."

Veronique raised her eyebrows. "You didn't know the entire story, Callie. Jacques is quite wonderful."

When a dimple puckered her cheek, Callie was instantly transported to a memory when Francois' cheek reacted the same way. He was Veronique's father after all. Callie stared at her dimple.

"I see…" She fought a grin.

Veronique timidly asked, "The *santons*. He makes them for other events, not only for Christmas. When you told me they should sell well in my shop, you were right. He is working harder now than before he met me."

"Oh, I'll just bet he is…"

Olivia tapped Callie's cheek. "Well, isn't love grand?"

Callie rolled her eyes. "Tell me what we can do for the reception, *ma chère*. The flowers are taken care of. Janine hired a caterer to bring some of the food. Christianne is making the cake. We'll play music from my iPad through my Bose receiver and then…well, I'll be married again." She was overcome with that reality and stumbled a little.

FLAMENCO STRINGS UNCORKED

Veronique and Olivia wrapped their arms around her because it appeared she was ready to drop. The emotion of the past few weeks was taking its toll and the women felt her stress through their fingers.

"I hope the dress still fits you, Callie. You feel like you've lost more weight." Veronique squeezed her around the waist.

"No. I've just rearranged my fat because of all the walking I've been doing in Algodonales. In the past two weeks, my Fitbit shows that I've walked over fifty miles. Now we need to find shoes." Her dark hair bounced around her face and the silvery bangs slipped down to mar her view. With a swift flick of her hand, the strands were out of her eyes and Olivia pulled her from the shop.

After a quick wave to Veronique, they walked down the street. "Let's stop for a glass of wine. Shoes can wait."

"Olivia, we're on a schedule."

"Yes we are. Mine. Come on."

When the server delivered a small plate of grapes and fresh brie along with French Bordeaux, both women relaxed into their chairs. "Good idea, huh?"

"Always," Callie breathed as she slid a fat grape into her mouth.

Olivia leaned toward her friend. "Now tell me everything."

~

A few miles to the west, Michel sank into his easy chair. His belly didn't hurt. His head didn't hurt. He was hungry. He smiled at the thought because lately, that had been a new one. When he reached for the snack in front of him, his arm felt strange. He glanced at it and wondered why his fingers wouldn't close around the bread and cheese. A moment later, they wrapped around the food and he slowly brought the bread to his mouth. While he chewed, Michel stared at his fingers and then laid his hand in his lap.

Another secret he would keep from Janine. She was enjoying the chaos of planning Callie's wedding. His problems could wait until after the ceremony. He urged his fingers to make a fist. His hand didn't move.

At sunset the following evening, Bram, Olivia, Jules and Callie walked into *Gadoline's*. They'd chosen their favorite restaurant in Pertuis because of the food, music, and ambiance. Music was piped in softly amid glowing candles, linen tablecloths, napkins and real silver. The menu was small enough to fit into one hand, specials daily and always excellent.

The night felt magical to Callie, like a fairyland. When Jules had driven into the driveway and scooped her up into his arms, she had laughed like a school girl. It was their last night of singlehood. The air was balmy as she had smelled flowers along the stone pathway.

"Your carriage awaits," he said and lifted a hand in welcome to Olivia and Bram when they stepped outside the mill house. They were sleeping in the guest bedroom, one that had always been Olivia's when she'd come to visit Callie in those years when she'd lived in France before. Both when Francois was alive and after he died when Callie had lived in France for more than a year.

The men had opened their women's doors like gentlemen.

"Is this a bachelor and bachelorette party all wrapped into one?" Bram had slid in beside his wife and kissed her.

"It is." Olivia had turned to him and said, "We're letting you guys off at the corner. Callie and I have big plans and it's a ladies-only thing."

"Not on your life, Mrs. Carle." He'd snickered.

In the front seat, Jules had patted Callie's knee. "Ready, Cinderella?" His voice was just above a whisper.

She had nodded, too emotional to answer him.

Now, inside the restaurant, music enveloped them as the clink of glassware accompanied their quiet conversation. Callie had to keep her mind focused on the moment, so she wouldn't think about Michel's misery or Janine's sad eyes.

She'd thought of Jules and the wedding that would take place tomorrow from the moment she slipped the electric blue dress over her head earlier. When the silky fabric slid down her body, she'd loved the feel of it on her skin. It was warm, so she wore no pantyhose. Instead, she'd pushed her feet into matching blue stilettos, much higher than she normally wore. It was a special night, after all.

"Wow." Olivia mumbled something under her breath when Callie crossed her legs and she spied the blue shoes.

"What was that, Livvy?"

Olivia had laughed behind her hand. "I'll tell you later. It's about those remarkable stilettos. You must know their naughty name..."

A bottle of red wine was in the server's hand when he stood beside their table. He made a show of opening it, pouring about one inch of wine into the stemmed glass and handing it to Jules.

"Mmmm. Smells good." He twirled it gently round and round until he was certain it had reached the sides of the glass and then took a tentative sip. He grinned. *"Oui."*

The young man poured each glass half full and then bowed before he left the table. They lifted them in the air and whispered, *"À votre santé."*

"To you, my friend. May you find the peace and happiness I've found," Olivia said as her eyes brimmed over and she sniffed.

Bram slid the back of his finger down his wife's cheek.

"Thank you, Livvy." Callie turned to look at Jules and they shared a smile that carried them into a place where nobody else could go. His warm gray eyes shifted to her lips and held there.

"And you, Jules. Here's to having this fabulous, sassy woman at your side for the rest of your lives. May you be as happy with Callie as

I am with her best friend." Bram tapped the rim of Jules' glass and then felt Olivia's kiss on his cheek.

"We are sure getting mushy." Callie sniffed and watched her friends across the table, equally as happy with one another as she was with Jules. Still determined to keep her mind off of Michel and Janine for the evening, she slid off one shoe. When her toes found Jules' sock, she slid it down a little at a time without looking at him.

His ankle leaned into her foot. He took a sip of wine and gave her the eye beneath a raised eyebrow. She chuckled and lifted her glass.

Aromatic plates of food filled the table, more wine was poured and they talked late into the evening. The women had missed one another miserably and the men chuckled as they chattered nonstop.

"Dessert?" The server brought a large plate of various cheeses and a small dessert menu. They groaned, sure they could not eat another bite. But Olivia definitely wanted dessert. When the men saw her face, they laughed. Jules pointed to the menu and returned it to the man. Within minutes, four plates of *Gâteau Basque* was delivered. It was an exquisite tart; flaky crust surrounded a pastry cream dotted with brandied cherries. And they ate everything.

Callie and Jules felt each other's warmth all through dinner. The playfulness of their foot encounter added fire to the embers that never seemed to go out. He let his fingers dance over her shoulder. She lifted hers to assure him she enjoyed his touch.

She thought of all the conflicted self-talk she'd given herself the last few weeks after she arrived back from America and during her short sojourn in Spain. What had she been thinking? Of course, it was Jules for her all along. Maybe she was just afraid? But afraid of what? He was an honorable and kind man. He'd been Francois' best friend, hadn't he? Ah, therein lies the rub. She beat back the thoughts and slipped her toe into the top of his sock again. When she looked over at him, a muscle jumped in his jaw. A secret little smile slipped onto her face and she felt a tingle encompass her body.

Olivia clinked her glass and the last inch of red wine swirled around inside. "I think you are entirely too happy, lovey. And I also want to remind you that you have never had a poker face." She winked at Callie as she watched her friend's hands dance through the air.

When Callie burst out laughing, she felt the sacrifice again of missing Olivia, but the fullness of trading her for Jules made it better. She glanced at her friend fondly.

In the car afterward, Olivia leaned forward and tapped Callie on the shoulder. "Don't even *think* about inviting your fiancé into the cottage tonight because we'll be watching. You have a big day tomorrow."

Callie's swift intake of breath made Olivia laugh.

Jules rolled his eyes and turned toward Callie who raised an eyebrow toward him. "*Merde,*" he mouthed.

She kept her face as straight as possible except for the slight smile that slipped across her lips. She reached over and tapped his thigh in a promise. One more day and they'd be one in every way.

"Are you going to let your friend tell you what to do?" He was chuckling beside her.

She sighed heavily and turned around to look at Olivia who was smirking in the back seat. When she turned back to look out the front window, she said, "Well, no...actually, I'm not."

The car erupted in laughter and Jules slid his hand across the seat. She laced her fingers in his, needing him to push her past the worries that had swamped her about Michel's health. Tick tock. The fear of losing him was lodged inside her like a clicking pendulum.

Thirty Five

Callie's wedding day dawned without a single cloud overhead. She'd pushed Jules out after midnight with a kiss that left them weak again. The stars lit his way home. This morning, when she saw the bright blue sky from her kitchen window, she smiled as back flashes slipped through her mind from the night before. When she saw Olivia prancing over to the cottage in her nightie and robe, she laughed out loud all the way to her front door.

"Let me in or I'll blow your house down, said the big bad...."

"You don't look like a wolf to me, Livvy. You are too funny. Get in here. I have coffee. Where did you leave your husband? And why are you wearing your night clothes?"

Callie pushed her into a kitchen chair and poured her a cup of hot coffee. Knowing Livvy like she did, she opened the fridge and pulled out the half and half, poured in just the right amount and slipped it back into its spot on the door.

"Because I'm too lazy to get dressed twice and Cendrine told me it was all right, so I did it. Bram and Olivier have been chatting over their coffee for an hour already. The children are running around like wild Indians and Lulu peed all over me." She glanced down at her robe. "This is a new nightgown, not the one I didn't sleep in," she sniggered.

Callie was rejuvenated as she listened to Olivia's prattle. She sat down across from her with her own cup of coffee. She let out an exaggerated sigh. "I should throw some brandy in my coffee. You know that Jules' sister will be there. The last time I saw Aurore was at Veronique's open house. We managed to work together and I've forgiven her for the role she inadvertently played in Francois' death, but....ah...life is complicated. I will have a sister-in-law who slept with my husband before I married him. Since she is the mother of my step-daughter, what should I call her...?"

Olivia tapped Callie's hand. "Everything will be perfect. You'll see." She looked at her watch. "We have seven hours to change you from a pumpkin to Cinderella. What are you going to do with your hair? And..."

Callie held up a hand. "Livvy. You help Janine at the manse. I can get ready with Cendrine and Veronique. I will come to the big house early. I want to spend some time with Michel. It's important to me. You understand, don't you?" Her eyes pleaded with Olivia and nearly cried when her friend leaned in with a kiss on her forehead.

"Of course I understand, you goose. I'll go over there about ten o'clock. Janine has a list of things for me to do. I'm chopping up fresh lobster and salmon. She said something about making lobster oil." She dipped a spoon into her coffee, stirred it and then tested it with her tongue.

Callie raised her eyebrows. "Oh my God. *Maman* is making Salmon and Lobster *Tartare*. My absolute favorite French dish. She told me she was making *Carré d'gneau en croute d'herbes*. The woman is amazing. And with Michel so..." She took a big breath. "It's a lot of work. She has probably been cooking since dawn."

"Well, she's excited about the wedding and wants everything to be perfect. I think she's happy to have your wedding to take her mind off her husband's illness. You aren't surprised, are you?"

Shaking her head sadly, "I wouldn't be surprised under normal circumstances, but Michel..." She couldn't continue.

Olivia finished her coffee, knotted her robe and said, "Is there anything you want me to take with me?"

Callie shook her head, still unable to form the words.

Olivia hugged her and let herself out the front door.

~

Janine's apron was snugged around her body like a sheath. She stood back to survey her kitchen and smiled shakily. Looking at her watch, she counted the hours since she'd been in the kitchen. Three hours. Michel was sitting in the living room and she'd stood in the doorway every little while to watch him. He'd eaten a little cracker and cheese and washed it down with his coffee mixed with a big dollop of milk, just as he liked it.

When she heard the door knocker, she hurried to usher Olivia inside and then checked on him again. She handed Olivia an apron and a recipe after she'd spoken to Michel. Janine grinned at her eagerness; the woman was ready to work.

Two hours later, the wedding meal was nearly prepared. Bowls of freshly chopped lobster and salmon were filled to the brim. Chunks of red onion waited in the measuring cup beside them and the lobster oil was cooling. The rack of lamb was encased in its herb crust and the scallops had been grilled and were cooling in the refrigerator.

Christianne Deniau had just arrived with the small dishes of *Crème Brulee* and they were lined up in the extra refrigerator beside bottles of *Chloe Rosé* wine. Janine closed the door after counting everything and turned toward Bertrand, Christianne's husband, who was bringing in the wedding cake with Andre's help.

"The *Croquembouche* looks spectacular."

Christianne raised a cheek for her kiss and blushed. She had assured Janine she could make the French wedding cake and it was glorious. It was their wedding gift to Callie and Jules. Janine was shaking with excitement. Callie had no idea they planned to serve it at the reception. Janine knew she would be touched by the traditional cake on her wedding day.

Michel had insisted on the musicians too. No iPad was going to send music into the beautiful manse on Callinda's wedding day, he'd told her.

Several surprises waited for Callie. The hour was fast approaching when she'd walk into the front door as a widow and walk out as a bride. Janine's hand grabbed the back of the kitchen chair. She missed her son Francois with a pain so severe, she thought she must sit down. Her heart still ached from burying both of her children. It should never happen. Children are supposed to bury their parents, Janine's mind screamed. And then her hands stilled on the table top. She was afraid that is exactly what was going to happen and very soon.

When Callie arrived ten minutes later, Janine hadn't moved. She kissed her mother-in-law on the top of her head. "Tired, *maman*? I know you went to so much work to create our wedding feast. And I thank you from the bottom of my heart, but..."

Janine stood up slowly and took her daughter-in-law in her arms. "No buts," she whispered and squeezed her tightly. "I know you came early to visit with Michel and he waits for you."

Callie retraced her steps from the kitchen back into the living room and tiptoed toward him. His head was thrown back and his eyes were closed, but she was sure he wasn't asleep. When she reached him, he lifted a hand and she slipped hers inside his palm.

"Callinda. This is your day, *ma chère*. Sit beside me." His voice was soft. When he opened his eyes, a smile sat within their depths.

Her eyes swam with tears. "*Pére*. I love you dearly." Her nose started to run and she swiped the top of her hand beneath her nose, looking frantically for a tissue. He reached beside his chair and handed her the tissue box. She smiled through her tears.

"My darling. Soon, the old manse will be filled with noise, music and people. I love you as my daughter, you know that, don't you?"

She couldn't answer, so she nodded wordlessly. She sniffed again and blew her nose. His presence had always been like a deep-rooted oak tree. Her lips trembled and he reached a finger to still them as he continued.

"I know you will watch over *maman*..."

"But..." When she tried to stop him with a frantic shake of her head, he nodded with a look.

"Callinda, listen to me. I know my time to go away from here is near. I've lived a long life with beautiful people. When Francois died, you know the pain you had when it ripped out your heart."

She nodded desperately and blew her nose again.

"You are the perfect person to help *maman* after I'm gone. You will know how she feels. She loves you very much. She will listen to you. I want you to talk to her about something important. She can't stay here in this huge museum alone. It needs a big family."

Callie looked horrified. "You mean tell her to sell it?"

"*Non*. I want Cendrine and Olivier to move in here. You and Jules must move into the mill house and Janine should move into your cottage. I've thought this out very carefully and I've written down my wishes." He reached into his shirt pocket and pulled out a letter. "This is for you, darling. Just for you. Open it when I'm gone. Promise me?"

She caught the sob in her throat. When he placed it into her hand, his fingers froze for an instant. When she stared into his face, he nodded. "Yes, there's something wrong. I don't know what it is. For now, it is nothing. Just sit with me a little while and then go get fancy. Jules will want a smiling wife, not a crybaby on his hands."

"Oh, *Pére*. You are the father I never had. You know I will watch over *maman*. I am glad I will live in France. This is home. You and *maman* made it so." She blew her nose again. "I don't like this..."

"*Ma chère*. You've given us so much. You found the devil who killed Francois and you gave us Veronique. I bless the day Francois brought you to us. But, please be strong, my darling." His eyes smiled and he nodded as if he was answering all of her questions.

The sun was streaming into the window. She noticed he had several bright-colored cushions on the floor beside his chair as if he'd been holding them. She noticed three small vases on the table next to him. She was stunned to see white Lilies of the Valley. For mom. The enormity of their love to remember that for her was almost more than she could endure.

Michel saw the look on her face when she pulled her eyes back toward him. "Of course, we remembered, Callinda. We thought they would help bring your mother into the room to feel your happiness on this day. All for you." He pressed his lips together and glanced at the doorway. Janine stood there with her hand on her chest.

Callie gulped hard several times trying to dissolve the tears that were stuck in her throat. He closed his eyes and let out a long sigh. When he reached for her hand, she held it like a lifeline. She couldn't let him go. She wasn't ready. Dammit.

Michel's breathing changed within minutes and Callie knew he'd fallen asleep this time. She sat beside him holding his hand and didn't want to let go. It was warm, welcoming and sweet just as he'd been to her since the moment Francois had brought her into their home just before her thirtieth birthday.

When Olivia tapped her shoulder and pointed to the clock, Callie knew it was time to move.

"It's time, sweetheart. Are you ready?" Olivia's eyes swung from Michel to Callie, whose heart was reflected in her eyes.

Callie gently slipped her hand from his and swallowed hard again, not sure if it would work this time. Standing beside him, she stood motionless a moment before allowing Olivia to guide her into the back bedroom. She pushed the white envelope beneath the lamp base, assuring its safety. And then she turned around to dress for the second most important day of her life.

Thirty Six

Olivia slipped the vanilla-colored dress around Callie's shoulders and helped her button it from breast to hem. The soft shoulder pads were simple and small, just enough to create the elegance the dress deserved. A soft filmy scarf was fixed to the shoulders and swung around the back to drift down the front in a loose tie. Green, blue and pink flowers shadowed the froth and Olivia knotted it delicately as she looked into Callie's face.

"He wouldn't want you to wear your sadness like a veil, darling," she said gently. Olivia reached up to slip a satin covered headband around Callie's head that was entwined with silk flowers. The thin satin ribbons were tied at the back and rambled down the back of her head.

Callie brought her eyes up to her friend. "I know, Livvy. Help me make the pain go away before Jules sees me. I know I wear my emotions on my face."

Olivia grinned and pushed Callie onto the soft bedside chair. "Wait here. I'll be right back."

Callie watched her walk out the door and heard the soft click of the latch behind her. She turned to glance at Michel's white envelope beneath the lamp base and touched it with a finger. When the door opened again, she drew back her hand as if she'd been burned.

"Just what we need, hmmmmmm?"

Two fluted glasses were in one hand and a bottle of *Veuve Clicquot Champagne* was gripped in the other. The yellowish-orange label made Callie smile. Her favorite, but she rarely bought it since it was almost fifty dollars a bottle.

But today? Her smile changed to a grin when Olivia pushed the bottle between her knees and held a towel over the bottle. When they heard the cork pop out of the green bottle, they knew it was exactly what they needed to change the day from shit to flowers.

Olivia jumped up from the bed, still holding the towel over the rim of the bottle in case the foam rolled over the top. When she peeked under the towel, she danced in place and reached for the glasses.

"*Perfecto, mi amiga*," Callie proudly said in Spanish.

Two glasses later, Callie put her hand over the empty glass when Olivia lifted the bottle a third time. "I don't want to crawl across the floor to marry Jules, Livvy. I want to stand beside him. Thank goodness I didn't have to memorize words for the ceremony." She hiccupped.

When Callie giggled and covered her mouth with a hand, Olivia Carle knew the champagne had been the key to success. She reached up to rearrange the head wreath and pulled a couple of the flowers into her friend's hair. She lifted one silken, rose flower and slipped a strand of silver hair behind it.

Someone knocked on the door and Olivia opened it to peek into the hallway. Veronique and Cendrine slipped inside, each wearing matching pink gowns that whispered against their skin when they walked. It was a close pattern to Olivia's, only hers was a darker shade of pink.

"Your hot pink dress is beautiful. I guess I didn't notice it until now, Livvy." Callie glanced down at her friend's shoes and laughed. "Oh. My. God. You would wear those, wouldn't you?"

The younger women laughed when they spied Olivia's feet. Hot pink stiletto sandals were entwined around her ankles like grapevines. The heels were nearly four inches and pointed like ice picks.

"Of course I did. You know what they call these stilettos and when I wear them, it tells Bram what he can expect later." She lifted her champagne glass to her lips with a naughty grin and gave the bottle to the younger women.

Veronique and Cendrine laughed and took turns upending the bottle directly into their mouths. When some of the yellow bubbly leaked down Veronique's lips, she grabbed the box of tissues off the bed.

Cendrine finished the bottle and said, "God, I hope this doesn't flow into Lulu's breast milk." And then the women laughed again.

Callie plopped down on the bed. Her eyes were a bit tipsy, but she was sure she could say *I do*. When she heard guitar music, she raised her eyebrows. Both her Bose receiver and iPad still sat on the side table. Olivia had been instructed to place them on the tall stone mantle. "What is that music out there?"

The girls snickered and Olivia shrugged her shoulders innocently. It was one forty five. In fifteen minutes, Callie would give herself to Jules and she would become Callinda Beauvais Armand. She'd told him the name was important to keep and he'd readily agreed.

"Almost time, Callie."

She inhaled deeply and exhaled slowly. Lifting her mother's pearls to her neck, she clasped them tightly and added the matching earrings to her ear lobes. The women silently watched her, knowing it was a sweet moment for Callie.

The music volume increased. Callie's head came up quickly, somewhat mystified. "Spanish flamenco guitar? Who? How did..." She laughed quietly into her fist. "Maybe I should say *I do* in Spanish then. *Hago*. No, it sounds better when it's in English." She made a face and giggled, knowing the champagne was making her hazy.

FLAMENCO STRINGS UNCORKED

The women left Olivia and Callie alone. They hugged one another and then Olivia said, "Smile, Callie. You must smile even though your heart is breaking."

"I can't! I know I must, but...nobody can tell me how to feel."

"Yes. You. Can."

The women stood nose to nose.

Callie dropped her gaze and nodded solemnly.

"Now would be a good time. I am not opening that door until I get at least one smile from you."

When Callie spread her lips, Olivia hissed, "You call *that* a smile?"

"Dammit. It's the best I can do." Callie marched to the bedroom door and pulled it open. The hallway was empty. Olivia moved in front of her. When Callie reached the large entryway for her small, intimate wedding, she heard the rustle of conversations. She walked further through the opening and nearly fell into Olivia.

Michel was there to greet her. He stood in the doorway, leaning on his cane and reached out a hand to pull Callie into the room. She was so stunned, she couldn't move. Looking into the room blindly, she saw Rafael Bernal sitting on a chair in front of the fireplace holding his flamenco guitar. He grinned at her shocked face and began playing the beautiful strains of *Malagueña*.

"*Pére.* How...?"

"But of course, darling. This is your day and no one else's. We flew Rafael and four of your friends here for a surprise." His veined hand clutched hers and held her fingers tightly.

Dazedly, she whispered, "Four friends?"

Olivia followed Veronique and Cendrine slowly into the room, stepping in time with the cadence of the sensuous guitar music. They'd been so excited about Michel and Janine's surprise, they'd nearly let it slip when the champagne was flowing.

Michel leaned on her slightly. She smelled his aftershave cologne as he guided her further into the room. Her heart was beating so wildly, she felt like a bird in a cage. She saw Jules at the end of the room and focused on him. When Callie saw him beam at her, she held onto Michel and caught her breath. She didn't dare try to talk or look at his old face. Was she floating? Was this a dream? Was Michel actually walking her across this large room?

When they arrived beside Jules, she watched him help Michel to the waiting chair next to Janine. She was sure her heart was going to explode in her chest as the emotion swelled and ran over.

There were so many candles glowing on the massive, stone mantle in front of her, she thought she was seeing double. Her bottle of *Sueño España* sat among grapevines, woven through bright, red poppies. They were strewn across the hearth in so many vases, she couldn't count them. When she thought she couldn't take one more surprise, Jules reached for her. She grasped hold of his fingers and didn't let go.

She grinned at Rafael and closed her eyes as the beautiful Spanish music filled her with the thrill of Spain and the friendships she'd made. Jules whispered beside her, "Callie, are you all right?"

"No, I'm certainly *not* all right," she whispered back to him.

"Who gives this woman to this man today?"

Callie heard the soft voices behind her and turned to see Janine and Michel's hands tightly clasped. They were looking at her with so much love on their old faces that she thought she would surely faint.

But she didn't. Jules held her up. They lit the large, white candle with its satin streamers touching the floor. The minister lifted a hand, palm out toward them, as the candle's flame glimmered.

It was their turn.

Jules lifted Callie's hand to his lips and kissed her palm. "With this ring, I vow to love you and care for you always." His eyes said so much more than the simple, beautiful words as he slipped the diamond and emerald ring onto her finger.

She lifted their clasped hands to her lips and looked deeply into his gray eyes. She saw a kiss in its depths and nearly lost her next thought. Oh, yes. She pulled his hand to her lips, kissed it and touched the tip of her tongue to its warmth for just an instant. His eyes opened wide and he fought the smile that hovered there. "With this ring, I vow to love you and care for you always."

When Olivia put the gold band into Callie's hand, she winked at her. Callie tried not to roll her eyes and instead brought them back to Jules while she tried to slip it onto his finger. It wouldn't fit. She pushed and tugged the ring on and he kept pulling his hand away from her. What? Fog clogged her brain. She knew this ring should fit perfectly. She tried again and Jules pulled his hand away again.

When she heard Olivia say, "The other hand, Cal," she looked down at the ring. The guests laughed bemusedly. She was holding Jules' right hand in hers. She'd been trying to force the ring on the wrong hand. Oh, god. This time, he did roll his eyes and the lightened mood filled her with relief. He shook his head with a smile in his eyes and gave her his left hand.

"I knew that ring should fit..."

The room erupted in laughter again.

"I now pronounce your Mr. and Mrs. Jules Armand." The minister motioned them to turn around and face the room behind them. The gleaming candles added a soft glow to the room and Callie received her second shock of the day.

Javier was there holding Mari's hand. Mateo stood next to Loli and then Rafael began strumming *Besame Mucho*. Her heart lifted and she turned to Jules.

"Kiss me a lot. That's our song. She reached up and their lips connected in a long, drawn out kiss that left them breathless. And the crowd clapped their approval as if she really was Cinderella. Of course she was, she'd just married her Prince Charming.

The crowd surrounded them. Rafael continued to play in the background with short, rapid beats as his fingers rippled over the flamenco strings. Veronique and Cendrine hugged her and then Olivia grabbed her and held her there in a tight embrace.

Walking over to Janine and Michel, she leaned down to kiss their cheeks. They were so dear. She still couldn't quite believe they'd flown her friends to the wedding with the flamenco guitarist too.

"*Merci beaucoup.*" Thank you.

And then she saw Aurore walk slowly toward them. They stared at one another for a heartbeat and then Jules' sister put her arms around Callie. She kissed both of her cheeks and she said, "You are now my sister. Who would have ever guessed such a thing could happen?" She smiled and gave Jules a mock slap on the arm. "And you, my beautiful brother, have chosen well."

It was exactly the words they both wanted to hear. Bernadette and Francois threw their arms around Callie's legs. Cendrine returned to Olivier's side and reached for Lulu who was making hunger noises.

Her Spanish friends gave Callie the hug she needed. When it was Mateo's turn, he gave Jules a look. "You need to watch this one, Jules." He kissed her on both cheeks.

Jules grinned.

And then it was Loli's turn. Her gold dress sparkled in the candle light; a small red flower in her hair looked very Spanish.

Callie whispered into her long hair, "Well?"

Loli blushed and said, "Working on it."

"Good," Callie kissed her on both cheeks and gave Mateo a look.

Andre held his daughter's arm and tickled his new granddaughter's cheek while the older children circled around him. He tried to grab one of them but they were too fast.

The food aromas on the massive dining room table made Callie's mouth water. Cold scallops sat on top of crisp lettuce leaves, cold salmon and lobster nearly burst from several bowls. Lobster oil glistened beside them. An encrusted leg of lamb was golden brown.

Rafael played his guitar, so Jules filled a plate of food for him. "You better eat now or the table will be empty when you get in there."

He thanked Jules, braced his flamenco guitar carefully against the stone fireplace and picked up his fork.

Janine inched her way toward Callie and Jules. When she reached them, she placed a small box into Callie's hand and a larger box into Jules' hand. "From both of us. You are now our son, Jules. And I know Francois would be happy for it."

Callie's fingers tightened on his arm and she leaned into him to kiss his lips. His arms caressed her back as he pulled her off her feet. When they parted, the room erupted in applause.

Veronique and Aurore left early to return to the shop, Hybrid Designs. It would be a smaller reception party without Michel and Janine. The wedding party would sadly miss them, but they were not surprised. Michel's condition had remained an unspoken worry for everyone.

The beautiful French cake was at Veronique's shop waiting for the bride and groom. Christianne's son would take photographs. And a case of chilled *Chloe Rosé* was ready to pour.

In the large, manse's living room, Michel let Jules help him into his favorite easy chair. He held Jules' hand a moment. "*Merci*, Jules. You will have your hands full very soon. Help her be strong."

Jules studied Michel a long minute and then leaned down to embrace him. "You take good care now, Michel. We all need you." When Jules walked away to find his new wife, he wasn't sure if Michel had been talking about Janine or Callie.

Thirty Seven

Three miles away, the cars began to assemble on the street in front of Hybrid Designs. Pink sparkling wine bubbled in fluted glasses and the traditional cake was oohed and aahed over. Callie's friends from Spain mingled with her family and friends in Pertuis. She'd been delighted to introduce them to Jules. And Cupid's arrow had found one mark for sure and was circling a second one.

Callie and Jules were the last to arrive. After the group disbursed from the manse, they had opened the boxes Janine had given them. And then they'd held one another, too drained with emotion to go to their wedding party just yet.

Inside Callie's box was the broach Janine wore, one she'd loved since the first day she saw it, when Francois married her. Three inches tall and two inches wide, the woman's beautiful porcelain face stared at her. Her eyes were sapphire stones just below painted eyebrows and eyelashes. Her face was set at an angle. A diamond was embedded in her earlobe and her nineteen-twenties, wide-brimmed hat was trimmed with black onyx stones and diamond chips. Her lips were, of course, three small rubies set in a wide smile. And the small flowing scarf around her porcelain neck matched her hat. Callie had promptly burst into tears and couldn't stop them from coursing down her cheeks.

Jules held Callie's hand and gently outlined the pin with his finger. "Do you want to wear this to the reception?"

Callie huffed out a ragged breath. "Yes."

His hand shook as he lifted the bodice from her collar bone and tightened the clasp that held the beautiful broach in place. She covered his hand with her own and then her fingers slipped over the woman's jeweled face.

"I'm afraid to open my box." His voice wavered.

She laughed shakily. "I don't blame you."

When he pulled it from his pocket, he was relieved to remove the bulkiness. The white box had a bright blue ribbon wrapped with a bit of raffia.

Callie watched his face instead of trying to look beneath his hands into the box. When his eyes began to pool with tears, she dropped her eyes to look at the gift inside. And then she swallowed hard several times and touched his cheek with her left hand. Her wedding ring sparkled as the sun shone through the window at exactly the right angle.

"He would have wanted you to have this and they knew it."

Jules lifted the gold pocket watch from the blue velvet bed and raised his eyes to Callie. "Michel's father gave this to him the day he married Janine. He gave it to Francois the day he married you. And now..." His voice broke as he popped the button on top to release the gold door to view the watch face. The second hand was moving, moving, moving.

But, time stood still.

Callie reached for the double gold chain that was hooked to the top golden loop. She removed it from the palm of his hand and helped him attach it to his belt loop. And then he pulled her hand into his pocket as it dropped within its depths. Their warm hands held it together, both lost for a heartbeat in past memories.

He leaned forward and touched her lips, soft as butterfly wings.

Now, sometime later, they stood inside Hybrid Designs.

Rafael had found a chair and played his flamenco guitar with wild abandon. Spanish tunes filled the shop and several couples danced in the small front area on parquet tiles, making it easy to slide around. The bubbly, sparkling wine gave the party a festive air and the beautiful cake was a sight to behold.

Jacques took several photographs of the bride and groom, the cake and the people that surrounded them. He sought out Veronique often and it was obvious they were besotted with one another. His father, Bertrand, stood over the small table with the wine and didn't stop smiling. When Christianne joined her husband, they introduced the cake.

More laughter. More photos. More memories.

Veronique pulled Callie aside. "You know, of course, that you and I have the strongest family tie of anyone in this room, *oui*?"

Callie raised her wine flute toward her. "Because I'm your step-mother?"

Veronique giggled as the sparkling wine sailed through her blood stream. "*Non.* More."

Callie looked at Veronique quizzically.

"You just married my uncle. You are now my aunt *and* my step-mother." The young woman giggled again. "I am the luckiest girl in the world now." Her golden, brown hair glistened a perfect contrast against her light pink dress. Her eyelashes were long and curled nearly to her eyebrows. Just like Francois.

Callie raised her fluted glass to Veronique. When the young woman hugged her, they nearly spilled their wine all over the parquet tiles.

"Ah, so what shall I call you now? Niece or daughter?"

"You are a Beauvais Armand and I am an Armand Beauvais. I can't call you *maman.*" She glanced around to find her mother, Aurore. She was talking with Jules near the front window. "I've tried to create a combination of the two words and nothing sounds right. And I don't want to call you Callie or Aunt Callie." She put a finger to her chin a moment and raised an eyebrow. I will call you *tante maman,* Auntie Mama."

Callie threw her head back and laughed. "That's a mouthful. It sounds better in French." When she looked at Veronique again, she whispered, "*Tante maman vous aime.*" Auntie Mama loves you.

They were still laughing when Jules and Aurore joined them.

"Jules tells me you are postponing your honeymoon. I know you are worried about Michel." She glanced at Veronique. "I am happy Paul Havre took care of him. He is an excellent doctor. If anyone can help him, Paul can."

Callie didn't want to talk about it. She knew Aurore was only trying to ease her mind over Michel's health condition, but her words brought it all back to her like a mudslide falling off a mountain.

Nobody responded.

Callie saw everything in slow motion.

The revelry in the room sounded distorted. Rafael's lilting guitar music enticed people to sway and tap their feet. Cendrine held onto Olivier, happy to be there, but anxious to get home to their children. Dry lavender bouquets littered the tables and hung from the ceiling by brass hooks. Mari and Javier were dancing. Mateo was leaning against the wall listening to something Loli said and then he laughed down at her.

Veronique put an arm around her mother's shoulder. "*Maman*, your glass is empty. Let's get more for you."

Callie forced a smile and lifted her own half-full glass and watched the women walk away.

Jules touched her lips with a finger and caressed it lightly. "Cake, *ma petite*. I think we need cake."

She tried to keep her heart in one piece, but it was difficult. The cake tasted delicious and the cherries were a perfect combination. Callie thought that was her last surprise and when the cake melted on the tip of her tongue, she was sure of it.

But she was wrong.

Thirty Eight

The house was empty, quiet and spotless again.

Janine stood in the doorway for the hundredth time to look at her husband. Removing her soiled apron, she smoothed her hands over the new dress she'd bought for Callie's wedding. It made her feel pretty and she'd needed the happy feelings it gave her when she tried it on. She doused all the lights except those on the mantle. One large candle burned among several smaller tapers. She left them.

"Michel, do you want a coffee?"

"Non. Come sit with me."

Janine slipped onto the couch near him and was surprised when he lifted himself from his easy chair to join her. She'd put on soft music after the musician stopped strumming his flamenco guitar. Sweet music floated through the air around them.

Michel lifted her hand and pulled it onto his lap. Their veined hands laced together and they didn't speak for a time. Their heads leaned back on the cushion and they closed their eyes.

"This is nice."

Michel let out a long, satisfied breath. "Wonderful."

"Our girl is now married and Francois would be glad it is Jules."

"Uh-hmmmmmm."

"She loved seeing her surprise guests and the music, *oui*?"

"Uh-hmmmmmm."

They sat in silence with their hands tightly woven together.

"Janine. You remember the day we got married?"

"Oh, yes I do. You had those funny pants on and you wouldn't button your shirt up or wear the tie I bought for you."

He chuckled. "I mean the ceremony."

"Ah, but of course. I remember smelling the flowers and the scent of burning candles. There were only two candles and my bouquet. I wanted more candles and flowers for Callie."

"Flowers and candles do not make a marriage, Janine."

She huffed. "I know that. It's just...well, I wanted more something. Our wedding was beautiful though. I remember the way you winked at me when I walked down the aisle and my face got hot. I wanted you and I was intensely proud that you wanted me too."

"Oh, I wanted you all right. Remember that time out in the barn?" His voice turned husky with the memory.

Janine chuckled and bumped his shoulder with hers in mock reprimand. "You were a sweet talker, Michel. I was so naïve then, but I knew you were the man for me. I'd never been so attracted to a man. I felt it the minute I looked into your face.

Michel chuckled again. "And you had that long curly hair that flowed around your face like an angel. In the barn that day when the sun was sending points of light through the door, I saw fairy dust. When I looked at you, it looked like it was floating around your head. It was magical and I couldn't wait to hold you close."

"Close and naked, you mean," Janine whispered.

"Darling, we're alone. Nobody is going to hear you. Why are you whispering? We have nothing to be ashamed of. We were in love. It was natural…"

She grinned as she remembered the straw in the loft. She couldn't stop kissing him and when they had their clothes off, their hands explored every inch of each other. She'd found straw in her clothes for days afterward. She blushed with the memory.

"We've had a good life, Janine."

She stiffened.

"And then that time when Francois was sitting on my shoulders and he saw you across the vineyard pulling that cow? The way he laughed and jumped with excitement and I almost dropped him? When you saw us, you started running. Your hair was flying around your head like a halo. I don't think I ever loved you so much than when you rounded that corner and slid across that pear cactus."

"You laughed. I remember that. Francois wanted down to help his *maman* up and all you could do was bend over and laugh."

"The look on your face stayed with me for days."

"So did those damn cactus stickers."

"I pulled them out for you. Don't you remember that part?"

"Oh, yes…I remember afterward. You always had a special way of celebrating notable events."

"And you loved it."

"Of course, I did, darling. You know I've always loved your touch." Her face softened with emotion.

Michel smoothed the soft folds of her dress across her thigh. He rubbed the cloth as if he was caressing the memories, over and over again.

"Michel?"

"Janine, always remember the time in the barn. Never forget how much we loved each other and the good life we've lived together. Our children, their children." He breathed deeply and exhaled.

Janine's hand tightened and squeezed his old fingers. "I'll remember all the parts of our life together except what old age makes me forget. You are melancholy tonight, my dear."

"Remember the barn, my darling. And always remember that I love you." He smiled in the near darkness of the room and watched the largest candle begin to sputter.

Janine moved closer to the man she'd been married to for nearly sixty years. She felt his warmth seep through his shirt and into her soul. It had always been that way for them. A touch. A spark. A smile. Laughter. And the grapevines.

They sat in the dark for a long time after one of the candles sizzled and sputtered on the mantle. Music still wrapped around them; each soft tune brought a new memory of time and place like a slow-motion movie. Their hands remained clasped and then Janine whispered, "And don't forget the time Chloe couldn't sleep and slipped into the bedroom when we were in a delicate situation…"

Michel laughed out loud. "Yes. I remember she asked you what I was doing to you and you said, "Papa is tickling me." Their laughter drowned out the song that drifted through the room."

They sat, hands entwined, for a long time as the candle's wicks grew shorter and Michel's breathing grew shallower. After Janine guided her husband into bed and she knew he had fallen asleep, she lay awake for a long time.

She tightly clasped her hands over her breasts and tried to swallow the tears that fought their way upward. Her heartbeat seemed to echo in the large bedroom, leaving her emotions bare. Where would she be without Michel? How could she live without seeing his smile each morning, his kiss each night? She let her mind wander and poke into the vast memory vault of her mind and her face crumpled in the darkness.

Her foot caressed his calf and she gathered the warmth to herself like a baby kitten curling around her master's leg. Never in her life had she felt so lonely and frightened. Her hand reached toward Michel and closed over his fingers, loose in sleep. She felt her shadow fly to the future, but refused to see past their linked hands under the covers.

The room enclosed her; their vineyard, the living room, kitchen, fireplace mantle he lovingly carved, the gardens, the man beside her. She clutched his hand again, willing health into his body. And then she felt the room begin to spin and knew she'd never sleep.

When Janine returned to the living room, she lit two more candles, sat in the dark to watch them burn, and twisted the belt of her robe with her fingers until they felt like confetti. She watched the shadows on the wall cast by the glow. Her mind sped to the pain in

Michel's eyes, the throbbing in his body, weakness in his legs. How could she wish for him to continue living with this horrible pain? Was she so selfish? Could she only think of herself, her life without him? Would she continue to justify her need for him without caring for his comfort? "*Merde*," she whispered into the emptiness…"Hush, Janine, hush."

She strained to see into the night sky where stars must be shining, stars they used to stare at for hours through his telescope. Where was his telescope now? They hadn't done that for a long time. Yes, she knew a great change was coming. Whispering "*Merde*" again, she drew in her belt, pushed herself out of the chair and blew out the sputtering candles.

When she slid beneath the covers after midnight, she reached to touch Michel's chest. Still breathing. She moved closer to him and spooned against him. When his warmth pervaded her soul, she finally allowed the tears to fall until she fell asleep.

Just before the vineyard's rooster crowed at dawn, Michel Beauvais was dead. When a breathless sound like a hiccup woke Janine, she rolled into the bed covers toward him. After she touched his cheek, she knew it instantly.

And she felt her world die without her permission.

FLAMENCO STRINGS UNCORKED

If you enjoyed this book.....

One of the most powerful gifts a reader can give an author is recommend a writer's work to a friend. So, if you have friends you think will enjoy reading about Callie and her escapades, please tell them.

I don't have shelf space in airports or many book stores, so your reviews help more readers discover my work. When you have a moment or two, and would like to spread the word, please jot down your thoughts and reactions in an honest review. I would be very grateful.

Just go to the internet site where you purchased the book, click on the cover image and scroll down to "leave a customer review."

NEXT PAGES:
Excerpts from Books 1, 2 and 3

Excerpt – Shoot the Moon: Book one of Callinda Beauvais Series

"Callie. I think I just shot Hunter."

"You *think* you shot him? Oh, my God!!" Callie heard Olivia crying and Hunter yelling in the background. Her mind froze only a second before she screamed into the phone. "I'm not far away. Stay away from him if you can." She blew her nose loudly, stunned at the turn of events as curiosity married fear. She listened breathlessly.

"Yes, hurry! He's so angry, I have a bad feeling. He's a little bit crazy, Cal, I just know it. He keeps ranting about our new prescription drug contract that will upgrade all of Larkspur's health insurance policies. He sounds seriously as if his life depended on it. He is angry I want to use another company for the drug coverage. We can save our policyholders so much money with the new contract! But he isn't focusing on the people we insure at all....Here he comes again, Callie."

"Oh God, Olivia..... I'm coming!" She tossed the phone onto the seat and heard a sharp blast. Horrified, her brain went into overdrive knowing her car was not backfiring; her foot slipped off the accelerator and then quickly adjusted as she tromped downward and sped toward the Milwaukie exit, raced a few blocks and twisted the wheel right onto Carlyle and left on 13th. Her little car careened into Olivia's driveway at 40 mph, bumping the edge of the curb, jerking her body like a rag doll and banging her head into the headliner. Oblivious, she downshifted, turned off the engine, ripped the door open as the Audi rocked wildly on its tires and slammed the door before making a bead toward Olivia's front door.

Skipping up the condo's sixteen cedar steps, the tantalizing perfume of lilacs bombarded her. She reached the door but was dismayed when it wouldn't open. Everything was silent. Rushing around the wide deck to the bay window, she looked into the living room, shading her eyes with her hand. *Now what? Call 911. That's it.*

Why didn't I do that first? Dammit!! Blindly, she rushed back to her car and reached inside for her cell phone still lying on the passenger seat. Her fingers didn't want to work as she clutched it, finally thumbed the button and frantically dialed 911.

At the sound of a woman's voice, Callie's voice shook so badly, she could barely get out controlled sentences. "I'm sure she's in danger; please send the police because I am outside her house right now, afraid to go inside. She called just a few minutes ago and told me Hunter Roget had threatened her..." Callie glanced at the house again.

"What is your name, ma'am?"

"Callinda Beauvais. Can't you ask me that later?"

"What is the address, Ms. Beauvais?"

Callie reeled off the house number and rubbed the stinging tears from her eyes with a jerk of her fingers. "Can you find out if there is a police cruiser close? We may need an ambulance too. I just don't know what to do!" Callie sniffed before placing one hand on the side of her car to lean against the door. For a moment, she pressed her head against the cold steel before slumping down on the seat inside her car.

"Please remain in your car, ma'am. I'm checking now and will send the police and an ambulance right away." The woman hung up.

Ok. The ambulance and police. That's good. That's good. A few seconds later, her hand jerked the car door open and she bolted for the house once again. *Remain in my car? Hell no, I can't remain in my car.*

Lunging toward the front door a second time, she rammed herself against it, pushing hard with the palm of her hand. The heavy, leaded glass door lurched open, stunning her momentarily. She grabbed the knob before it banged against the wall, fearing the noise, damage and the broken glass. She was so sure it had been locked.

Callie heard a whimpering sound and realized it was her own...

~

FLAMENCO STRINGS UNCORKED

<u>Excerpt – Wine, Vines and Picasso: Book two of Callinda Beauvais Series</u>

In Portland the following morning, a warm glow flowed through Callie as she sat in her best friend's office at Larkspur Insurance. "Cendrine left another message. I should fly to Pertuis. I can help and just……."

"………run away?" Olivia struggled with irritation.

"I don't need to run away, Livvy. We're trading phone calls and frankly, I'm worried."

"Well, take Nate with you…after my wedding." Olivia's diamond earrings glimmered as the sun shifted through her office window. Her green eyes stared at Callie with a question.

"No, François' ghost would be between us. Of course it would."

Olivia Phillips bit her lip and heaved a heavy sigh.

Callie grinned. "Nate and I had a long talk last night after I'd falsely accused him of…well. You know why. We spent time under the stars…"

"You mean, in your hot tub?" Olivia perked up.

"He is really a lovely man, Livvy. Now back to work," she teased without answering. With a small wave, she left the office.

At dawn the next day, the phone woke Callie from a deep sleep. Her eyelashes fluttered and she jerked awake with a gasp. Twisting both hands beneath her pillow, she nuzzled deeper into its folds. The phone jangled again. Callie's tousled head lifted off the pillow a few inches, a swath of chestnut and silver bangs covered one eye.

"François? François, are you awake?" An eerie silence met her question as December's morning sun streamed through the bedroom window. Empty space met her questing fingers. And then her eyes popped open and reality swooped down like a hammer. She heaved herself onto her back. "Of course, François can't answer the damn phone." She was sick with the struggle within her. *I'm a widow. Say it!*

Flipping the covers off her small, satin-clad body, she jerked the coverlet upward. Goose bumps crawled over her arms; she swore she saw the indentation of François' head on the other pillow. Would she ever adapt to widowhood? The morning's slip confused her. *It's Cendrine's phone messages. They've taken my mind back to Provence and of course, to François.*

A niggle of alarm wormed its way through her mind when ringing split the air again. Making a mad dash for the phone, her niece's words crashed together like a racing freight train. Listening intently to the garbled story, Callie's chin sank to her chest. "Slowly, *ma chérie.* And please, in English. My French needs some practice....."

"Callie...I cannot tell *grandmère* and *grandpère.* Olivier took money from the vineyard's account. I do not know why. I'm scared and I do not know what to do and he...has disappeared. Please come help me."

Book Three:
<u>Excerpt – Thorny Secrets and Pinot Noir of Callinda Beauvais Series</u>

She tried to shake the panic that was rioting within her. Why was it so important? And wasn't it odd that Bryan wouldn't know the woman. Their firm had not been large and she knew they often shared their cases, often brainstormed over the phone at night. This one, François had evidently kept secret from his partner. Maybe that should make her feel better?

The next few days, Callie worked in a blur of activity. Boxes were strewn all over her house, the debris from the break-in was long gone, but packing papers and bubble wrap still filled the corners of each room. She'd procrastinated about looking for Mae Haydon to learn who Lily was. She did, however, know that she couldn't put off going to the office to say her goodbyes and to see Nate Leander. He'd been an important part of her life as he'd helped her get past her grief after losing François. He showed her she could love again. It just wouldn't be with Nate and she was sorry for that. She thought a lot of the man and his family. She blew her nose, fighting the tears that wanted to escape. He deserved more. But then she'd found Jules.

A few boxes were set aside in the garage with France boldly written on each one. The others sat for Alexis' estate agents to go through, tag and prepare for the sale set for ten days from now. The plan was set in motion to finish at the lake house the following week.

WHO WAS LILY?

Her ordered life was in quicksand again and she didn't like it. Maybe Olivia was right and it didn't mean anything. But, maybe it did and Callie knew there was no ignoring it. Words scrambled around in her head like marbles and she kept hearing, 'who was Lily?' over and over again. Holding her hands over her ears, as if to stop the questions ripping through her brain, she sank down into a chair filled with packing debris.

Refusing to believe Lily might be someone important in François' life, she turned, instead, to thinking out other scenarios. A friend? A client? Someone's sister? She was driving herself nuts and she couldn't stop herself. Who would know about these people? Mae Haydon must be a local resident and once she spoke with her, she could clear up the gloom and then Callie could finish packing, sell the houses and get back to France. The obvious person to call had been Bryan Martos, the old partner at the firm. She was stumped when he didn't recognize the name, so maybe the woman wasn't a client at all? There she was, back again, to the furtive, unspoken fear that Lily was more to François than an acquaintance. He'd done it before and they say the first time is the easiest when you start hiding secrets from your wife.

She thought of her friend, Valerie Blume, the paralegal who worked closely with François in the Beauvais Martos Law Firm. She might know who Mae and Lily were. Why hadn't she thought of her before? They'd been friends for years. They'd lost track of one another and Callie had missed her.

Arguing with herself about the note for a few days as she stuffed boxes and pulled items off shelves she hadn't thought of in years, she decided to call Valerie. Callie admitted to herself that she wasn't sure if she wanted to know the answers. She'd already gotten past the secrets in France. Did she really want to face more secrets in America? In the end, she needed to make a decision because the constant barrage of arguments between herself and her alter ego kept blasting through her head day and night.